Finland as a Knowledge Economy 2.0

DIRECTIONS IN DEVELOPMENT
Science, Technology, and Innovation

Finland as a Knowledge Economy 2.0

Lessons on Policies and Governance

Kimmo Halme, Ilari Lindy, Kalle A. Piirainen, Vesa Salminen,
and Justine White, Editors

1818 H Street NW, Washington DC 20433
Telephone: 202-473-1000; Internet: www.worldbank.org

1 2 3 4 17 16 15 14

ISBN (paper): 978-1-4648-0194-5
ISBN (electronic): 978-1-4648-0195-2
DOI: 10.1596/978-1-4648-0194-5

Cover photo: © Team Finland/Riitta Supperi. Used with permission. Further permission required for reused.
Cover design: Debra Naylor, Naylor Design, Inc.

Library of Congress Cataloging-in-Publication Data has been requested.

Contents

Boxes

Figures

Tables

Foreword

The technology and innovation landscape has changed considerably since 2006 when *Finland as a Knowledge Economy: Elements of Success and Lessons Learned* was first published by the World Bank Institute (WBI). In the intervening years, the rise of information technologies and of innovation as a vehicle for development have transformed knowledge economies the world over.

In Finland today, technological connectivity is excellent, but the innovation landscape poses certain challenges. Evaluations of the Finnish innovation system show that while it is effective, it only has a moderate level of international research collaboration and needs to link its well-educated immigrant population to the innovation economy. Recognizing this, the Finnish Government is exploring partnerships, cooperation frameworks, and more inclusive engagement with international experts to promote entrepreneurship, links with leading international innovation hubs, and learning with innovation communities, regardless of their location.

Finland's path is unique to its own history and not a readily replicable blueprint for other countries. However, valuable lessons can be drawn from Finland's policies and governance framework, including processes that underpin policy implementation. Therefore, the report is devoted to analyzing not only the substance of such policies (*the what*) but also the policy-making process (*the how*) addressing the challenges of globalization. It is the understanding of the marriage of these two – process and substance – that truly reveals the underpinnings of Finland's success and provides food for thought for policymakers and practitioners globally.

The report's approach is very practical and presents the challenges first and then explains the concrete actions taken, as well as the thinking behind those actions. As is often the case, building a knowledge economy is never a straightforward process but is more a continuous renewal of policy responding to the challenges of globalization. The Finnish story is one of both hope and pragmatism, filled with many interesting lessons and case studies for countries of all income levels, aspiring to build a more competitive economy. The Finnish experience shows that it is possible to make significant changes in a relatively short time. It also shows the value of keeping long-term core investments in key sectors while continuously course-correcting and experimenting with new approaches to overcome obstacles.

I hope that all readers will share my enjoyment in reading this report and will take away the many rich lessons in order to experiment in building their own knowledge economies.

Sanjay Pradhan
Vice-President for Change, Leadership & Innovation
The World Bank Group

Acknowledgments

This report is the result of collaboration of several organizations and individuals. A small team of experts coordinated by Ramboll Management Consulting Oy carried out the research and writing of the report. The team was headed by Kimmo Halme and members included Tarmo Lemola, Katri Haila, Kimmo Viljamaa, Kalle Piirainen, Kaisa Lähteenmäki-Smith, Vesa Salminen, and Hannes Toivanen (VTT Technical Research Centre of Finland). Luke Gheorghiou (Manchester Business School), Minna Halme (Aalto University Finland) and Petri Rouvinen (Research Institute of the Finnish Economy ETLA) reviewed the interim content. The WBI team responsible for completion of the report consisted Kurt Larsen, Justine White, Derek Chen, Natalia Agapitova, Ilari Lindy, and Adela Antic under the guidance of Yugandhar Raj Nallari.

An international advisory board formed by Marko Laiho (Ministry of Employment and the Economy), Bengt-Åke Lundvall (University of Aalborg/ Sciences-Po Paris), Stefano Negri (The World Bank), Jyrki Pulkkinen (Finnish Ministry for Foreign Affairs), Pekka Ylä-Anttila (Research Institute of the Finnish Economy ETLA), Reinhilde Veugelers (Katholieke Universiteit Leuven), and Tiina Vihma-Purovaara (Ministry of Education & Culture) provided valuable guidance and direction to the authors. The scope, focus, and content of the report were extensively discussed, debated, and reviewed in regular feedback sessions throughout the writing process. The clarity and focus of the final report is very much a result of the thoughtful input by the advisory board.

The content was presented for discussion in several events including SAIS workshop organized in the context of InfoDev Global Forum 2013, South Africa; "The Road from R&D to Commercialization—Better Productivity Better Jobs" organized by FPD Mena Region in Cambridge, the United Kingdom; "Making Growth Happen: Implementing Policies for Industries" organized by FPD/ITE practice in Washington D.C. and in "Case Study: Knowledge & Learning Workshop" organized by KDI School & WBI in Seoul, South Korea. Comments to the drafts from the users' perspective were provided by Dr. Tran Ngoc Ca (National Council for S&T Policy Vietnam) and Laurens Cloete (CSIR Meraka Institute South Africa) as well as Esperanza Lasagabaster from the World Bank. Timothy John Charles Kelly, Natasha Kapil, and Anubha Verma all from the World Bank reviewed the text through the lens of technical experts focusing on key sectors, namely information communications technologies, innovation policy, and education.

Acknowledgement is extended to Carl J. Dahlman, Jorma Routti, and Pekka Ylä-Anttila who were the editors of the first "Finland as a Knowledge Economy: Elements of Success and Lessons Learned" report published by the World Bank Institute in 2006. The authors are also grateful for the administrative support of the World Bank Institute partnership team including Seth Ayers and Ellen De Vreede as well as Johanna Karanko, Markku Kauppinen, Matti Kiisseli, and Laura Torvinen from the Ministry for Foreign Affairs of Finland. Publication and dissemination process was managed by Stephen McGroarty, Paola Scalabrin, and Rumit Pancholi from the Publishing & Knowledge Division of the World Bank, while Elizabeth R. Forsyth did proofreading and editing of the final manuscript.

The book was co-financed by the World Bank Institute and Finnish Ministry for Foreign Affairs. Final acknowledgement goes to those numerous colleagues and individuals from the World Bank staff, public and private sectors, academia, and civil society whose insights and comments have guided and inspired the thinking of the authors throughout the project.

Contributors

About the Authors

Katri Haila works as a senior consultant at the Ramboll Management Consulting. Her areas of expertise include evaluation, science, technology, and innovation policies, and biosciences. Recently, she has worked on a number of projects concerning the Finnish science and innovation system, for example, a study on the Finnish strategic centers for science, technology, and innovation (SHOK), an evaluation of the Technical Research Centre (VTT) of Finland an evaluation of Finnish participation in the European Union's Sixth Framework Programme, and evaluation of Finland's National Fund for Research and Development (Sitra) and its programs. In 2004–06, she was the Head of the Evaluation Office of the research assessment exercise of the University of Helsinki. In 1999–2003, she worked at the Academy of Finland on science administration and science policy. In the 1990s, she undertook different posts as a researcher and teacher at the University of Helsinki and in Denmark. Haila has published 44 publications, of which 11 peer reviewed scientific articles in international journals.

Kimmo Halme is the managing director of Ramboll Management Consulting in Finland. He has more than 20 years of experience in the design, management, and evaluation of innovation policy–related activities at the international, national, and regional levels. Halme has in-depth experience in Finnish innovation policy planning, governance, and implementation mechanisms, having earlier worked for the Science and Technology Policy Council of Finland. He worked as a consultant and an innovation policy expert for the European Commission, the Organisation for Economic Co-operation and Development, the European Research Area and Innovation Committee, the United Nations Industrial Development Organization, the European Parliament, and the World Bank, among others.

Kaisa Lähteenmäki-Smith has worked on research and development (R&D) and evaluation projects in the Finnish public sector since finalizing her PhD in political science at Turku University in 1999. She has focused on program management, evaluation, and governance issues for research and innovation policies, as well as territorial aspects of policies. Between 2000 and 2007,

Lähteenmäki-Smith worked on Nordic issues and European evaluations at Nordregio, Stockholm, and thereafter as a consultant at Net Effect Ltd. and Ramboll Management Consulting, Helsinki. In her evaluation projects, she has developed assessments for the evaluation of strategic centers for science, technology, and innovation (SHOK) in Finland (2012–13), the Finnish National Fund for Research and Development (Sitra, 2010–11), evaluation of three research, development, and innovation programs implemented in collaboration with Portuguese universities and research organizations and universities in the United States (2011), the Technical Research Centre (VTT) (2010). From November 2013 until October 2014, she is working on an assignment establishing a new funding instrument for policy-relevant strategic research in the Prime Minister's Office, Finland.

Tarmo Lemola is a senior advisor of Ramboll Management Consulting, Finland. He has worked as the director and chairman of the board of a Finnish consulting company, Advansis Ltd., and as the director of the Group for Technology Studies at Finland's Technical Research Centre (VTT). As a researcher and consultant, he has been working on technology foresight, monitoring and evaluation of science, technology, and innovation (STI) policy, development of innovation systems at international, national, sectoral, regional, and local levels, as well as design and management of STI instruments. Lemola's expertise has been used by the European Commission, Organisation for Economic Co-operation and Development, the World Bank, and governments and regional authorities in Finland and other European countries, emerging economies in Latin America (Chile, Peru, Uruguay), Asia (Vietnam), and Africa (South Africa, Tanzania). He has published several books and articles on innovation, STI policy, and related topics. Lemola holds a master of science in social sciences from the University of Helsinki. He has been a visiting scholar at Stanford University.

Kalle A. Piirainen works currently as a postdoctoral researcher on a cluster development project in the North Sea offshore wind service sector. His main areas of expertise are innovation and technology management and foresight as well as research, development, and innovation (RDI) policy. Piirainen holds a doctor of science, accepted with honors, from Lappeenranta University of Technology in technology and innovation management.

Vesa Salminen is a consultant at Ramboll Management Consulting, Finland. Salminen has focused on evaluating the implementation and effectiveness of different funding instruments and programs, especially in the field of research, development, and innovation policy.

Hannes Toivanen is a principal scientist at the Technical Research Centre of Finland (VTT) in the Knowledge Economy and Innovation unit. At VTT, he leads research groups that investigate globalization of innovation, innovation in the emerging economies and developing countries, and quantitative analysis of science and technology. He was a Fulbright fellow during 2000–2004 and received his PhD from the Georgia Institute of Technology in 2004. He previously worked at the Finnish Ministry of Employment and the Economy and the Lappeenranta University of Technology, where he continues to serve as an adjunct professor. Toivanen has more than 15 years of experience in Finnish and several European innovation systems, as well as international organizations, including the European Commission, Organisation for Economic Co-operation and Development, United Nations Economic Commission for Africa, the African Union Commission, the World Bank Group, and several African countries as well as Brazil. He served as the European co-chair for the joint expert group in support of the information society track of the Africa–European Union partnership for 2011–12 and advises governments on innovation, information and communication technology, and development.

About the Co-Authors

Kalle Lamminmäki works as an analyst at Ramboll Management Consulting, specializing in regional policy, regional development, and innovation policy. Lamminmäki's responsibilities cover evaluations, studies, and impact assessments.

Maria Merisalo works in Ramboll Management Consulting as a consultant. She has experience in public management, especially municipality mergers, service development and electronic governance, and knowledge economy, knowledge-based development, information society, and knowledge work. Her doctoral study (degree in progress) is related to electronic governance and social media.

Kimmo Viljamaa works as a business development manager for the City of Vantaa, Finland. He has participated in several Finnish and international research and development projects in the field of research, innovation, and economic development policy. He also worked for several years as the Finnish country correspondent for the European Union information service on national research and innovation policies.

Key Definitions

Knowledge economy. As distinct from agrarian, resource-based, or traditional industrial economies, a knowledge economy is essentially driven by the creation, distribution, and use of knowledge and information. In this respect, it reflects the latest stage of development in the evolution of modern economies, often characterized by an increased use of ICT, globalization, active networking, and various forms of innovation.

Innovation policy. Innovation is the application of new solutions that meet emerging requirements, unarticulated or existing market needs. This is accomplished through more effective products, processes, services, technologies, solutions, or ideas that are available to markets, governments, and society. Hence innovation policy consists of all those policy actions that aim to help individuals, companies, and any other organization to perform better and therefore that contribute to wider social objectives such as growth, jobs, and sustainability.

Innovation policy tools. Typical innovation policy tools include supporting education, science, and research, building conducive framework conditions (such as intellectual property rights), facilitating access to finance, benchmarking policy, and stimulating collaboration and demand for innovations through standards, regulations, and public procurement.

Innovation systems and ecosystems. Innovation systems are concepts for understanding the dynamics and collaborative nature of innovation in societies and economies. According to innovation system theory, innovation is the result of a complex set of relationships among actors in the system, including enterprises, universities, research institutes, and government. Innovation systems are often observed at the national, regional, and local levels or at sectoral or technological levels.

The systemic nature of the environment for innovation is sometimes referred to an innovation ecosystem, highlighting its uncoordinated or autonomous character and the amorphous nature of system development.

Abbreviations

ACE	Aalto Center for Entrepreneurship
BOP	bottom of the pyramid (also base of the pyramid)
BRICS	Brazil, Russia, India, China, and South Africa
COFISA	Cooperation Framework on Innovation Systems between Finland and South Africa
ECTS	European Credit Transfer and Accumulation System (a standard for comparing the attainment and performance of students of higher education)
ELY Centers	centers for economic development, transport, and the environment
ETLA	Research Institute of the Finnish Economy (Finland)
EU	European Union
FINHEEC	Finnish Higher Education Evaluation Council
FISC	Finnish Information Security Cluster
GDP	gross domestic product
HDI	Human Development Index
ICT	information and communication technology
INKA	Innovative Cities
IS	information society
IT	information technology
MEE	Ministry of Employment and the Economy (Finland)
OECD	Organisation for Economic Co-operation and Development
PISA	Program for International Student Assessment
R&D	research and development
RDI	research, development, and innovation
RIC	Research and Innovation Council (Finland)
SADe	Action Program on eServices and eDemocracy
SHOK	strategic centers for science, technology, and innovation
Sitra	National Fund for Research and Development (Finland)
SLL	Siyhakhula Living Lab (South Africa)

SME	small and medium enterprise
STI	science, technology, and innovation
STPC	Science and Technology Policy Council (Finland)
Tekes	the Finnish Funding Agency for Innovation
TINTO	RIC Action Plan
VTT	Technical Research Centre (Finland)

Overview

Finland is known for its consistent economic progress, competitiveness, and egalitarian society. Yet the challenges experienced by Finland at the beginning of the twentieth century are similar to those experienced by many countries today. Finland emerged as an independent nation in the midst of international economic and political turbulence. In spite of its remoteness, relatively scarce natural resources, small domestic market, and recent history of wars and social cleavages, Finland transformed itself from an agriculture-based economy in the 1950s to one of the leading innovation-driven, knowledge-based economies and high-tech producers of the twenty-first century. The development was rapid and involved determined action and sometimes drastic decisions by the government and other key actors.

Finland as a Knowledge Economy 2.0 presents some of the key policies, elements, initiatives, and decisions behind Finland's path to becoming a knowledge economy of today. It aims to provide readers with inspiration, ideas, and insights that may prove valuable in another context. The authors have identified six areas of lessons, described in chapters 3 through 8 (see also figure O.1). The report should not be seen as a scientific, all-encompassing study, but rather as a "knowledge economy cookbook," with cases, links, and insights provided for further exploration. This Overview presents the key issues and findings of the full report organized by chapters.

Figure O.1 Areas of Lessons

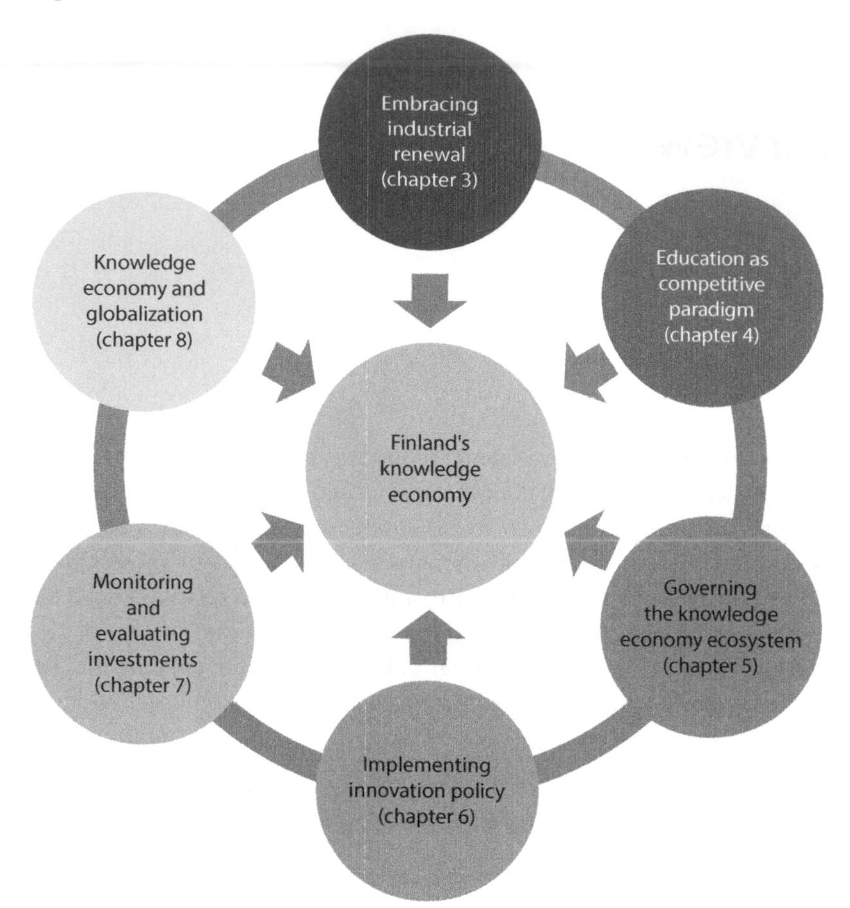

Introduction: Finland's Economic Transition

Industrial Transformation until the 1990s

Within the European context, Finland was among the late developers. In the mid-nineteenth century, Finland—an autonomous grand duchy of Russia between 1809 and 1917—was a backward agrarian economy with approximately 1.6 million people. The mid-nineteenth century marked the beginning of Finnish industrialization and brought about key reforms in infrastructure, banking, education, and financial institutions.

During the interwar years, Finland was catching up with the Western economies. However, these years were marked by national, political, and social dispersion, which culminated in civil war in 1918. The country was divided along the lines of the conflict and was reunited only during the Second World War. As late as the 1950s, Finland, recovering from the war, was still an agriculture-based economy. Substantial war reparations—largely paid in the form of goods as well as machinery, equipment, and vessels—provided the impetus for industrialization during the postwar years. Postwar industrialization and the rise of the welfare state help to explain why Finland was able to raise the education levels of the population and to become one of the most educated countries in the world. Since then, social cohesion has remained high, the policy environment predictable, and basic infrastructure in good condition. The seeds for transition to knowledge intensive economy were planted at the time.

The early 1990s were characterized by the collapse of the Soviet Union and a national economic crisis in Finland. The recession Finland suffered was particularly deep for two reasons. First, the Soviet Union was its main export market for consumer goods, so the collapse affected large portions of the Finnish economy. Second, financial crises hit the overheated Finnish economy, which took steps to liberalize financial markets, resulting in major credit defaults and a banking crisis.

Against this background, the 1990s marked a turning point in the shift from an investment-driven to a more innovation-driven economy. Important decisions affecting the future of the economy were also made during these troubled years. First, the economy was opened up in an effort to reposition Finland in the world market. Second, more emphasis was placed on microeconomic policies to enhance competitiveness. Third, the newly established Science and Technology Policy Council (STPC) set an agenda for economic growth led by information and communication technology (ICT) and for creation a "national innovation system." As a consequence of the STPC agenda, more funding was made available for research and development (R&D) and higher education institutions.

Role of the ICT Sector and RDI Investments

During the recession in the 1990s, public investments were targeted at the ICT sector, as mobile communications were among the few sectors growing at the time. These decisions were made in the midst of a severe economic crisis, when the government implemented austerity measures, cutting all other public expenditures except those for education and for research, development, and innovation (RDI). Later on, these decisions proved to be instrumental in enabling growth of the ICT sector. From the mid-1990s onward, Finland enjoyed extraordinary growth (figure O.2). The ICT sector, with Nokia as its flagship, was at the center of this development.

The Finnish government had taken an active role in developing digital and mobile communications in the 1970s and 1980s. During these decades, the state invested heavily in the development of domestic technology and production capabilities through funding for collaborative research involving private enterprises, public agencies, and universities. The state also had a role in expanding university degree programs in electronics and information technology and in directing technologically demanding government procurement to domestic firms (Sabel and Saxenian 2008, 55). Moreover, the ICT sector benefited from public financial support as well as the extensive collaboration among public research institutes, state technology agencies, universities and other educational institutions, and private companies. As this development work coincided with the opening of the Nordic telephone markets (the first in the world, followed by the European and global telephone markets), the Finnish ICT sector (especially Nokia) was in an

Figure O.2 GDP Growth (Expenditure Approach) in Finland and OECD-Europe, 1971–2011

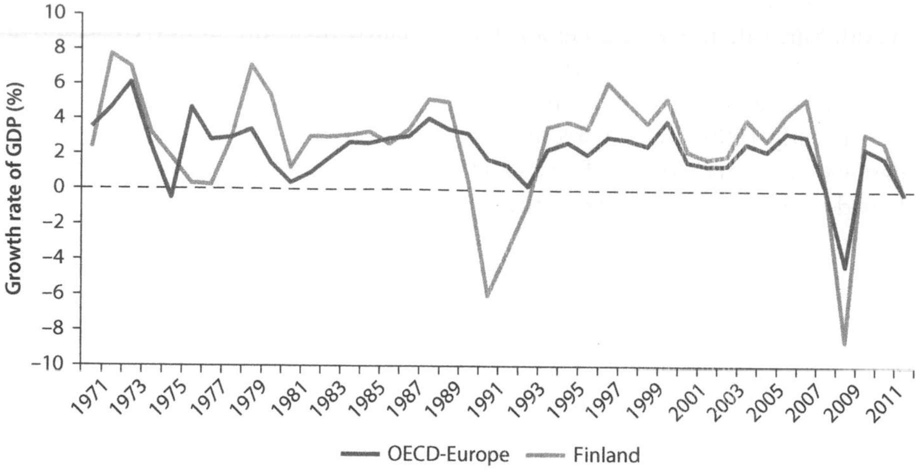

Source: OECD data (stats.oecd.org).

advantageous position (Sabel and Saxenian 2008, 55). The government had a clear role both as a developer of technology (government as client) and, primarily, as a creator of conditions (infrastructure, funding, and regulation).

The New Knowledge Economy

The main characteristics of Finland's economic development in the 20 years leading up to the worldwide economic crisis in 2008 were radical increases in intangible investments (education, RDI, and the organization of work) and the comprehensive building of the national base of knowledge. These contributed to increasing productivity, redirecting and refocusing employment into more productive and knowledge-intensive sectors, and more efficient use of financial resources. The miraculous growth of the Nokia-led electronics industry to become Finland's largest industrial sector and biggest exporter is the best-known example from these years. However, electronics and ICT were not the only sectors that developed during this time. Practically all industrial and other sectors improved productivity, developed new products, and increased their exports.

For the past few years, Nokia's phone business had been declining rapidly due to the growing importance of the smartphone segment, where competitors like Apple and Samsung caught Nokia by surprise. In the summer of 2013, Nokia sold its mobile phone business to Microsoft at a significantly lower price than its value only a few years prior. At this point, many questions were raised about what would happen to Finland's knowledge economy and whether Finnish policies had been too focused on a few leading industrial sectors.

Luckily the ecosystem is broader and deeper than just one company or industry. During the last few years, the Finnish ICT sector has moved from manufacturing products to producing services and software. Hardware production has been transferred to low-cost countries, while the knowledge-intensive expertise

Figure O.3 Employment in Primary and Secondary Production and Services as a Percentage of Total Employment in Finland, 1900–2010

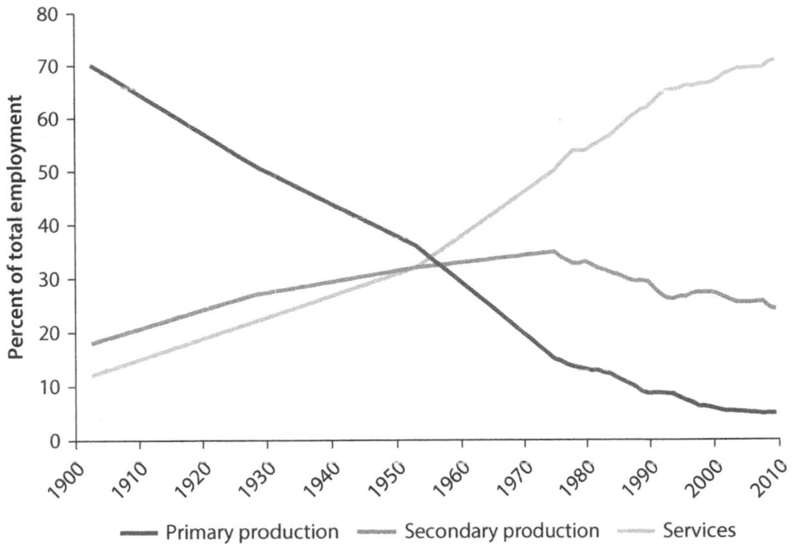

Source: Pajarinen, Rouvinen, and Ylä-Anttila 2012.

requiring higher education has maintained its position or even grown. The traditional manufacturing industries, especially machinery and equipment, have undergone a similar transformation, and many leading enterprises focus on both services and tangible products (figure O.3).

Background: Evolution of Finland's Knowledge Economy Policy (Chapter 2)

The development of the Finnish knowledge economy has gone through different phases, each with its own foundations, objectives, actors, and instruments (table O.1). Most of the key policy decisions behind this development were made in the mid-1960s, and initiated an era of *reform of basic structures* of education and R&D followed by an era of *technology push* with a focus on intensive development and use of ICT. This period of optimism, national networking, and robust economic development ended unexpectedly when the Finnish economy plunged into an exceptionally severe crisis in the early 1990s. From a knowledge economy point of view, the era started in the late 1990s was characterized by attempts to get Finland *out of recession*. *Globalization* began in the early 2000s and still dominates thinking on knowledge economy policy and operations in Finland today.

Is there a Finnish model of innovation policy or a formula for success in innovation-driven economic development? There is, but with a couple of provisos. First, Finland's success is not only or mainly thanks to government policy and intervention. Finnish companies have been at the forefront of innovation-driven development. Second, Finland's history, culture, administrative traditions,

Table O.1 Phases of Development of the Finnish Knowledge Economy

Indicator	*Reform of basic structures (1960–)*	*Technology push (1980–)*	*Out of recession (1990s)*	*Knowledge economy in a globalizing world (2000–)*
Foundations for policy operations	Liberalization of international trade	"Microelectronic revolution"	Recovery from recession	Globalization
Main objectives	Creation of a new policy sector	Use of new technological opportunities	Intensification of knowledge-based growth	Creation of growth companies
Focus of policies	Education, science	Technology	National innovation system	Innovation, innovation ecosystems
Key actors	Ministry of Education and Culture, Academy of Finland	Tekes (Funding Agency for Technology and Innovation)	STPC	Several actors
Expected outcomes or impacts	National competitiveness	Growth in high-tech products	Growth in employment	New innovative growth companies
Level of intervention	National	National, regional	Regional, transnational (European Union)	National, local
Representative instrument	Project financing	National technology programs	European Union sources of R&D financing	Strategic centers for science, technology, and innovation (SHOKs)

Box O.1 Key Messages from Chapter 2

- Major economic transitions and renewals in industrial structures and public and private institutions are possible, but usually require strong political will and consensus among stakeholders. Such a joint commitment is usually triggered by necessity in times of economic turbulence or crisis. Hence economic crisis also provides an opportunity to initiate change and renewal.
- Achieving economic transition takes time, patience, long-term vision, and consistency from all stakeholders of the knowledge economy.
- The transitions in the Finnish system have been driven by largely by private sector needs, in close collaboration with the government. The government has had an important role as a coordinator and facilitator of change, as well as a builder of shared platforms for making decisions and setting priorities for the knowledge economy.
- Finland has monitored closely how more advanced countries are performing and what can be learned from their development. To a large extent, Finland has adopted its policy doctrines and institutional and organizational models from other organizations and countries.
- Making progress toward a knowledge economy has many positive side effects. A full-fledged welfare state is very much supportive of, or even based on, technological innovation, with development of an information society, and a dynamic, competitive society.
- Due to national characteristics, no one-size-fits-all solutions exist, However, there are areas where interesting lessons can be drawn.

political contexts, and industrialization process have influenced the country's policy and approach. However, Finland has adopted policy doctrines and institutional and organizational models largely from other organizations and countries. Third, because innovation policies have to address competition in a globalized world, innovation policies of various countries are becoming more alike. Good practices, not to mention "best practices," are moving fast from country to country. Innovation policies of nation states are converging.

The role of government has been important and even central in some cases, but all in all, the Finnish system has not been strongly government led. It has been very much company led and company centered. The government has mainly been a coordinator, a facilitator, and a builder of shared platforms for making decisions and setting priorities for R&D. Box O.1 presents the key messages from chapter 2.

Embracing Industrial Renewal (Chapter 3)

As a small, knowledge-based economy, Finland has been increasingly subject to global influence and international competition. In addition to its strengths, Finland faces considerable challenges both domestically and internationally in an effort to maintain its position in world markets. Global competition has intensified significantly, and emerging economies are challenging Finland's role as a competence- and knowledge-driven economy. These challenges are the subject of chapter 3.

The Finnish ICT sector has changed from manufacturing products (hardware) toward producing services (software, digital services). As noted, hardware production has been transferred to low-cost countries, while the role of knowledge-intensive expertise requiring higher education has maintained its position or even grown (Hernesniemi 2010).

What remains of the ICT sector after this structural change? First, despite structural changes and a heavy loss of jobs in some sectors (and geographic regions), the ICT sector is still strong in Finland. In fact, due to growth in software and ICT services, the ICT sector remains a significant employer (figure O.4).

A good example is the rapidly growing game industry, with its two leading companies, Rovio and Supercell, the latter of which is a company established in 2010 and sold to Japanese investors for around US$1.5 billion (approximately a third of Nokia's selling price) in November 2013. Although this industry is still

Figure O.4 Employment in the ICT Sector in Finland, by Subcategories, 1990–2012

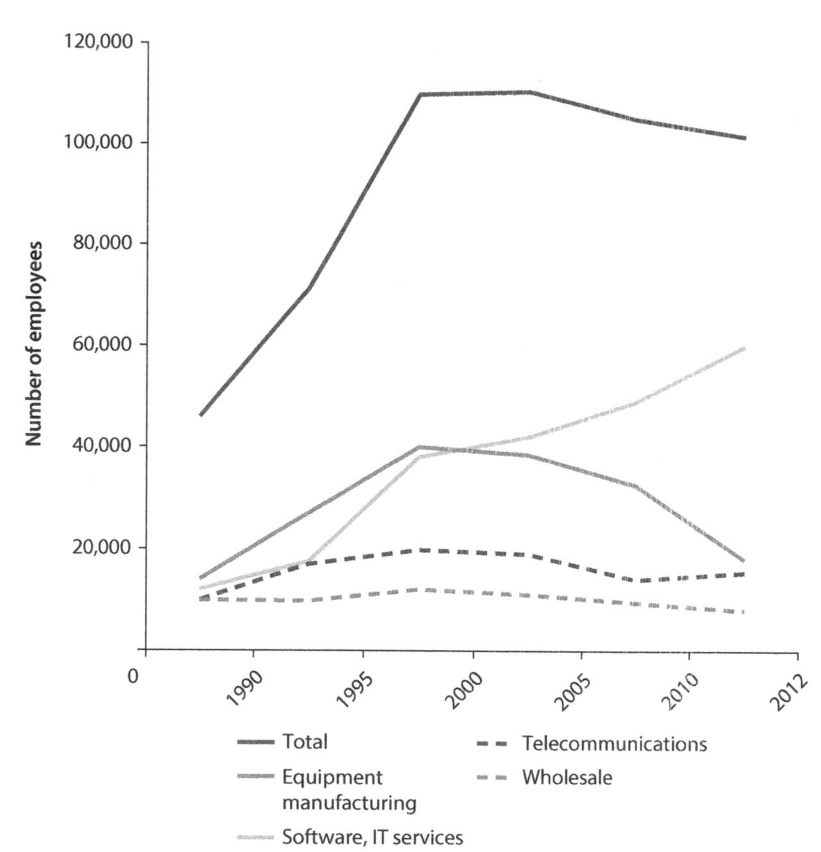

Sources: Based on Ali-Yrkkö *et al.* 2013; Statistics Finland data (https://www.tilastokeskus.fi/index_en.html).

young (average age three years), it is growing quickly, at around 200 percent in 2012 and with an estimated turnover of €800 million in 2013 (€250 million in 2012). Moreover, multinational corporations such as Electronic Arts, Ericsson, Google, Huawei, Intel, Microsoft, and Samsung have established part of their operations or R&D in Finland. For software and game industries, Finland is being called the next Silicon Valley, but this remains to be realized.

The key message of chapter 3 is that crises and structural transformations occur, affecting all economies that are integrated into the global markets. Hence, understanding global trends and seeing changes as opportunities are important for policy planning. The fortunes of countries are determined by how they prepare for and respond to the challenges. What is important in such times of change is that national systems (research, innovation, education, economic policy) are prepared and ready for the upcoming transformation. A country should not emphasize a single sector of the economy without preparing for alternative scenarios. Conditions that promote and support entrepreneurship are hard to create through direct state action, but, as this report shows, the public sector can create a desirable climate that supports multifaceted forms of entrepreneurship and encourages novel innovative companies to seek international growth. Hands-on examples of how this has been addressed in Finland are illustrated through cases on collaborative initiative Innovation Mill, the business accelerator Vigo, and the open innovation platform Demola. Box O.2 presents the key messages from chapter 3.

Box O.2 Key Messages from Chapter 3

- All open economies are increasingly subject to global influence and international competition. This is particularly true for small, knowledge-based economies. The objective is not to avoid competition, but to improve and sustain competitiveness. Hence understanding global development trends and seeing changes as opportunities are important for policy planning. Countries should seek and be prepared for constant economic renewal.
- Improving the overall productivity of the economy and building its competitiveness and attractiveness for investors is a long-term process. In general, the relevant planning horizon should be a few decades rather than a few years, and there are no obvious shortcuts.
- Several characteristics are typical of this transformation (such as the increase in intangible investments and knowledge-based services) and can be used to indicate stages of change, progress, or development.
- Sometimes changes in technological paradigms offer opportunities for fast growth. ICT, in broad terms, has played an important role in Finland's transformation to a knowledge economy. During the 1990s, Finland was able to support the tremendous growth of the ICT sector and harness it to develop the knowledge economy. ICT still plays an important, but not an instrumental, role in the Finnish economy.

Education as Competitive Paradigm (Chapter 4)

Investment in education is the basis for the knowledge economy. In order to build a foundation for the education system, Finland has systematically and heavily invested in education since its independence. Besides this "big picture," key elements of the Finnish educational success include legislation, guidance, teacher education, and a comprehensive education system.

Competent teachers are the starting point of a high-quality education. Teaching is an attractive profession in Finland. Only 10 percent of all applicants are accepted to pursue degrees in teacher education. Teachers are highly educated and highly respected.

Education is available to everyone. All citizens are offered equal opportunities to receive an education regardless of age, domicile, financial situation, sex, or mother tongue. Education is provided free-of-charge at all levels, from pre-primary to higher education. Women are highly educated, and there are no separate schools for males and females.

Basic education is a comprehensive concept. Basic education includes school materials, school meals, health care, and dental care, all free-of-charge.

The school network is regionally extensive. Finnish education is of uniform quality irrespective of the location of the school. The local authorities have a statutory duty to provide basic education for children living in the municipality. Most pupils attend the nearest school.

The Finnish education system focuses on lifelong learning. This means that Finns may continue their studies at an upper level of education after the obligatory level has been completed. There are no dead ends in education.

Educational achievement among the population is high. Finland's population is highly educated, and the employment rate is especially high among highly educated people. In 2010, 69 percent of the population 15 to 64 years of age were employed. Approximately 84 percent of persons with tertiary-level degrees were employed. The employment rate of those with polytechnic and higher-level university degrees is at record levels. For example, in 2010 more than 90 percent of doctors were employed.

The governance of the education system has developed from control toward autonomy. Autonomy is high at all levels of education. School inspections, were important for the development of Finnish schools, but they were stopped in the 1990s. Quality assurance is now based on objectives laid out in legislation, the national core curriculum, and qualification requirements. In Finland, educators have a statutory duty to evaluate their own activities and participate in external evaluations.

In the future, actions are needed to address the needs of the aging population, enhance the efficiency of the education system, speed up transition points, and shorten study periods. The increasingly global labor market calls for closer international cooperation to develop models to anticipate future needs for education and skills. Moreover, better entrepreneurship education is needed at all levels. Box O.3 presents the key messages from chapter 4.

Box O.3 Key Messages from Chapter 4

- A strong educational base is the backbone of a knowledge economy.
- Finnish education policy emphasizes comprehensiveness and equality (regardless of age, domicile, financial situation, sex, or mother tongue). A knowledge economy needs a vast pool of educated professionals.
- Quick results should not be expected: improving the educational base requires systematic and long-term investments.
- Competent teachers are the starting point for a successful education system.
- A strong legal basis and effective steering—without weakening the autonomy of schools—are important in guaranteeing a high quality of education.
- The education needs of an economy and society can change relatively rapidly: the education system should be flexible and able to adjust quickly. Opportunities for lifelong learning should be supported and promoted at all education levels.
- Promoting entrepreneurial elements in all areas of education and encouraging the interplay between businesses and education are increasingly vital.

Governing the Knowledge Economy Ecosystem (Chapter 5)

For a small country with relatively limited resources, Finland has an inherent need to pool scarce resources both across sectors and ministries and across the public and private sectors. This requires consensus and collaboration among all actors, from strategic-level agenda setting to hands-on governance. One of the key characteristics of Finland's approach to development of a knowledge economy has been its systemic, coordinated, and engaging approach to an education, research, and innovation policy agenda.

There is a broad consensus that the success of the country depends on its ability to create and use new information, to build high-quality technological and business competence, and to understand markets. Consequently, Finland has chosen to invest in developing knowledge and know-how. Moreover, the development of education, research, technology, and innovation has been a "national project." One of the key strengths of the policy agenda has been the persistence of a long-term policy from government to government.

In addition to strong R&D- and ICT-oriented activities, which dominated the strategy earlier, a more horizontal approach has been taken for innovation activities covering all of society. In this approach, the key to building a successful knowledge economy is combining material, intellectual, and social capital.

From the agenda-setting perspective, a few issues are important. First, achieving a wide consensus in support of the national strategy of making Finland a knowledge economy has been important. Consensus has been maintained for the past two decades, and the basic approach has been relatively stable as successive governments have assumed power. Despite significant budget cuts in recent years, the relative importance of education, research, and innovation policies has remained stable.

Second, the long-term perspective is visible in how the government, parliament, and different agencies use forward-planning (foresight) processes to support policy making. Foresight is used to guide not only individual policies but also the broad national agenda. This is a definite strength of the Finnish approach.

Third, the strong coordination of education, research, and innovation policy at the national, strategic level, especially through a high-level coordination body—the Research and Innovation Council—has significantly enhanced the development of Finland's knowledge economy. Box O.4 presents the main actors and institutions in this process.

Box O.4 Actors and Institutions in the Finnish Knowledge Economy

The actors and institutions of the Finnish knowledge economy can be divided into three rough categories: (a) those responsible for setting policy and strategy, (b) those responsible for providing funding and support ("enablers"), and (c) research and education institutions (see figure BO.4.1). There are also different types of "platforms" for facilitating the collaboration of various actors.

The *Research and Innovation Council* is responsible for the strategic development and coordination of Finnish science and technology policy as well as the national innovation system as a whole. It is chaired by the prime minister and comprises all key ministries and representatives from various actors.

Sitra is an independent public foundation, or think tank, reporting directly to the Finnish parliament. *Tekes*—the Funding Agency for Technology and Innovation—is responsible for financing R&D and innovation activities (for both companies and research institutions). It reports to the Ministry of Employment and the Economy. The *Academy of Finland* is responsible for funding academic research and reports to the Ministry of Education and Culture. *Finnvera* provides banking and loan services for companies seeking to grow and internationalize. Its affiliates—*Veraventure* (funds), *Seed Fund Vera* (direct investments), and *Finnish Industry Investment*—provide public venture capital investments to private equity funds and companies. The *15 centers for economic development, transport, and the environment* (*ELY centers)* are responsible for the regional implementation and development tasks of the central government. They handle financing and development services for enterprises and employment-based aid and labor market training. *Finpro* and *Team Finland* promote trade, investments, and internalization of companies abroad.

Research and education institutions include close to 20 *public research organizations*—for example, the Technical Research Centre (VTT), Statistics Finland, and the Finnish Environment

box continues next page

Box O.4 Actors and Institutions in the Finnish Knowledge Economy *(continued)*

Figure BO.4.1 Finnish Knowledge Economy System

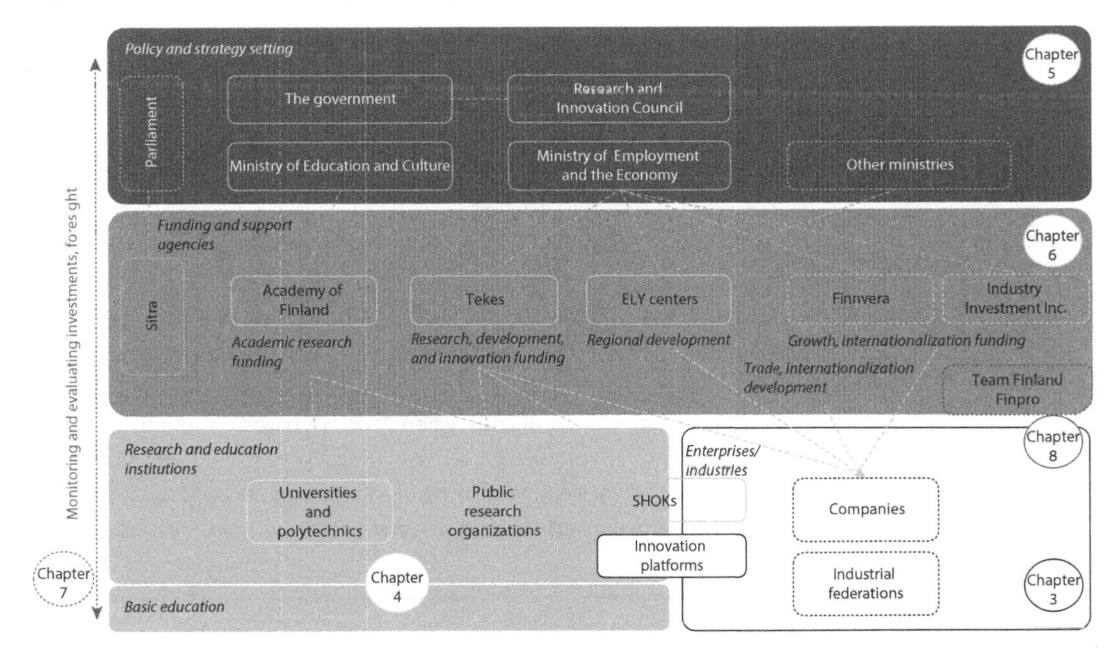

Institute—as well as 14 *universities* and 25 *polytechnics*. The *strategic centers for science, technology, and innovation (SHOKs)* are public-private partnerships for speeding up innovation processes and bringing together academic research and private R&D activities. The Innovative Cities (INKA) program aims to create internationally attractive local innovation hubs and to intensify cooperation between the public and private sectors.

A list of actors appears at the end of the report.

A fourth key aspect is the emphasis on integrating education policy into the national strategy. Education has been a high priority in terms of both the high levels of education attained by the population as well as the high-quality basic education that is available for everybody. Box O.5 presents the key messages of chapter 5.

Implementing Innovation Policy (Chapter 6)

Knowledge economy policies spread across different sectors, and putting them efficiently into practice, requires an effective organizational structure and appropriate policy instruments. In Finland, the policy-making role of ministries has been separated from the "professional implementing role" of agencies and their specific instruments.

Finnish innovation policy is built on a model of decentralized implementation, although financial resources are relatively centralized (in particular

Box O.5 Key Messages from Chapter 5

- The Finnish approach to governing the knowledge economy emphasizes the importance of having a shared vision of the future and a collaborative policy-planning process, as well as stakeholder engagement in all parts of the process. This approach is likely to enhance the consistency, stability, and predictability of policies, too.
- Finland is a small country, and the scarcity of available resources further highlights the importance of a broad consensus, collaborative preparation, and stakeholder engagement on a strategic level. Also the adoption of a long-term perspective and the integration of education policy in the national strategy are crucial.
- An implicit challenge is the question of whether an approach based on strong consensus allows sufficient "out-of-the-box" thinking—hence the emergence of radical changes and innovations and, equally, radical decision making when such is needed. Bold political decisions are typically made during times of crisis, when decisions based on consensus are not sufficient.
- Putting a broad-based strategy into practice requires systemic and engaging practices and processes for coordinating across ministries as well as within individual policy sectors.

through Tekes). For a geographically diverse country, this model of centralized financing is probably the most feasible and ensures a strategic overview.

While the concentration of resources is important in light of their increasing scarcity, and efficiency and effectiveness are important assessment criteria, the diversity and multiple sources of innovation are clearly valued in Finland. Multiple funding modes and sources are likely to contribute to the diversity and viability of the research and innovation community; for this reason, implementation should not be streamlined excessively. Tekes and the Academy of Finland have different strategies, and rightly so, but to ensure the best use of all sources of innovation and expertise, dialogue and close collaboration between them are essential.

The dualism between industrial and academic interests has been dealt with largely through the distribution of responsibility between Tekes and the Academy of Finland, as exemplified by the centers of excellence, the SHOKs, for instance. If academic and industrial interests are to be reconciled, this should be attempted through the implementation of programs and projects; in this area, SHOKs have been the first test case, where the two sources of financing and the two strategies could meet. This is still very much a work in progress, but providing sufficient financial incentives as well as opening the relevant governance structures to both parties are means of achieving this. The Research and Innovation Council can play a key role here.

The degree of Finnish government intervention is traditionally high, though not without debate. Main issues have involved the nature of intervention and the

Box O.6 Key Messages from Chapter 6

- An essential element of Finnish policy implementation has been in finding and keeping a good balance between science, research, and innovation funding and policy implementation, with respect to the following: (1) private financing vs. public funding, (2) competitive vs. basic funding of research organizations, (3) top-down (strategic) vs. bottom-up (free) funding, as well as (4) centralized (national) vs. decentralized (regional or provincial) funding and implementation.
- In Finland, policy making related to the knowledge economy has been separated from policy implementation. The latter function has been given to implementation agencies, with sufficient professional experience and a set of instruments. Such a clear distinction between roles and responsibilities has proven to be an effective way to implement policy and ensure that all aspects and policy objectives are pursued.
- The Finnish SHOKs provide an interesting example of an attempt to combine the objectives of organizing large-scale public-private partnerships with strong industrial leadership, strong strategic prioritization with high scientific ambitions, as well as development of long-term competence with medium-term industrial renewal.

extent to which government should restrain itself to dealing with market failure or indeed involve itself in a more proactive role, even picking winners. SHOKs are illustrative in this regard: the structure is clearly more encompassing than selective, enabling the ability of committed actors and organizations within the RDI system, from companies to research organizations, to determine success.

The overlapping roles of expert organizations and public authorities have continued to be a source of lively debate. While the Finnish system is far from perfect, the Finnish experiences provide ample lessons learned with regard to the need for transparency, for clear roles and responsibilities, as well as for striking a balance between implementation (chapter 6), planning and guidance (chapter 5), as well as monitoring and evaluation (chapter 7). Box O.6 presents the key messages from chapter 6.

Monitoring and Evaluating Investments (Chapter 7)

For policy making to be effective, policies have to be well focused and implemented efficiently. In practice, improving the effectiveness of policies is realized largely through systematic monitoring and evaluation and the willingness of policy makers to learn and understand from their own and others' experiences and to adapt policies accordingly. Moreover, monitoring and evaluation are crucial for transparency and legitimacy of the whole system.

Policy learning is a part of Finnish policy making at different levels, from the institutional to the individual. Perhaps the most important way of learning is to conduct periodic evaluations of different institutions and programs.

While Finnish policy-learning practice may not be theoretically or technically perfect, the system and practices have developed over time. By taking a big-picture perspective and developing national statistics, assessment of the big picture of the innovation system lays important groundwork for developing more intricate monitoring and evaluation systems. Moreover, developing an open evaluation culture takes time. In the Finnish case, evaluations started slowly in the 1970s, became common practice in the 1980s and 1990s, and were institutionalized in the 2010s. Involving key stakeholders in evaluations through, for example, a steering group or a participative evaluation strategy may constitute a good start (figure O.5).

Finnish policy making is enhanced largely by drawing lessons from one's own and others' experience. As discussed, lesson drawing in Finland happens both at the institutional level and through direct benchmarking. Benchmarking forms part of the design of many interventions; for example, preparation of the SHOKs program included a rather comprehensive benchmarking of similar centers of excellence around the world, to find best practices for implementation. Benchmarking, or lesson drawing, during the design of policy interventions has also become important. The significance of interacting with international organizations at the ministerial and individual levels is harder to assess, but Finland is active in European Union (EU) policy preparation, the Organisation for Economic

Figure O.5 Evaluation and Foresight in Policy Making

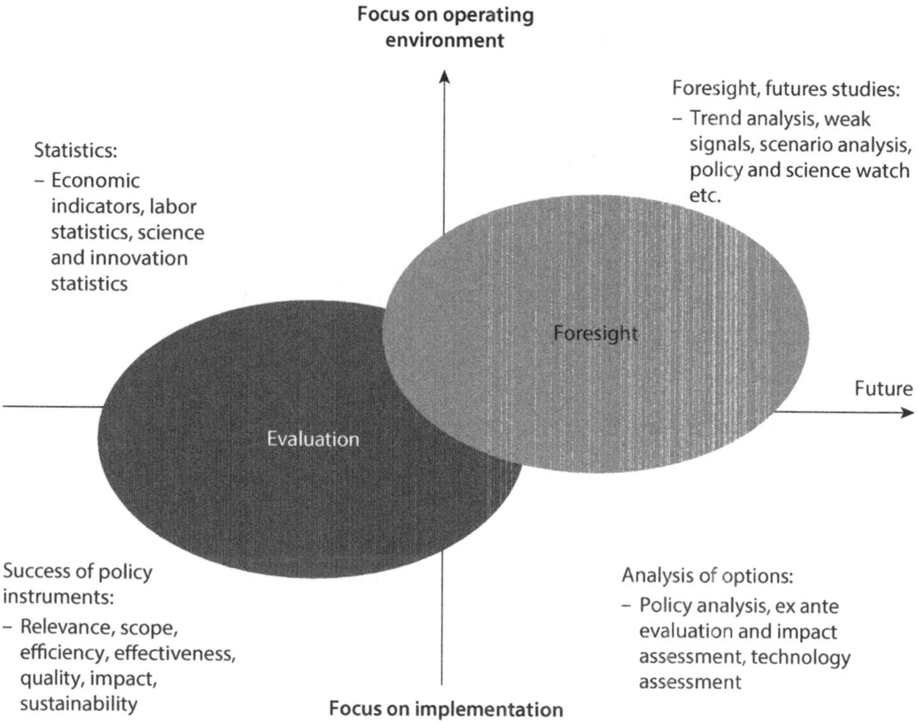

Source: STPC 2007.

Co-operation and Development (OECD), as well as in the United Nations, and various officials commonly visit one of these organizations during their career.

There are two final, overarching lessons. First, impartial evaluations of institutions, policies, instruments, and programs are potentially valuable, as they offer feedback on actions. Further, evaluations potentially improve the transparency of government, if they are impartial, candid, and published afterward. Second, building the opportunities for evaluation into structures can support policy learning. For example, evaluation can be built into the governance of institutions and agencies, visits to international organizations can be plotted into officials' career paths, and joining international organizations and committees can open up paths for inserting new ideas and feedback into policy making. Box O.7 presents the key messages from chapter 7.

Box O.7 Key Messages from Chapter 7

- Monitoring and evaluation of progress toward a knowledge economy and investments are important for policy learning. They enhance transparency, effectiveness of public investments, and good governance.
- In Finland, all areas of public expenditure are the subject of systematic monitoring and evaluation.
- Investing in building an open evaluation culture pays in the long run: evaluations make little contribution to learning from experience if they are not genuinely insightful and openly critical.
- Systematic data collection and monitoring are instrumental. Comprehensive and reliable basic data are the foundation of all evaluations.
- Building policy learning into structures is essential (for example, steering documents, key performance indicators, international benchmarking visits).
- When drawing lessons, the evidence and political agendas should be separated: policy learning, lesson drawing, and evaluation aim to gather evidence about how best to achieve the political objectives and implement the political agenda.
- Evaluation and monitoring should be planned carefully in advance, before the start of programs or other initiatives. Lack of clear goals and indicators attached to the underlying logic of the intervention, backed by systematic collection of monitoring data, makes evaluation and impact assessment costly and inefficient and does not support program implementation or corrective actions.

Knowledge Economy and Globalization (Chapter 8)

Since the early 2000s, the proliferation of emerging economies and developing countries as central sources of global economic growth has been transforming these states' relationship with the developed countries, which remain mired in a mix of slow growth and other financial problems. One central theme in this unfolding transition, called here the "new globalization," is the increasing development of innovations aimed at low-income markets across the developing world. Facilitated by efforts to reconceptualize the role of the private sector in global poverty alleviation and to underscore its ability to leverage change and reduce aid dependency, a range of new approaches to developing business and innovation for low-income markets has emerged.

To succeed in creating and introducing innovations for and in the low-income markets, a deep understanding of highly diverse user needs and requirements is needed. For developing countries, this phenomenon may offer a new competitive advantage, which they can exploit by upgrading their national innovation ecosystems and capabilities, and foster a new type of global network with innovation leaders. For developed countries, the challenge is to reorient their traditional internationalization strategies and establish new types of innovation co-creation models with partners from the developing world.

The economic importance of emerging economies and developing countries as sources of global economic growth and hosts to market segments that are growing rapidly is recasting the process of globalization, including the relationships between innovation leaders and those catching up. The international orientation of countries changes gradually, but the transition inevitably involves wide-ranging processes. It is yet to be seen whether the increasing importance accorded to emerging economies and developing countries in the global reach of rich-country innovation systems amounts to a substantial and lasting change, but an important turning point has been passed. Firms, universities, and governments around the world are placing great importance on the development of innovative products and services that can succeed in the global low-income market; they have realized that they must include the intended users in innovation processes.

The emergence of a new type of global innovation network presents specific opportunities and challenges for developed and developing countries, and both groups of countries need to adopt comprehensive public policy strategies in order to reap the benefits.

The *incumbent global innovation leaders*, such as Finland, must reevaluate their overall internationalization strategies and approaches and foster new policies, capabilities, and instruments enabling co-creation innovation and business models that extend between rich and low-income countries.

As for *emerging economies and developing countries*, low-income markets may gain a new competitive advantage. Firms, universities, and governments around the world are rushing to understand this market and develop innovations that best serve its needs and preferences. It is essential that governments recognize this development and use it to leverage national innovation systems and capabilities.

Participation in co-creative innovation processes is premised on securing mutual benefits, and in this regard developing countries have a lot to gain by opening up for collaboration. Yet carefully planned policies and regulation must be in place to insure against exploitation and harmful practices. More important, and probably more difficult, is to devise policies and practices that contribute to upgrading developing-country innovation systems and capabilities.

The best way for developing countries to benefit from innovation collaboration with rich-country partners is to implement active and forward-looking innovation policy, which includes a range of implementation instruments aimed at localizing benefits. These may include active scouting and selection of international collaboration partners, a strong vision and strategy to create locally strong living labs, harmonization and coordination of collaboration activities, and alignment of broader social objectives as well as higher education programs with collaboration programs. Global companies and universities are scouting for the best places to develop innovations for the low-income market, and national governments can make a big difference in setting up the right environment to innovate for the poor.

The character of developing countries' global interaction is critical in determining the extent to which they can exploit the growing interest in developing and marketing new services and products to low-income markets. With an increasing number of actors based in developed countries interested in developing technologies, products, and services for low-income markets, there is an important potential for forging new types of partnerships between developing and developed countries, ones that go beyond traditional links between donor and recipient.

The promise of such innovation partnerships lies in mutual interest. Developed countries need to learn—and it is easy to underestimate the amount of learning required—to develop and introduce innovations in low-income markets. Developing countries need to upgrade their innovation ecosystems and capabilities. However, to gain momentum, the build-up of such collaborative mechanisms will take time and require considerable policy making from both developing and developed countries. Box O.8 presents the key messages of chapter 8.

Box O.8 Key Messages from Chapter 8

- The traditional roles of advanced economies as well as emerging and developing economies are changing rapidly. This development has prompted Finland, among other innovation leaders, to reconsider its strategies and approaches to developing countries.
- Development collaboration is about joint learning processes in which both sides should have an active role. Successful implementation of knowledge partnerships presupposes a deep understanding of user needs.
- The role of the various collaboration programs should be seen as a coordinated, systematic set of complementary measures leading, step-by-step, toward common strategic ends.

References

Ali-Yrkkö, J., M. Kalm, M. Pajarinen, P. Rouvinen, T. Seppälä, and A.-J. Tahvanainen. 2013. "Microsoft Acquires Nokia: Implications for the Two Companies and Finland." ETLA Brief 16, Research Institute of the Finnish Economy, Helsinki. http://pub.etla.fi/ETLA-Muistio-Brief-16.pdf.

Hernesniemi, H., ed. 2010. *Digitaalinen Suomi 2020 [Digital Finland 2020]*. Helsinki: Teknologiateollisuus ry. http://www.teknologiainfo.net/content/kirjat/pdf-tiedostot/Sahko_elektroniikka_ja_tietoteollisuus/digitaalinen_suomi-ekirja.pdf.

Johnson, C. 1982. *MITI and the Japanese Miracle: The Growth of Industrial Policy, 1925–1975*. Stanford, CA: Stanford University Press.

Kniivilä, M. 2007. "Industrial Development and Economic Growth: Implications for Poverty Reduction and Income Inequality." In *Industrial Development for the 21st Century: Sustainable Development Perspectives*, edited by J. A. Ocampo, 295–333. New York: United Nations, Department of Economic and Social Affairs.

Kokkinen, A. 2012. *On Finland's Economic Growth and Convergence with Sweden and the EU15 in the 20th Century*. Research Report 258. Helsinki: Statistics Finland. http://tilastokeskus.fi/tup/julkaisut/tiedostot/978-952-244-334-2.pdf.

Nørmark, D. 2013. *Cultural Intelligence of Stone-Aged Brains: How to Work with Danes and Beyond*. Copenhagen: Gyldendal Business.

Pajarinen, M., P. Rouvinen, and P. Ylä-Anttila. 2012. *Uutta arvoa palveluista*. ETLA Series B256. Helsinki: Taloustieto Oy.

Sabel, C., and A. Saxenian. 2008. *A Fugitive Success: Finland's Economic Future*. Sitra Report 80. Helsinki: Edita Prima. http://www.sitra.fi/julkaisut/raportti80.pdf.

Stiglitz, J. E. 1996. "Some Lessons from the East Asian Miracle." *World Bank Research Observer* 11 (2): 151–77.

STPC (Science and Technology Policy Council). 2007. "Vaikuttavuuden arviointi ja ennakointi [Evaluation, Impact Assessment, and Foresight]." Background memorandum for the Council Statement on Development of Evaluation and Foresight, August 17.

CHAPTER 1

Introduction: Finland's Economic Transition

Kimmo Halme, Vesa Salminen, and Kalle A. Piirainen

Finland is known for its consistent economic progress, competitiveness, and egalitarian society. Yet the challenges that Finland experienced at the beginning of the twentieth century are similar to those experienced by many countries today. Finland emerged as an independent nation in the midst of international economic and political turbulence. In spite of its remoteness, relatively scarce natural resources, small domestic market, and recent history of wars and social cleavages, Finland transformed itself from an agriculture-based economy in the 1950s to one of the leading innovation-driven, knowledge-based economies and high-tech producers in the twenty-first century. The development was rapid and involved determined action and sometimes drastic decisions by the government and other key actors.

At the end of 2013, Finland faced considerable challenges both domestically and internationally in efforts to maintain its societal sustainability and economic competitiveness.

Industrial Transformation until the 1990s

Within the European context, Finland was among the late developers. In the mid-nineteenth century, Finland—an autonomous grand duchy of Russia between 1809 and 1917—was a backward agrarian economy with approximately 1.6 million people. The mid-nineteenth century marked the beginning of Finnish industrialization and ushered in some key reforms in infrastructure, banking, education, and financial institutions.

During the interwar years, Finland was catching up with the Western economies. However, these years were marked by national, political, and social dispersion, which culminated in civil war in 1918. The country was divided along the lines of the conflict and was reunited during the Second World War. As late as the 1950s, Finland, recovering from the war, was still an agriculture-based economy. Substantial war reparations—largely paid in the form of goods as well as machinery, equipment, and vessels—provided the impetus for industrialization during the postwar years. Postwar industrialization and rise of the welfare state help to explain why Finland was able to raise the education levels of the population and to become one of the most educated countries in the world. Since then, social cohesion has remained high, the policy environment predictable, and basic infrastructure in good condition. Indeed, the seeds were sown for the economy's transition to knowledge-intensive products.

The early 1990s were characterized by the collapse of the Soviet Union and a national economic crisis in Finland. The recession Finland suffered was particularly deep for two reasons. First, the Soviet Union was its main export market for consumer goods, so the collapse affected large portions of the Finnish economy. Second, financial crises hit the overheated Finnish economy, which took steps to liberalize financial markets, resulting in major credit defaults and a banking crisis.

Against this background, the 1990s marked the turning point in the economy's shift from an investment-driven to a more innovation-driven economy. Important decisions affecting the future of the economy were also made during these troubled years. First, the economy was opened up in an effort to reposition Finland in the world market. Second, more emphasis was placed on microeconomic policies to enhance competitiveness. Third, the newly established Science and Technology Policy Council (STPC) set an agenda for economic growth led by information and communication technology (ICT) and for creation of a "national innovation system." As a consequence of the STPC agenda, more funding was made available for research and development (R&D) and higher education institutions.

Role of the ICT Sector

During the recession in the 1990s, public investments were targeted at the ICT sector, as mobile communications were among the few sectors growing at the time. These decisions were made in the midst of a severe economic crisis, when the government implemented austerity measures, cutting all public expenditures except those for education and for research, development, and innovation (RDI). Later on, these decisions proved to be instrumental in enabling growth of the ICT sector. From the mid-1990s onward, Finland enjoyed extraordinary growth. The ICT sector, with Nokia as its flagship, was at the center of this development.

The Finnish government had taken an active role in developing digital and mobile communications in the 1970s and 1980s. During these decades, the state invested heavily in the development of domestic technology and production capabilities through funding for collaborative research involving private enterprises, public agencies, and universities. The state also had a role in expanding university degree programs in electronics and information technology and in targeting technologically demanding government procurement to domestic firms (Sabel and Saxenian 2008, 55). Moreover, the ICT sector benefited from public financial support, the extensive collaboration of public research institutes, state technology agencies, universities and other educational institutions, and private companies. As this development work coincided with the opening of the Nordic telephone markets (the first in the world, followed by the European and global telephone markets), the Finnish ICT sector (especially Nokia) was in an advantageous position (Sabel and Saxenian 2008, 55). The government had a clear role both as a developer of technology (government as client) and, primarily, as a creator of conditions (infrastructure, funding, and regulation).

The New Knowledge Economy

The main characteristics of Finland's economic development in the 20 years leading up to the worldwide economic crisis in 2008 were radical increases in intangible investments (education, RDI, and the organization of work) and comprehensive building of the national base of knowledge. These contributed to increasing productivity, redirecting and refocusing employment into more productive and knowledge-intensive sectors, and using financial resources more efficiently. The miraculous growth of the Nokia-led ICT and electronics industry to become Finland's largest industrial sector and biggest exporter is the best-known example from these years. However, electronics and ICT were not the only sectors that developed during this time. Practically all industrial and other sectors improved productivity, developed new products, and increased their exports.

For the past few years, Nokia's phone business had been declining rapidly due to the growing importance of the smartphone segment, where competitors like Apple and Samsung caught Nokia by surprise. In summer 2013 Nokia sold its mobile phone business to Microsoft at a significantly lower price than its value only a few years prior. At this point, many questions were raised about what would happen to Finland's knowledge economy and whether Finnish policies had been too focused on a few leading industrial sectors.

Luckily the ecosystem is broader and deeper than just one company or industry. During the last few years, the Finnish ICT sector has moved from manufacturing products to producing services and software. Hardware production has been transferred to low-cost countries, and knowledge-intensive expertise requiring higher education has maintained its position or even grown. The traditional manufacturing industries, especially machinery and equipment, have undergone a similar transformation, and many leading enterprises focus on both services and tangible products.

Despite structural changes, the ICT sector is still strong in Finland. Due to growth in software and ICT services, the role of the ICT sector as an employer is hardly diminishing (see, for example, Ali-Yrkkö *et al.* 2013). A good example is the rapidly growing game industry, with two leading companies, Rovio and Supercell, a company established in 2010 and sold to Japanese investors for around US$1.5 billion (approximately a third of Nokia's selling price) in November 2013. Although this industry is still young (average age three years), it is growing fast, at around 200 percent in 2012, with an estimated turnover of €800 million in 2013 (€250 million in 2012; see box 1.1 and the Neogames

Box 1.1 Finland Fact File

Basic information

- *Land area:* 338,145 square kilometers (approximately the size of Germany)
- *Population:* 5.4 million; population density, 15.7 people per square kilometer (European Union average, 116)
- *Ethnic composition:* Finnish-speaking Finns (93.4 percent), Swedish-speaking Finns (5.6 percent), together forming 99 percent of the population, and ethnic Russians (0.5 percent)
- *Religion:* Predominantly Christian (79.9 percent Lutheran, about 1.1 percent Finnish Orthodox); in practice, a fairly secular society
- *Urbanization:* 85 percent living in urban areas
- *Life expectancy:* 79.55 years (total population), slightly above the Organisation for Economic Co-operation and Development (OECD) average
- *Age composition:* Rapidly aging population, with more than 255,000 persons 80 years of age and older at the end of 2010, a fivefold growth in the past 40 years
- *Literacy rate:* 100 percent
- *Climate:* Great contrasts, with cold winters and fairly warm summers (2012 extremes: low of –42.7°C and high of 31.0°C).

Political system

- *Political organization:* A parliamentary democracy with a multiparty political system and a president as the head of state. The president is elected for a period of six years. The constitution, adopted in 2000 and further amended in 2012, moved the political system in a more parliamentary direction, by increasing the amount of power that parliament and the government wield. The parliament (Eduskunta in Finnish) has 200 members elected every four years. Voter turnout was 70.5 percent in 2011 parliamentary elections (OECD average, 72 percent).
- *Stability:* The political system is stable. The last time that the government was replaced during a four-year term was in 1975.

Economy and working life

- *Unemployment rate:* 8.8 percent in April 2013
- *Gross domestic product (GDP) per capita (purchasing power parity):* US$37,642 (OECD average, US$35,058) in 2011
- *Current account balance:* Negative since 2011
- *Inflation:* 3 percent for 2012; government loans of around US$10 billion a year, equal to 6 percent of GDP
- *Income:* Average household net adjusted disposable income, US$25,739 a year (OECD, US$23,047 a year)
- *Work:* 69 percent of people 15 to 64 years of age have a paid job (men, 71 percent; women, 68 percent, OECD average, 66 percent) average number of working hours a year, 1,684 (OECD average, 1,776 hours).

box continues next page

Box 1.1 Finland Fact File *(continued)*

Research and education

- *Educational attainment:* School life expectancy (primary to tertiary education), 17 years for the total population
- *Compulsory schooling:* Starting in the year when a child turns 7 and ending after the basic education syllabus has been completed or after 10 years. There has been discussion on lengthening compulsory education to the age of 17 for all youth.
- *High school equivalency:* 83 percent of adults 25–64 years of age have earned the equivalent of a high school degree (men, 81 percent; women, 85 percent; OECD average, 74 percent)
- *R&D expenditure:* Surpassed €7 billion (approximately US$9.19 billion) in 2011, of which €5 billion was spent by corporations, €1.4 billion by the higher education sector, and €0.7 billion by the public sector. Total R&D expenditure as a share of national GDP, 3.78 percent (second highest in the world).

For additional information, see Findicator 2013 (www.finland.fi), Statistics Finland, Finland in Figures (https://www.tilastokeskus.fi/index_en.html), and OECD Better Life Index (http://www.oecdbetterlifeindex.org).

website, http://www.neogames.fi/en/). Moreover, multinational corporations such as Electronic Arts, Ericsson, Google, Huawei, Intel, Microsoft, and Samsung have established part of their operations or R&D in Finland. For the software and game industries, Finland is now expected to become the next Silicon Valley, but this remains to be seen.

Aim and Structure of the Book

In 2006 the World Bank Institute published *Finland as a Knowledge Economy* (Dahlman, Routti, and Ylä-Anttila 2007), which explained the key elements of Finland's transition to a knowledge economy. The book was well received by policy makers and practitioners World Bank client countries. It detailed the active role that government can take in managing a significant transition of the economy. Several years have passed since publication of that book, and the country's economic situation and government policies have evolved. Hence, it is time to take a second look at Finland's knowledge economy.

Finland as a Knowledge Economy 2.0 presents some of the key policies, elements, initiatives, and decisions behind Finland's path to the knowledge economy of today. The book aims to provide readers with inspiration, ideas, and insights that may prove valuable in another context. In order to provide a useful account of Finland's transition to a knowledge economy, the book provides a detailed explanation of the policy choices, the thinking behind them, and the relevant actors in the country. As the topics discussed are often widely debated and even controversial, room is left for readers to come to their own conclusions about the value and worth of the Finnish approach. In doing that, they should keep in mind that the book is written mainly in the spirit of "appreciative inquiry." It focuses on positive experiences and best practices, recognizing that cultural and social issues play different roles in different contexts. Some implications of these issues are discussed briefly in the conclusions of the report.

The report is structured as follows: chapter 2 sheds light on the key decisions taken during various phases of development of the Finnish knowledge economy and identifies key areas for learning from specific policies. Based on this account of the development of the Finnish knowledge economy, the authors have identified six areas of lessons, described in chapters 3 through 8. Together the chapters offer a "knowledge economy cookbook," providing cases, links, and insights for further exploration. Figure 1.1 outlines the structure of the book.

Figure 1.1 Structure of the Book

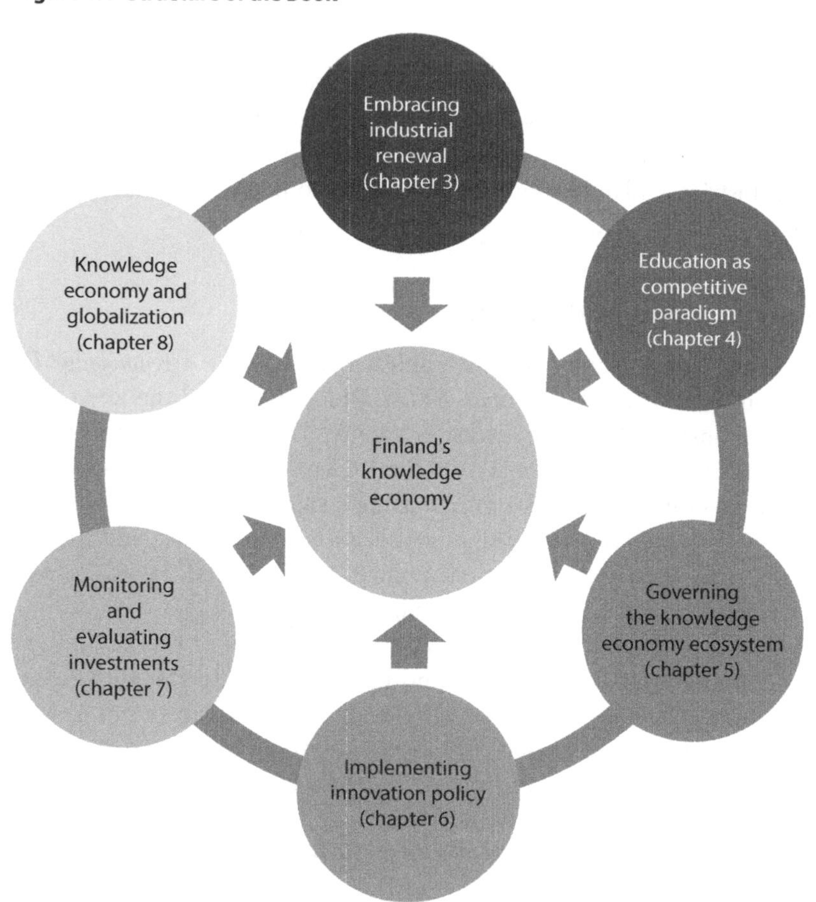

References

Ali-Yrkkö, J., M. Kalm, M. Pajarinen, P. Rouvinen, T. Seppälä, and A.-J. Tahvanainen. 2013. "Microsoft Acquires Nokia: Implications for the Two Companies and Finland." ETLA Brief 16, Research Institute of the Finnish Economy, Helsinki. http://pub.etla.fi/ETLA-Muistio-Brief-16.pdf.

Dahlman, C., J. Routti, and P. Ylä-Anttila. 2006. *Finland as a Knowledge Economy: Elements of Success and Lessons Learned.* Washington, DC: World Bank.

Findicator. 2013. http://www.findikaattori.fi/en.

Sabel, C., and A. Saxenian. 2008. *A Fugitive Success: Finland's Economic Future.* Sitra Report 80. Helsinki: Edita Prima. http://www.sitra.fi/julkaisut/raportti80.pdf.

References

CHAPTER 2

Background: Evolution of Finland's Knowledge Economy Policy

Tarmo Lemola

Finland transformed itself from an agrarian society in the 1950s to one of the leading knowledge economies in the world. This development has been very much company led and company centered. However, the government has had an important role in setting national strategies and coordinating and facilitating their implementation, building shared platforms for making funding decisions, and setting priorities for research and development (R&D). This chapter sheds light on the key decisions taken during different phases of the Finnish knowledge economy and identifies key areas for learning from specific policies.

The Finnish knowledge economy developed in phases, each with its own foundations, objectives, actors, and instruments. Most of the key policy decisions behind this development were made in the mid-1960s, which initiated an era of *reform of basic structures* of education and R&D followed by an era of *technology push* with a focus on intensive development and use of information and communication technology (ICT). This era of optimism, national networking, and robust economic development ended unexpectedly when the Finnish economy plunged into an exceptionally severe crisis in the early 1990s. From a knowledge economy point of view, the era that began in the late 1990s was characterized by attempts to get Finland *out of recession*. *Globalization* began in the early 2000s and still dominates knowledge economy policy thinking and operations in Finland today.

Reform of Basic Structures (1960–)

Up until the early years of the twentieth century, Finland had only one university, the University of Helsinki. By the end of the 1960s, it had 15. Universities were established not only in southern Finland but also in eastern and northern parts of the country in the 1960s. At that time, government research institutes formed a significant component of Finland's public research system. The first government research institutes were established in Finland at the end of the nineteenth century. The biggest Finnish companies had R&D units, but their R&D intensity as well as that of other components of the research system were low. Specialized funding mechanisms for R&D were still in the very early stages of development in Finland.

In the 1960s science and technology and R&D and their economic significance became a topic of debate and an area of government activity. This occurred later in Finland than in larger and more developed member countries of the Organisation for Economic Co-operation and Development (OECD). The late start was counterbalanced by the fact that the development of education as well as research and innovation policies proceeded quickly, particularly after the early 1980s (Lemola 2003b).

The policy doctrines and institutional and organizational models that Finland adopted reflected national historical, cultural, political, and administrative specificities, but many came from other countries and organizations. Sweden was a significant source of inspiration and imitation up until the late 1980s. For decades, the OECD has played a large role in the formulation of policy guidelines (Lemola 2002).

During the first phase, emphasis was placed on constructing and expanding the machinery of innovation policy. The main driver was the intensifying internationalization and liberalization of trade. This placed new strains on Finland's structure of production, which was one-sided (high dependence on forest-based industry, particularly the paper industry), and on its level of technology, which was low compared with that of Finland's main competitors (Vartia and Ylä-Anttila 1996).

Finland had an urgent need to widen the industrial base and to increase productivity and value added. Investment in R&D and education was considered an important building block of the Finnish national modernization project. Catching up with industrially and technologically more advanced countries became the goal that would shape Finnish activities and structures in science and technology for more than a few decades.

Four important changes occurred in Finland's innovation policy in the 1960s and early 1970s (Lemola 2002, 2003b):

1. Improved capabilities and operating conditions of universities
2. Increased and improved (technical) research
3. Public support for firms' R&D
4. Establishment of high-level coordination.

First, the capabilities and operating conditions of the *universities* were improved. The measures were targeted directly at the teaching and research appropriations of universities and at the Academy of Finland (a system of research councils). The large postwar (baby boom) generation began to reach maturity at this time, making expansion of the institutions of higher education a social and political necessity.

Second, research that would raise the level of industrial technology was undertaken and improved. Above all, this meant developing the Technical

Research Centre (VTT), Finland's biggest research institute. The VTT was comprehensively reorganized in 1972. In addition, the Ministry of Trade and Industry received an appropriation from the state for goal-oriented technical research. This gave rise to the first "national technology programs" in technology universities and the VTT.

Third, the government began to support firms' research and product development directly by means of R&D loans and grants. A new fund under the authority of the Bank of Finland—the National Fund for Research and Development (Sitra)—was established for this purpose. In addition, the Ministry of Trade and Industry began to support the research and product development of firms. The impulse for these measures originated in concern about the lack of firms' own R&D.

Fourth, a ministerial committee on science—the Science Policy Council, which became the Science and Technology Policy Council (STPC) and then the Research and Innovation Council (RIC)—was established in 1963 as a high-level political body for the formulation of science (and technology) policy guidelines and for interministerial coordination of R&D activities. In 1973 the council introduced an ambitious plan for increasing the share of R&D expenditure in gross domestic product (GDP) from 0.9 percent in 1971 to 1.7 percent in 1980. It was a big disappointment to Finnish R&D communities that this plan was not realized. In 1979 Finnish R&D expenditure amounted to only 1.1 percent of GDP, one the lowest figures among the OECD countries.

Technology Push (1980–)

A new era in Finland's innovation policy began at the turn of the 1980s. The factors behind the transition from research orientation to technology orientation were economic and social. The oil crisis of the late 1970s led to a slowdown in economic growth and to high unemployment and inflation. These were the years of the "microelectronics revolution," which offered new productive and other opportunities, but threatened to cause social problems. In particular, it was feared that the increase in the use of automation in industry and services would cause mass unemployment and greater social inequality.

At the beginning of the 1980s, key actors in the business sector concluded that economic development in Finland could no longer be based on cost-effectiveness (the competitive advantage of the forest industry) but should focus on knowledge intensity (Schienstock 2004). The creation of a knowledge base was seen as crucial for Finnish companies to survive in the increasingly globalized economy. This change in approach was evident in the rapid growth of private sector R&D expenditures throughout the decade (Ormala 1999).

A national consensus was reached on the necessity for technological development and its basic objectives (Finnish Technology Committee 1982), leading to formation of the Funding Agency for Technology and Innovation (Tekes) in 1983 (see box 6.1 in chapter 6). The tasks formerly carried out by the Ministry of Trade and Industry—R&D loans and grants and appropriations for goal-oriented technical research—were assigned to Tekes, which became the key planner and implementer of the new innovation policy.

In the 1980s in Finland, as in many other OECD countries, government shifted from promoting science to stimulating and supporting industrial innovation. In particular, science and technology policy actively focused on the development and application of emerging (science-based) technologies, primarily information technology, materials technology, and biotechnology. Finland gave priority to information technology (Lemola 2003a).

National technology programs, which had already proven their worth in countries such as Japan and Sweden, were developed at the beginning of the 1980s to promote and control research activities. They took a more selective and strategic approach, but they were generated by a decentralized strategic planning mechanism. Initiatives for new programs came from universities, research institutes, firms, and industry associations, and they were dealt with informally or semi-informally in various cooperation bodies with representatives from a range of organizations. The programs were an important catalyst for national cooperation. An important new feature of these programs was that bilateral cooperation was transformed into multilateral cooperation. Firms, research institutes, universities, and the government through Tekes began implementing the programs together.

Another significant change within national science and technology policy at this time was the creation of new programs and organizations associated with the transfer, diffusion, and commercialization of technology. Nationwide networks of technology parks and centers of expertise were set up in Finland (although there was no national policy on technology parks). The technology parks initiated spin-off projects and incubators. Technology transfer companies were established to commercialize the results generated in universities and research institutes. Public and private venture capital operations also increased, although the venture capital market has long been less developed in Finland than in many other European countries, not to mention Israel and the United States. Some of these arrangements were created at the national level, but many were the result of local and regional initiatives, albeit with national funding.

As a symbol of the technology orientation of the 1980s, the Science Policy Council was transformed in 1987 into the STPC (see chapter 5). The polarization of Finnish science and technology policy into science policy administered by the Ministry of Education and Culture (universities and the Academy of Finland) and technology policy administered by the Ministry of Trade and Industry (Tekes, the VTT, and some other government research institutes), which had existed since the early 1970s, was thus settled in the 1980s. Tensions between the blocks were unavoidable, but were moderated fairly successfully by the STPC.

Out of Recession (1990–)

The next transition in Finnish innovation policy occurred in the recession years of the early 1990s. Economic development in Finland in the 1980s was faster than in most other industrial countries (Tainio, Pohjola, and Lilja 1999; see figure 2.1).

Figure 2.1 GDP Growth (Expenditure Approach) in Finland and OECD-Europe, 1971–2011

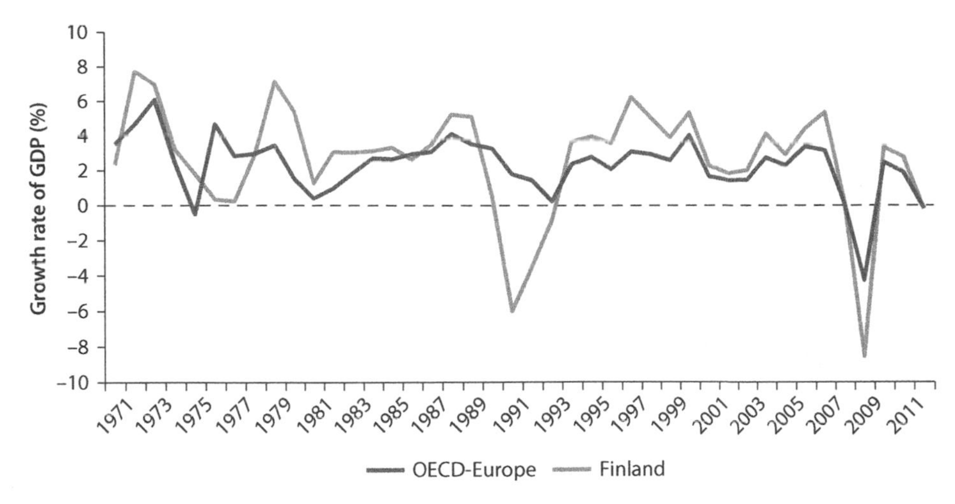

Source: OECD data (stats.oecd.org).

Knowledge-intensive production, technological development, and productivity grew quickly. Finland was transforming into a knowledge economy, as knowledge became the main driving force of societal and economic development.

However, due to the collapse of Soviet trade and bursting of the domestic banking and real estate bubbles, the Finnish economy was plunged into an exceptionally severe crisis in the early 1990s. Finland's GDP declined more than 10 percent during 1991–93, the stock market collapsed, the value of the Finnish currency (the markka) plummeted almost 40 percent from the level prevailing at the beginning of the decade, foreign debt and budget deficits grew rapidly, unemployment approached 20 percent at its height, and the country's banking system was thrown into deep crisis.

Severe social and economic crises often lead to radical changes in policy. This was the case in Finnish science and technology policy, but not as much as would be expected. The basics remained almost unchanged. This was very much due to the fact that Finland recovered from the recession as quickly as it had plunged into it. This was achieved largely on the back of rapid growth in exports. The strongest growth was in the ICT cluster, and a major part of this growth was explained by one company, Nokia. Thanks to Nokia, Finland became highly specialized in ICT equipment in a short period of time (Rouvinen and Ylä-Anttila 2003). As a relatively small and industrially specialized economy, Finland has felt the fluctuations of the global economy more drastically than OECD economies on average. However, it has been quicker to recover from economic crises.

The years of recession and recovery involved changes in Finnish innovation policy. However, these changes did not stem directly from the recession. The process of change had already started in the late 1980s. The main thrust of Finnish innovation policy in the early 1990s came from a strong need to develop R&D as a means to address the country's high rate of unemployment. The recession created a favorable environment for the adoption of new concepts and modes of operation and for the acceleration of R&D and innovation-driven growth.

An important milestone in formulating the "new" innovation policy was the 1990 review by the STPC (STPC 1990; Miettinen 2013). The report of this authoritative body, led by the prime minister, elevated the concept of a national innovation system as an instrument of Finland's innovation policy. The Finnish system was based on the ideas of Freeman and Lundvall (Freeman 1987; Lundvall 1992) as well as the OECD's Technology and Economy Program, which had been launched in 1988 (OECD 1992). The transfer of knowledge to Finland and Finnish application of it were undertaken by the STPC secretariat in collaboration with the Finnish academic community.

The following became key principles of Finland's national innovation system:

- A national innovation system is a whole set of factors influencing the development and use of new knowledge and know-how. The concept allows these factors and their development needs to be examined in aggregate.
- A national research system forms an intrinsic part of a national system of innovation. Education is another important element.
- The general atmosphere prevailing in society has a profound influence on the production and application of new knowledge. An efficient innovation system is characterized by close interaction and cooperation between different actors.
- Internationalization influences the activities of an innovation system in many ways, but also emphasizes the need to improve national conditions for creating innovations.

A crucial aspect the new approach was the emphasis put on learning and the link between employment and innovation policies. This was based on the growing awareness among policy makers that knowledge-intensive growth is of undeniable significance for the national economy and that macroeconomic or labor market measures alone do not create the preconditions for knowledge-intensive growth. Above all, the promotion of knowledge-intensive growth requires innovation policy measures relating to R&D, education, competition, intellectual property rights, national and international cooperation networks, and technology transfer and exploitation.

During the 1990s, the mind-set of innovation policy makers changed, but no significant changes occurred in the basic instruments of innovation policy. From the point of view of the importance of R&D and innovation, the most important single act was the government's decision in 1996 to increase state funding for research by €250 million in 1997–99. This meant an increase of about 25 percent in the state's annual research appropriations from the 1997 level. Most of these additional funds were channeled to competitive R&D projects through Tekes and the Academy of Finland. Yet, as figure 2.2 shows, the increase in the share of industries' R&D expenditure was even more significant. (Industries spent more than €2 billion on R&D in 1999 and almost €5 billion in 2012.) R&D in the ICT sector accounts for a major share (approximately 50 percent)

Figure 2.2 R&D Expenditure in Finland, 1992–2012

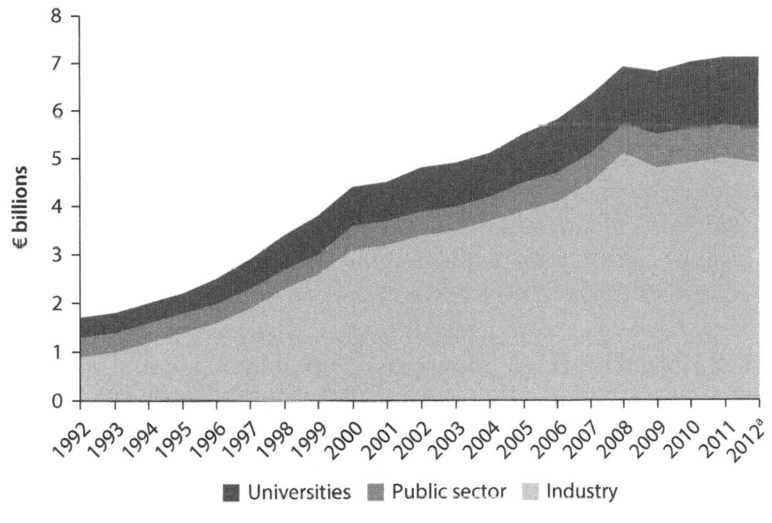

Source: Statistics Finland data (https://www.tilastokeskus.fi/).
a. Estimated.

of all R&D. Extensive public investments, especially in education, were an important prerequisite for the rise of industries' R&D (see chapter 4).

Members of the Finnish R&D community have always had direct personal links and cooperation with their colleagues in the Nordic countries, elsewhere in Europe, and in the United States. One of the first steps to institutionalizing international R&D cooperation was Finland's participation in Eureka in 1985 (Ormala *et al.* 1993). Finnish participation in Eureka was promoted and organized by Tekes, which played an important role in Finland's preparation for participating in the European Union's research framework program.

Finland became a member of the European Union (EU) in 1995, and Finnish researchers and developers markedly increased their participation in EU R&D programs, which quickly became an integral part of the country's science and technology operations and policy. Besides providing participants with financial resources to carry out their R&D projects, EU programs helped foster internationalization and globalization of R&D and innovation networks as well as value chains (Luukkonen and Hälikkä 2000; Kuitunen *et al.* 2008).

Regionalization of innovation and policy operations, which had started in the 1980s, gained strength in the 1990s as a result of national as well as regional and local initiatives. This development was aided by the EU's general emphasis on developing regions within member countries in conjunction with financial aid from the EU's structural funds. Without the influence and financial resources of the EU, Finnish regions would have had a modest role in innovation policy activities. The most significant single national initiative for regional innovation was the Center of Expertise Program, which was started in 1994 (see box 6.3 in chapter 6).

Knowledge Economy in a Globalizing World (2000–)

In the early 2000s, Finland was one of the most innovative and competitive countries in the world. Finland enjoyed the advantages of being an early producer of ICT and of setting technology standards. Nokia, the flagship of Finnish technology, had grown in conjunction with a great number of its Finnish subcontractors into a world leader in mobile communications (Ali-Yrkkö 2010). Finland had become an economy based on education, research, and innovation (Dahlman, Routti, and Ylä-Anttila 2006).

The issue of globalization dominated the discussion and formulation of policy (Prime Minister's Office 2004). Finland was one of the winners in the globalization process. As an open, competence-based, small economy with a small domestic market, Finland benefited from opening up to international trade. Expansion of global markets sped not only the growth of the Finnish ICT sector, but also the development of Finnish engineering industries and many other industrial sectors. Both the business enterprise sector and Finnish research communities benefited from globalization.

However, globalization also posed challenges for the national economy (RIC 2010). Global competition intensified. Companies began competing for customers, and nation-states competing for companies. The threshold for business enterprises to transfer not only industrial production but also product development and service production closer to final markets and to countries with cheaper production costs became significantly lower. Changing the locus of global specialization in the provision of goods and services did not imply that everything moved to Asia or other emerging off-shore locations. It did however, mean that innovation and other business activities would tend to become geographically dispersed more often and more easily (MEE and Ministry of Education and Culture 2009).

Despite being relatively competitive, Finland has suffered from a slowdown in production, exports, as well as tangible and intangible investments. Traditional companies, industries, and instruments for innovation can no longer guarantee economic development, which is needed to maintain the current level of welfare services. New resources are needed. The call for taking a broad-based, systemic approach as well as for focusing on demand and users has been among the key elements of Finnish innovation policy since publication of Finland's national innovation strategy in June 2008 (MEE 2008). This approach is described in more detail in chapter 5.

One of the main concerns of Finnish innovation policy that is related directly to the challenges of globalization is the need to create and internationalize innovative growth companies (Autio *et al.* 2013). The future of Finland will depend less on a few leading companies in traditional industrial sectors and more on widespread entrepreneurial activity. This realization has led to the establishment of many new types of incubators and enterprise accelerators, such as Demola, Protomo, and Vigo (described in box 3.3 in chapter 3) within universities and research institutes as well as in a few enterprises (for example, Nokia's Innovation Mill, described in box 3.2 in chapter 3). In addition, mechanisms for funding new innovators have been initiated, with the aim of increasing investments in equity funds substantially in the coming years.

At the same time, Finland has sought to develop traditional industrial sectors. The biggest Finnish R&D investment for some time—the strategic centers for science, technology, and innovation (SHOKs, discussed in chapter 6)—seeks to improve productivity and induce radical innovations in Finland's key industrial clusters. Realizing this ambitious scheme has been more demanding than expected. According to the interim evaluation of the SHOKs, published at the beginning of 2013, the centers have not yet achieved their goals. Concerns remain about the concept as a whole, its functionality, and its ability to add value (Lähteenmäki-Smith *et al.* 2013).

One obvious consequence of globalization pressures and the recent financial crisis has been a stronger belief in the need for critical mass and economies of scale. Universities have been merged (see box 4.5 in chapter 4 on Aalto University), structural changes continue to take place in the polytechnic sector, and a proposal for a radical structural reform of government research institutes is awaiting implementation (RIC 2012). The structure of research institutes will be reformed by merging existing institutes into bigger and stronger ones. The plan is to reduce the number of institutes from 17 to 9 by 2016. In addition, some of the financial resources of institutes are going to be pooled into a new competitive funding instrument for strategically targeted research supporting government decision making.

Finnish innovation policy is now focusing on services (see chapter 3) as a potential source of economic growth and societal well-being (Niinikoski 2011). Business services are the fastest-growing sector in Finland, but many opportunities exist in public services as well. A particular challenge is that half of service companies are not engaged in innovation activities. The R&D intensity of Finland's service sector has not reached the level of that in the leading OECD countries (Pajarinen, Rouvinen, and Ylä-Anttila 2012). The wide-ranging use of ICTs is again seen as a major enabler of new kinds of services and service systems as well as for the cooperation and operational and administrative practices that support them (MEE 2013).

In regional innovation policy, Finland is moving from a policy that has distributed national resources to various parts of the country to a model that will give a bigger role and more resources to a much smaller number of vital metropoles. The flagship of Finnish regional innovation policy—the Center of Expertise Program—is being replaced by the Innovative Cities (INKA) program (box 6.3 in chapter 6), and a new procedure is being used to encourage the most significant urban regions to construct attractive innovation centers and to strengthen the Finnish innovation system. Putting such strong emphasis on catalyzing the role and initiatives of major cities and their metropolises is a new development in Finnish innovation policy (box 2.1).

Box 2.1 Actors and Institutions in the Finnish Knowledge Economy

The actors and institutions of the Finnish knowledge economy can be divided into three rough categories: (a) those responsible for setting policy and strategy, (b) those responsible for providing funding and support ("enablers"), and (c) research and education institutions (see figure B2.1.1). There are also different types of "platforms" for facilitating the collaboration of various actors.

The *Research and Innovation Council* is responsible for the strategic development and coordination of Finnish science and technology policy as well as the national innovation system as a whole. It is chaired by the prime minister and comprises all key ministries and representatives from various actors.

Sitra is an independent public foundation, or think tank, reporting directly to the Finnish parliament. *Tekes* is responsible for financing R&D and innovation activities (for both companies and research institutions). It reports to the Ministry of Employment and the Economy. The *Academy of Finland* is responsible for funding academic research and reports to the Ministry of Education and Culture. *Finnvera* provides banking and loan services for companies seeking to grow and internationalize. Its affiliates—*Veraventure* (funds), *Seed Fund Vera* (direct investments), and *Finnish Industry Investment*—provide public venture capital investments to private equity funds and companies. Centers for economic development, transport, and the environment, *ELY centers* (15), are responsible for the regional implementation and development tasks of the central government. They handle financing and development services for enterprises and employment-based aid and labor

Figure B2.1.1 Finnish Knowledge Economy System

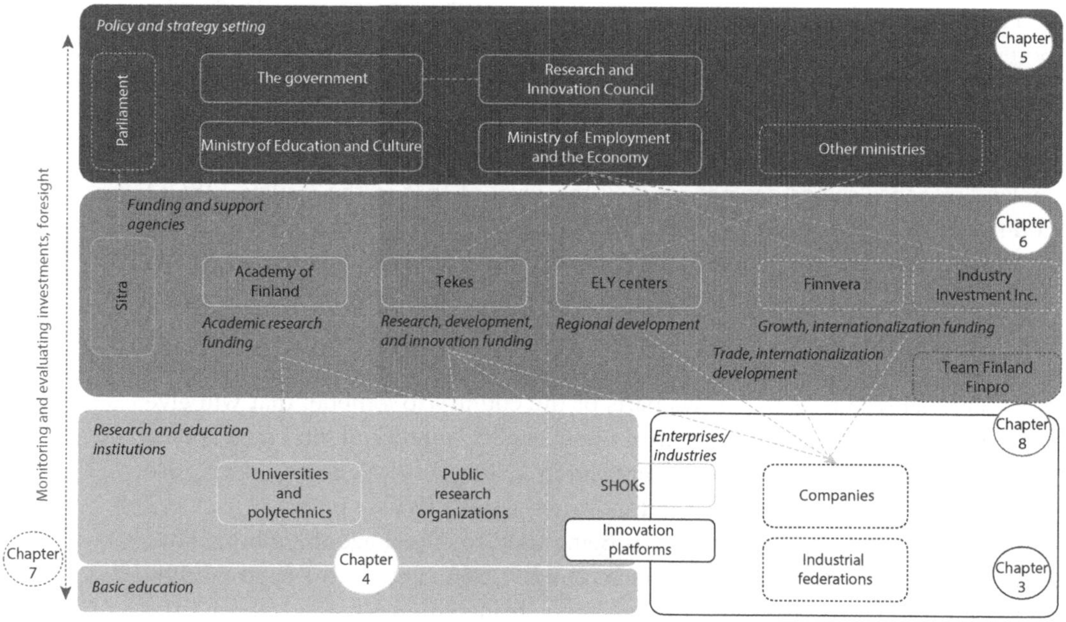

box continues next page

Box 2.1 Actors and Institutions in the Finnish Knowledge Economy *(continued)*

market training. *Finpro* and *Team Finland* promote trade, investments, and internalization of companies.

Research and education institutions include close to 20 *public research organizations* (for example, the VTT, Statistics Finland, and Finnish Environment Institute) as well as 14 *universities* and 25 *polytechnics*. The *SHOKs* are public-private partnerships for speeding up innovation processes and bringing together academic research and private R&D activities. The INKA program aims to create internationally attractive local innovation hubs and to intensify cooperation between the public and private sectors.

A list of actors appears at the end of this report.

Conclusion

The Finnish transformation into a knowledge economy started in the 1960s. Innovation policy—referred to as science & technology policy in earlier years—and education policy have formed the core of Finnish government policy aiming to change Finland from a resource-driven to a knowledge and innovation-driven economy. The transformation has had very positive economic and social effects.

Finland has shown that a full-fledged welfare state is not incompatible with technological innovation, with the development of an information society, and with a dynamic, competitive economy (Castells and Himanen 2002). On the contrary, being a welfare state has contributed to the stable growth of the Finnish economy. It has provided the human foundation for the renewal of industries and the growth of labor productivity, and it has brought institutional and social stability, which is a necessary condition for intensive long-term economic and social development. The success of Finland's knowledge-based, innovation-driven policy has made possible the continuous financing of Finland's welfare society, which has created new potential for developing and mobilizing competencies, skills, creativity, and financial, institutional, and social mechanisms for promoting the development, transfer, and implementation of technological and social innovations.

The role of government has been important and even central in some cases, but all in all, the Finnish system has not been strongly government led. It has been very much company led and company centered. The government has mainly been a coordinator, a facilitator, and a builder of shared platforms for making decisions and setting priorities for R&D.

During the early development of the Finnish knowledge economy in the 1960s, the basic structures of education and R&D were strengthened. New universities were established. Old universities and existing government research institutes were reformed, and new funding instruments for R&D were implemented. This era was followed in the 1980s by an era of technology push with a focus on intensive development and use of ICT. The seeds of Finland's success

Table 2.1 Phases of Development of the Finnish Knowledge Economy

Indicator	*Reform of basic structures (1960–)*	*Technology push (1980–)*	*Out of recession (1990s)*	*Knowledge economy in a globalizing world (2000–)*
Foundations for policy operations	Liberalization of international trade	"Microelectronic revolution"	Recovery from recession	Globalization
Main objectives	Creation of a new policy sector	Use of new technological opportunities	Intensification of knowledge-based growth	Creation of growth companies
Focus of policies	Education, science	Technology	National innovation system	Innovation, innovation ecosystems
Key actors	Ministry of Education and Culture, Academy of Finland	Tekes	STPC	Several actors
Expected outcomes or impacts	National competitiveness	Growth in high-tech products	Growth in employment	New innovative growth companies
Level of intervention	National	National, regional	Regional, transnational (EU)	National, local
Representative instrument	Project financing	National technology programs	EU sources of R&D financing	SHOKs

in ICT in the 1990s and 2000s were sown in the 1980s. In later phases, the common denominator for Finnish innovation policy has been globalization, including both its threats and its opportunities. So far, Finland has responded to the challenges of globalization by searching for new sources of growth (new innovative companies, services) and achieving economic benefits and better results by merging R&D institutions and mechanisms. Table 2.1 summarizes these phases and their characteristics.

Is there a Finnish model of innovation policy or a formula for success in innovation-driven economic development? There is, but with a couple of provisos. First, Finland's success is not only or mainly thanks to government policy and intervention. Finnish companies have been at the forefront of innovation-driven development. Second, Finland's history, culture, administrative traditions, political contexts, and industrialization process have influenced the country's policy and approach. However, Finland has adopted policy doctrines and institutional and organizational models largely from other organizations and countries. Third, because innovation policies have to address competition in a globalized world, innovation policies of various countries are becoming more alike. Good practices, not to mention "best practices," are moving fast from country to country. Innovation policies of nation states are converging. See box 2.2 for the key messages of this chapter.

Box 2.2 Key Messages

- Major economic changes in industrial structures and cooperation between public and private institutions are possible, but usually require strong political will and consensus among stakeholders. Such a joint commitment is often triggered by economic turbulence or crisis. Hence, economic crisis also provides an opportunity to initiate change and renewal.
- Achieving economic transitions will take time, patience, long-term vision, and consistency from all stakeholders of the knowledge economy.
- The transitions in the Finnish system have been led largely by private sector needs, in close collaboration with the government. The government has had an important role as a coordinator and facilitator of change as well as a builder of shared platforms for making decisions and setting priorities for the knowledge economy.
- Finland has monitored closely how more advanced countries are performing and what can be learned from their development. To a large extent, Finland has adopted its policy doctrines and institutional and organizational models from other organizations and countries.
- Making progress toward a knowledge economy has many positive side effects. A full-fledged welfare state is very much supportive of, or even based on, technological innovation, development of an information society, and a dynamic, competitive society.
- Due to national characteristics, no one-size-fits-all solutions exist. However, there are areas where interesting lessons can be drawn. These experiences are described in more detail in the following chapters.

References

Ali-Yrkkö, J., ed. 2010. *Nokia and Finland in a Sea of Change.* ETLA Series B244. Helsinki: Taloustieto Oy.

Autio, E., H. Rannikko, P. Kiuru, K. Luukkonen, R. Orenius, J. Handelberg, A. Bergenwall, and E. Berglund. 2013. *The Vigo Program: Mid-Term Evaluation.* MEE Report 4/2013. Ministry of Employment and the Economy, Enterprise and Innovation Department, Helsinki. http://www.tem.fi/files/35626/TEMrap_4_2013.pdf.

Castells, M., and P. Himanen. 2002. *The Information Society and the Welfare State: The Finnish Model.* New York: Oxford University Press.

Dahlman, C., J. Routti, and P. Ylä-Anttila. 2006. *Finland as a Knowledge Economy: Elements of Success and Lessons Learned.* Washington, DC: World Bank.

EUREKA Secretariat 1993. *The Evaluation of the Industrial and Economic Effects of Eureka.* Brussels: Eureka Secretariat, International Evaluation Group.

Finnish Technology Committee. 1982. *Report of the Finnish Technology Committee.* Report 1982:1. Helsinki: Prime Minister's Office.

Freeman, C. 1987. *Technology Policy and Economic Performance: Lessons from Japan.* London: Pinter.

Kuitunen, S., K. Haila, I. Kauppinen, M. Syrjänen, J. Vanhanen, P. Ahonen, I. Tuomi, P. Kettunen, and T. Paavola. 2008. *Finns in the EU 6th Framework Programme: Evaluation of Participation and Networks.* Report 6/2008. Helsinki: Tekes.

Lähteenmäki-Smith, K., K. Halme, T. Lemola, K. Piirainen, K. Viljamaa, K. Haila, A. Kotiranta, M. Hjelt, T. Raivio, W. Polt, M. Dinges, M. Ploder, S. Meyer, T. Luukkonen, and L. Georghiou. 2013. *Licence to SHOK? External Evaluation of the Strategic Centers for Science, Technology and Innovation.* MEE 1/2013. Helsinki: Ministry of Employment and the Economy. http://www.tekes.fi/u/Licence_to_SHOK.pdf.

Lemola, T. 2002. "Convergence of National Science and Technology Policies: The Case of Finland." *Research Policy* 31 (8–9): 1481–90.

———. 2003a. "Innovation Policy in Finland." In *Innovation Policies in Europe and the US: The New Agenda,* edited by P. S. Biegelbauer and S. Borrás, 77–92. Burlington, VT: Ashgate Publishing.

———. 2003b. "Transformation of Finnish Science and Technology Policy." *Science Studies* 16 (1): 52–67.

Lundvall, B., ed. 1992. *National Systems of Innovation: Towards a Theory of Interactive Learning.* London: Pinter.

Luukkonen, T., and S. Hälikkä. 2000. *Knowledge Creation and Knowledge Diffusion Networks: Impacts in Finland of the EU's Fourth Framework Program for Research and Development.* Publication 1/2000. Helsinki: Finnish Secretariat for EU R&D, Tekes Program.

MEE (Ministry of Employment and the Economy). 2008. *Finland's National Innovation Strategy.* Helsinki. http://ec.europa.eu/invest-in-research/pdf/download_en/finland_national_innovation_strategy.pdf.

———. 2013. *21 Paths to a Friction-Free Finland.* MEE 4/2013. Helsinki: Edita Publishing. http://www.tem.fi/files/35440/TEMjul_4_2013_web.pdf.

MEE and Ministry of Education and Culture. 2009. *Evaluation of the Finnish National Innovation System.* Policy report. Helsinki: Taloustieto Oy. http://www.tem.fi/files/24926/InnoEvalFi_POLICY_Report_28_Oct_2009.pdf.

Miettinen, R. 2013. *Innovation, Human Capabilities, and Democracy: Towards an Enabling Welfare State.* Oxford: Oxford University Press.

Niinikoski, M. 2011. "Innovation: Formation of Policy Field and Policy-Making Practice." Doctoral Dissertation 40/2011, Aalto University.

OECD (Organisation for Economic Co-operation and Development). 1992. *Technology and the Economy: The Key Relationship*. Paris: OECD.

Ormala, E. 1999. "Finnish Innovation Policy in the European Perspective." In *Transformation towards a Learning Economy: The Challenge for the Finnish Innovation System*, edited by G. Schienstock and O. Kuusi, 117–29. Sitra 213. Helsinki: Sitra.

Pajarinen, M., P. Rouvinen, and P. Ylä-Anttila. 2012. *Uutta arvoa palveluista*. ETLA Series B256. Helsinki: Taloustieto Oy.

Prime Minister's Office. 2004. *Strengthening Competence and Openness: Finland in the Global Economy*. Interim report. Helsinki: Prime Minister's Office.

RIC (Research and Innovation Council). 2010. *Research and Innovation Policy Guidelines for 2011–2015*. Kopijyvä Oy. http://www.minedu.fi/export/sites/default/OPM/Tiede/tutkimus-_ja_innovaationeuvosto/julkaisut/liitteet/Review2011-2015.pdf.

———. 2012. "State Research Institutes and Research Funding: A Proposal on a Comprehensive Reform." Prime Minister's Office, Helsinki.

Rouvinen, P., and P. Ylä-Anttila. 2003. "Case Study: Little Finland's Transformation to a Wireless Giant." In *The Global Information Technology Report, 2003–2004: Toward an Equitable Information Society*, edited by S. Dutta, B. Lanvin, and F. Paua, 87–108. New York: Oxford University Press for the World Economic Forum.

Schienstock, G. 2004. "The Finnish Model of the Knowledge Economy." In *Embracing the Knowledge Economy: The Dynamic Transformation of the Finnish Innovation System*, edited by G. Schienstock, 106–27. Cheltenham: Edward Elgar.

STPC (Science and Technology Policy Council). 1990. *Guidelines for Science and Technology Policy in the 1990s.* Helsinki: Government Printing Office.

Tainio, R., M. Pohjola, and K. Lilja. 1999. "Economic Performance of Finland after the Second World War: From Success to Failure." In *National Capitalism, Global Competition, and Economic Performance*, edited by S. Quack, G. Morga, and R. Whitley. Amsterdam: John Benjamin's Publishing.

Vartia, P., and P. Ylä-Anttila. 1996. *Kansantalous 2021*. ETLA Series B126, Sitra 153. Helsinki: Taloustieto Oy.

CHAPTER 3

Embracing Industrial Renewal

Vesa Salminen and Kalle Lamminmäki

As a small, knowledge-based economy, Finland has been increasingly subject to global influence and international competition. In addition to its strengths, Finland faces considerable challenges both domestically and internationally in efforts to maintain its position in world markets.

The key message of this chapter is that crises and structural transformations occur, affecting the economies of countries that are integrated into the global market economy. The fortunes of countries are however determined by how they prepare for and respond to the challenges. What is important in such times of change is that national systems (research, innovation, education, and economic policy, among others) are forward looking and prepared for the upcoming transformation.

Reasoning Behind: Current Economic Environment in Finland

The continuation of the Euro Area recession in 2013 and unstable global economic conditions are casting a cloud over Finnish prospects. Despite relatively good structural competitiveness, Finland is suffering from a slowdown in productivity growth (figure 3.1), a decline in its balance of payments (figure 3.2), and—by Finland's standards—relatively high unemployment (8 percent in 2012).

Industrial production has traditionally been the engine of growth for the Finnish economy. Up until the beginning of the new millennium, industrial production grew at a faster pace than total production. However, the level of industrial production also fell as a result of the 2008 economic crisis and has not recovered to pre-2008 levels (figure 3.3). In particular, the export of communication equipment and related services has declined due to problems in Nokia and structural changes in the industry. It can be expected that there are more years of slow growth to come (Pohjola 2010).

Simultaneously, Finland is experiencing yet another industrial transformation. Many contend that the Nordic model of the welfare state is under threat, as public sector debt rises and export sectors—forest industry, metal and machinery industry, electronics, and information and communication

Figure 3.1 Total Factor Productivity in Finland, 1975–2011

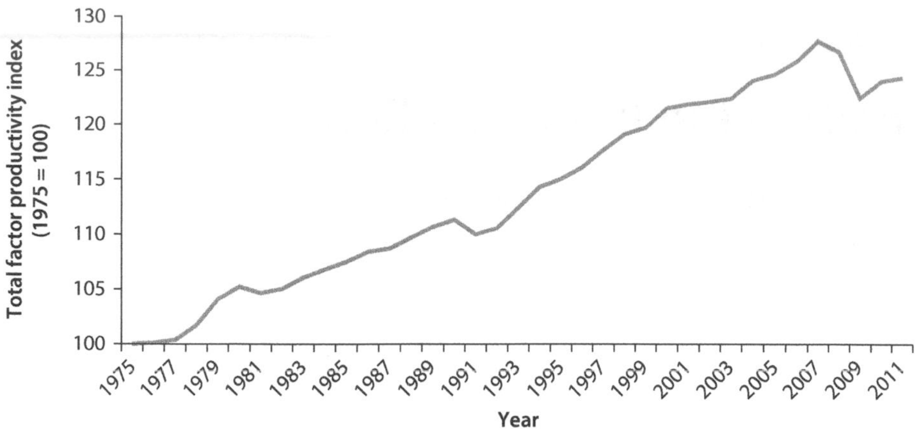

Source: OECD data (stats.oecd.org).

Figure 3.2 Balance of Payments (Main Economic Indicators) as a Percentage of GDP in Finland and Euro Area (17 Countries), 1990–2012

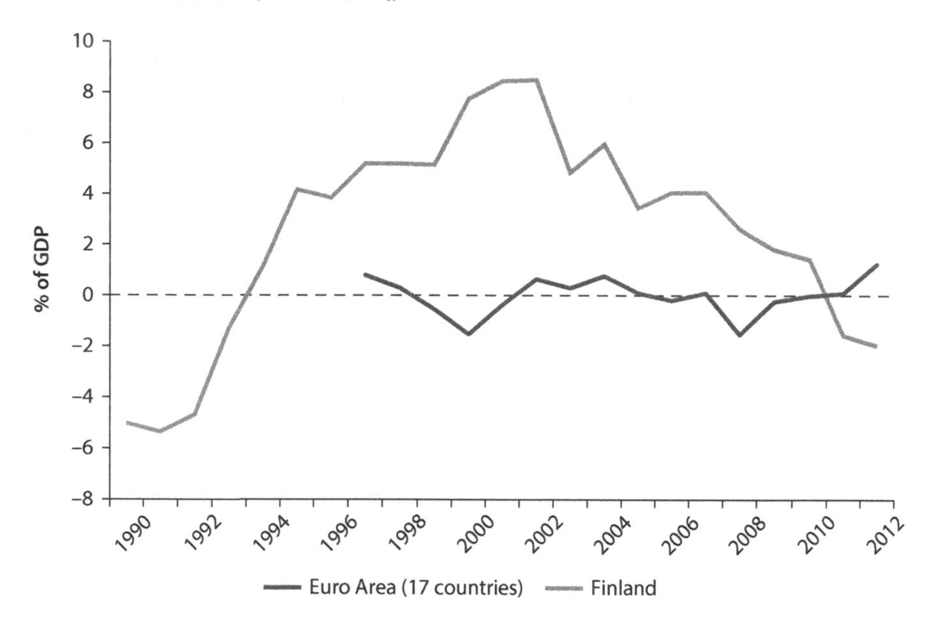

Source: OECD data (stats.oecd.org).

technology (ICT)—are in decline. Indeed, these central economic sectors formed 70 percent of the growth of value added of the Finnish economy in the 1990s, but only 50 percent in the 2000s (Pohjola 2010). This transformation is also evident in employment figures, as services account for more than 70 percent and secondary production for 26 percent of total employment.

Figure 3.3 Volume of Industrial Output in Finland, 1995–2013

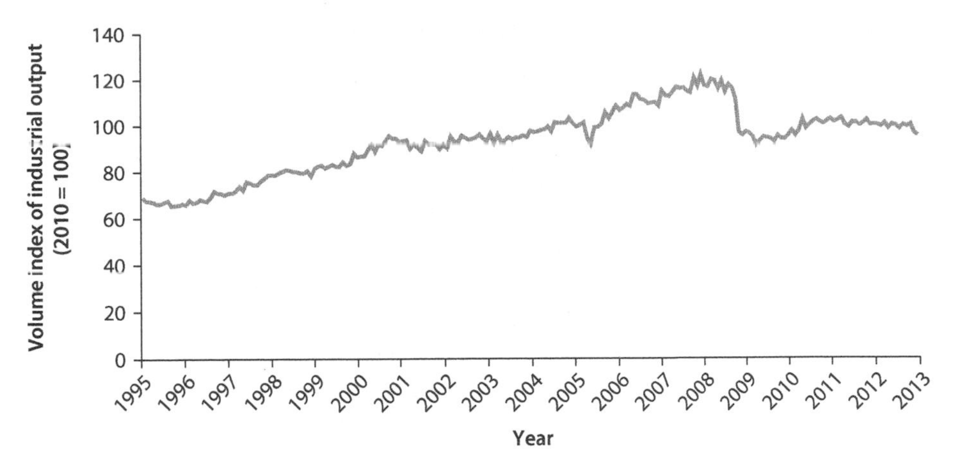

Source: OECD data (stats.oecd.org).

Figure 3.4 Employment in Primary and Secondary Production and Services as a Percentage of Total Employment in Finland, 1900–2010

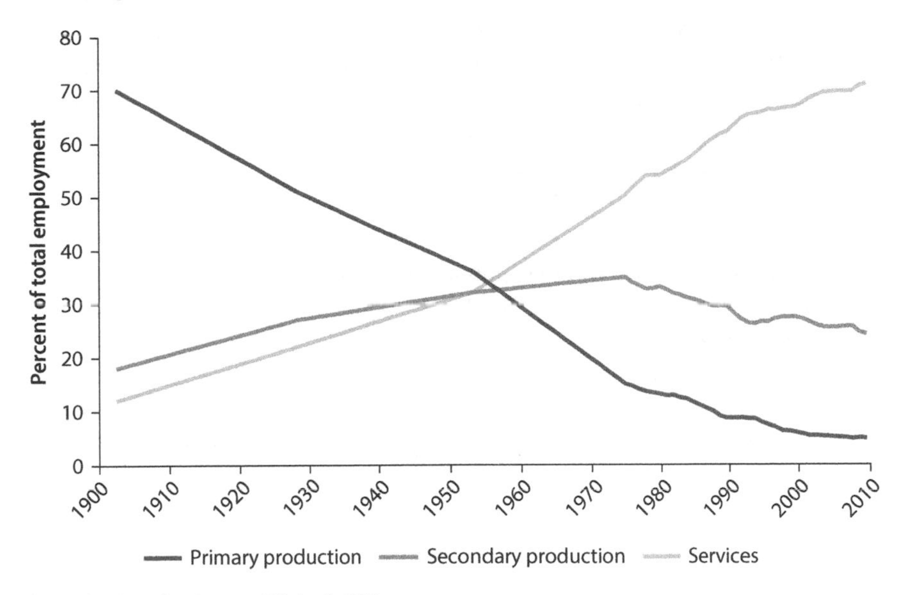

Source: Pajarinen, Rouvinen, and Ylä-Anttila 2012.

In 1950 the share of services in total employment was only 30 percent, compared to almost 40 percent for primary production (figure 3.4).

All of these changes (highlighted in box 3.1, which describes the case of Nokia) call for adjustments and new initiatives, especially regarding the promotion of entrepreneurial activities and industrial renewal. The following sections of this chapter describe some of the latest initiatives in this field.

Box 3.1 Nokia: Highlighting the Need for Constant Renewal

The story of Nokia is a great example of Finland's transition from a resource-based to a knowledge-based economy. The transition was marked by constant renewal and adaptation to global trends, showing that even major companies are vulnerable to changes in global markets and must constantly reinvent themselves.

Founded as a pulp mill company in 1865, Nokia has its roots in the history of another Finnish "big sector"—the forest industry. In 1967 Nokia merged with a cable works company and a rubber works company. During the following decades, rubber and cable formed the basis of Nokia's core knowledge and business.

In the 1980s Nokia acquired several electronics companies and began to shift its focus toward consumer electronics and telecommunications. The new strategy was not initially successful, as Nokia was hit by the 1990s recession. As a result, Nokia strengthened its emphasis on the electronics industry, especially telecommunications, and sold many of its former core business lines, including its forest, cable, television, and rubber businesses. During 1995–99, the company grew on average more than 30 percent a year, becoming the world's leading mobile phone manufacturer by 1998 and increasing its turnover to €31 billion.

During the past 10 years, Nokia has reinvented itself again, as the digital convergence of media, information technologies, and communications has proceeded and the trend has moved away from manufacturing hardware and toward producing services and content. Nokia was slow to develop a line of touch screen mobile phones and to turn its focus from hardware to software and mobile services. As competitors challenged Nokia's design, applications, and software platforms, Nokia tried to adapt. Since 2000, Nokia has acquired many companies related to services, including media sharing, music platforms, mobile advertising, and map data platforms. In 2007 a joint mobile network venture between Nokia and Siemens was launched. In 2011 Nokia announced a strategic partnership with Microsoft in February and released its first Windows phones in October.

However, the company's strategy of implementing the Windows operating system on its devices failed to bear fruit. On September 3, 2013, Microsoft announced that it had acquired Nokia's phone business (Ali-Yrkkö *et al.* 2013). In a sense, the sale of the phone business ended an era in Finland, with Nokia no longer the flagship of the Finnish economy. However, Nokia will continue to exist as a (smaller) company. It retains its operations in network devices with Nokia Solutions and Networks—Nokia acquired Siemens's share of the company in July 2013—and its location services through the HERE Unit. It also holds a portfolio of patents and other intellectual property rights.

Observations from the case:

- High productivity and growth are often found through innovations in new market segments.
- To maintain competitiveness and create jobs, companies, including established ones, mature companies, have to seek new opportunities for growth and adjust their strategies accordingly.
- Government policies should seek to encourage and facilitate industrial transformation, with the aim of creating more and better jobs and enhancing well-being in the future.

Increasing Global Competition

Finland, along with most national economies in the world, is in the middle of a new phase of globalization that started in the 1990s. The end of the Cold War and the electronic communication revolution fueled the relocation of industrial production to countries offering advantageous production costs combined with constantly improving infrastructure and increasingly skilled labor. The relative importance of the various factors of production was altered and in particular knowledge-intensive competencies grew in importance.

Finland is tackling the challenges of globalization largely in the same way as other developed countries where costs are high. However, being small and peripheral, Finland is in a very different position than Germany or France, for example. In comparison with small economies, big economies can use their home market more effectively to specialize in different products. The smallness of the Finnish home market forces small new companies to seek growth and expand to foreign markets early in their existence. In addition, small nations must be particularly active at transferring and diffusing knowledge and know-how from the knowledge centers of other countries.

Economic indicators based on gross domestic product (GDP) may be misleading in that they often fail to indicate the country's role in global value chains. It is crucial to identify where the value added of the product sold is created. Mobile phones produced in China are a case in point: only a few percentage points of the value added stay in China after the phone is sold, as most value added is created in the developed countries, where the brand, patents, design, service content, and other immaterial aspects of the mobile phone are developed (Pajarinen, Rouvinen, and Ylä-Anttila 2010). The share of value added that is created in the country is crucial. Hence every country should seek to identify its own industries' position in global value chains and, based on this assessment, identify in its innovation policy possible ways to increase the share of value added that stays in the country. As this book argues, investments in knowledge and knowledge-intensive industries are an important means of successful global competition.

The recent economic crisis has underlined the importance of shock absorption. Over the years, the Finnish economic environment had been considered one of the most competitive economies in the world. In particular Finland's long-term commitment to its educational institutions, the high level of welfare of the general populace, the equality of its labor market, and the efficiency of its public institutions were rated high in international comparisons, and the country has remained vibrant even in the face of economic crisis.

However, because of recent domestic and international economic and social developments, Finland constantly needs to reinvent its attractiveness and competitiveness. First of all, it is vital that the old welfare trajectory—and industries associated with it—not decelerate too fast. Finland has a diversified industrial structure with unique business, technological, and collaborative strengths supported by the Finnish education and research communities. This complexity still has a lot of development potential but faces increasing international competition. Without a sufficiently broad industrial base, Finland remains vulnerable to external shocks and adverse changes. This is evident not only from the experiences of Finland but also from those of several other developed and developing countries (Szirmai, Naudé, and Alcorta 2013).

At the same time, new resources and benefits should emerge, preferably in the near future. The Finnish industrial structure has been dominated by a small number of old, big companies. As production has been relocated abroad, the share of these companies in Finland's production, export, and employment has been quite low. Also business research and development (R&D) has been highly concentrated in Finland: the top 10 companies conduct about 60 percent of all R&D in the enterprise sector, and Nokia alone has been responsible for nearly half of Finland's business R&D.

In practice, globalization of innovation means that R&D conducted within the Finnish national borders is changing toward more challenging coordination, conceptual design, and managerial tasks, while routine tasks as well as market adaptation and customization are increasingly being located overseas. The same is true of predominantly Finnish-owned and -operated companies. Therefore, Finland has an acute and urgent need to create new businesses engaged in innovative activity and growth to compensate for losses generated by the bigger companies. The problem in Finland has not been the number of new companies, but the small number of "gazelles": small and medium enterprises (SMEs) that are able to grow and internationalize fast. Finland has a real gap between aspired and realized growth of new ventures. The reasons underlying the gap are not clear, but probably relate to low interest in high-growth entrepreneurship, aversion to risk, shortage of experience with high-growth ventures, and insufficient availability of funding (Autio *et al.* 2013). However, there has been some improvement in this regard, as Finland is doing increasingly better in international comparisons (Napier *et al.* 2012).

Recent years have shown that the future of Finland will rely less on a few leading industries and companies and more on widespread entrepreneurial activity. This poses a real challenge to Finnish R&D and innovation policies. Policies that supported the accumulation of wealth in the catching-up phase are not the same as those needed to support prosperity in a leading economy in the current global world (MEE and Ministry of Education and Culture 2009). A considerable part of Finland's success in the past was attributable to the long-term commitment to education and research. While this policy mix is still held dearly in Finland, increasing openness, R&D intensity, or educational attainment are in themselves insufficient for reaching the desired growth rates. The Innovation Mill program (box 3.2), the Demola open innovation platform (box 3.3), as well as the Vigo business accelerator program for start-ups (box 6.2 in chapter 6) are examples of attempts to spur more widespread innovation and entrepreneurial activity.

Box 3.2 Innovation Mill: Promoting Entrepreneurial Activity

Innovation Mill was founded in 2009 as a three-year joint project by Tekes, Technopolis (a Finnish operator of technology parks), and Nokia. Innovation Mill uses and creates new businesses that do not fall under Nokia's core business. The goal was to promote entrepreneurial activity by "screening" thousands of ideas to find approximately 100 new R&D projects for companies to acquire. The initial aim was to raise €8 million in project funding, including €4.5 million in public funding. Additional funds were allocated by eight Finnish cities. The project was coordinated and facilitated by Technopolis Ventures until 2013, when it was assigned to Open Innovation Management.

Due to its reliance on Nokia's immaterial rights, Innovation Mill cannot be totally open, and specific processes have been created to develop and commercialize Nokia's ideas. Tekes makes the final decisions on project funding.

When established, Innovation Mill was regarded as a groundbreaking and unique initiative in creating new businesses. Initial results have been encouraging. During its first years, Innovation Mill has created more than 250 new jobs and 50 new companies. The current project portfolio is about €30 million, including approximately €15 million in risk capital. In 2012 several other major Finnish companies joined Innovation Mill as anchor companies. For additional information, see the Open Innovation Management website (http://www.openim.fi/eng/services.php).

Observations from the case:

- Large, technology-based companies can be an important source of new enterprises.
- Efforts to transform an economy from traditional industries to a knowledge economy have consequences at the company level. New competencies are needed, and other competencies and business areas must be left behind.
- Innovative collaborative solutions (public-private partnerships), like Innovation Mill, can facilitate and smooth the transformation and provide a source of new growth and jobs.

The Ongoing Industrial Transformation

In Finland, as well as in most developed countries, services are expected to be one of the most promising sources of growth and well-being. The time of having many traditional industrial sectors is not yet over, but industrial employment in developed countries has been declining steadily. This development will continue and probably even accelerate in the future. At the same time, the importance of services to the economy, employment, productivity, and well-being has been increasing. For example, the percentage of employment in services rose from some 60 percent in 1991 (30 percent in 1950) to more than 70 percent in 2012 (figure 3.4).

Moreover, the old division of the economy into services and industry is no longer functional, as the distinction between them is increasingly blurred. Production processes are more and more dispersed globally. This enables companies to relocate certain tasks and functions, such as their physical

Box 3.3 Demola: Facilitating Open Innovation

Demola is a publicly funded, open innovation platform in which university students together with companies and education institutes develop product and service demonstration concepts (prototypes, or "demos") and apply them to real-life problems. The basic logic behind the platform is that student teams get the immaterial rights of the results, which then can be purchased in prefixed prices by the participating companies or developed further by new spin-off companies. Students receive experience working in real-life business projects as part of their studies, whereas companies get new perspectives and ideas.

In Finland Demola is coordinated by a private mediator company, Hermia, which conceptualized Demola in cooperation with Nokia. The first Demola was established in Tampere in 2008; since then, the concept has been extended successfully to Vilnius (Lithuania), Budapest (Hungary), and Oulu (Finland, in 2012). So far, approximately 1,500 students and 100 corporations have participated in approximately 250 projects, of which more than 90 percent have been claimed for business use.

Wider effectiveness and impacts of Demola have not been evaluated extensively, but initial results are promising and reactions have been positive. Demola offers a good example of open innovation between companies and universities. Demola's strengths are its neutral environment and facilities that are not dependent on any one participant, its cost-efficiency and agility, and its management of innovation ownership rights balancing the needs of students and companies. Demola also seems to be relatively easy to transfer to other settings. For additional information, see the Demola website (demola.net).

In Tampere, Demola has been integrated with two other open innovation concepts—Protomo and Suuntaamo. Together these form "New factory" platform provides students, self-employed entrepreneurs, researchers, and developers with an environment for open innovation, allowing them to process ideas into prototypes, pilot projects, products and services, new business, and new jobs." For additional information, see the following websites: Protomo (http://www.protomo.fi); Suuntaamo (www.suuntaamo.fi); new factory (http://newfactory.fi).

Observations from the case:

- Innovation processes in the knowledge economy are becoming increasingly complex and interdependent. They require the engagement of all available knowledge and competencies and active cooperation of various stakeholders.
- Platforms like Demola and others provide examples of how to design and organize platforms for collaboration that can facilitate open innovation processes.

production activities, more easily. Consequently, many traditional industrial companies have become service companies, and only a fraction of their production remains in physical production (Pajarinen, Rouvinen, and Ylä-Anttila 2012, 8). The leading Finnish industrial companies (for example, Nokia and the machinery industry) are, in fact, the most important exporters of services. Today, half of the industrial labor force works in service functions and tasks.

The traditional view was that productivity in services could not be increased at the same pace as productivity in industrial production and that the growth of services could hamper the growth of the economy (Baumol's cost disease). However, the digitalization of services changed this (Pajarinen, Rouvinen, and Ylä-Anttila 2012, 7) and the focus of research, development, and innovation activities is increasingly on services (box 3.4). As the emerging economies increase their production of traditional industrial products, services are forming a new asset in global competition (Pajarinen, Rouvinen, and Ylä-Anttila 2012, 7). Yet some have argued that the path to being a producer of services must be preceded by industrial manufacturing (Pajarinen, Rouvinen, and Ylä-Anttila 2010), in which services are added on top of the physical product.

Box 3.4 Forum Virium: Developing Digital Services

Forum Virium Helsinki was established in 2006 to promote cooperation with companies, the City of Helsinki and its residents in digital service creation. Operating on principle of openness, it nurtures radical, systemic innovations by engaging the user (city resident) to the innovation process and collaborative projects at early stage.

The cooperation starts by identifying development, service, and user needs. As the ideas start to form, Forum Virium rapidly launches pilot projects and tests the service concepts in practice. The focus areas are (1) well-being, (2) smart cities, (3) new forms of media, (4) environment and sustainability, (5) innovative procurement, (6) growth services, and (7) innovation communities. Forum Virium has different roles in the innovation process ranging from advisory position to the project executioner depending of the goals and set-up of the team.

Forum Virium has a diverse membership base including small and large actors. Plurality and diversity bring new angles and approaches to service creation process and reflects the challenges of cultivating urban innovation in a collaborative manner.

Operating as an innovation unit within the Helsinki City organization, Forum Virium is playing a key role in implementing Helsinki's Smart and Open City strategy. Forum Virium is active in international cooperation and has received recognition of its projects such as Helsinki Region Infoshare addressing opening of public data. For additional information, see the Forum Virium website (http://www.forumvirium.fi/en).

Observations from the case:

- Citizens and civil society are essential partners to engage when developing sustainable social innovations. Governments and municipalities can play a decisive role by including citizens to partnerships needed in the development of services, infrastructure and regulation.
- Open public-private partnership models and platforms, as piloted in Forum Virium, can be an effective way of organizing this collaboration.

Future Prospects of the ICT Sector

The electronics industry's success in the 1990s and beginning of the 2000s is now recent history. During the last 10 years, the industry has changed, and the Nokia cluster has shrunk significantly. Many of Nokia's subcontractors have been forced to reduce or move production to countries with lower production costs. Some 14,000 jobs have disappeared from the Nokia cluster since 2011, but many of those workers made redundant have found new jobs since then (see, for example, box 3.5 on the Nokia Bridge program). More jobs are created in SMEs than in larger companies. Indeed, more than 9 out of 10 new jobs are created in companies employing fewer than 250 people (MEE 2013, 13). These companies have a different market focus. They are less export oriented and more focused on the domestic market. Because expanding the customer base into other countries requires significant investments, small companies often choose to remain domestic.

In short, the Finnish ICT sector has changed from manufacturing products (hardware) to producing services (software, digital services). Hardware production has been transferred to low-cost countries, and the role of

---

Box 3.5 Nokia Bridge Program

Nokia set up the Nokia Bridge program in 2011 to help laid-off workers receive training and find new jobs. The program operated in 17 locations, of which four were in Finland. Nokia Bridge helps departing employees and employees under the threat of redundancy find new employment within or outside Nokia, provides continuing education and retraining, and helps participants start their own companies (Nokia 2011). The program has been relatively successful in reaching its goals, as 70 percent of the participants found new work in 2012 (Finnish Broadcasting Company 2012).

As part of the program, Nokia provides substantial funding to participants wanting to start their own companies. Each start-up can receive up to €25,000, with the limitation that no more than four former employees can come together for the start-up. In 2012 approximately 250 companies had received funding through the program. Approximately half of the new start-ups were in ICT and mobile applications. The business ideas often came out of projects that participants had pursued when still at Nokia, but that Nokia did not implement due to strategic or other reasons. For example, Jolla, a start-up formed by former Nokia employees, recently released its first mobile phone. The phone uses the MeeGo operating system, which Nokia set aside a few years ago.

Observation from the case:

- Governments should encourage large corporations, which are facing possible restructuring, to initiate innovative programs that encourage staff to establish spin-off companies and to create jobs.

---

knowledge-intensive expertise requiring higher education has maintained its position or even grown (Hernesniemi 2010).

In response to this structural change, the minister of economic affairs, Jyri Häkämies, set up a working group to examine the challenges that the ICT sector is encountering and to identify possible ways to address them.

The ICT 2015 Working Group noted that digital technologies and services could be better integrated with industrial products and that digital technology is underused in controlling global value chains (ICT 2015 Working Group 2013). In its analysis, the working group pointed to fractured public ICT infrastructure and proposed treating ICT not as a sector of the economy, but as a tool for the whole society. It urged Finland to involve both the public and private sectors in an effort to adopt and integrate elements of ICT in their operations and highlighted the role of ICT in bringing added value to products and services (MEE 2013).

What is left of the ICT sector after the structural change? First, despite structural changes and heavy loss of jobs in some sectors (and geographic regions), the ICT sector is still strong in Finland. In fact, due to growth in software and ICT services, the ICT sector remains a significant employer (see figure 3.5). According to Ali-Yrkkö *et al.* (2013),

> A dramatic structural change has occurred within the ICT sector. While ICT hardware manufacturers have shed their workforce, software firms have recruited more staff in Finland. Thus, the Finnish ICT sector does not rely only on Nokia anymore.
>
> The past few years have witnessed the birth and growth of new ICT companies. The most visible of those are game makers Rovio and Supercell. But there are also thousands of other software companies in Finland. The vitality of the Finnish ICT sector requires not only new establishments but also successful divestments of existing operations. Only the future will tell the total impact of the Microsoft–Nokia deal on the Finnish economy.

Second, Finnish companies have superior technologies in narrower sectors of ICT, such as mobile applications and services (MEE 2013, 17). Finnish companies have crucial skills, knowledge, and patents in these sectors. International ICT corporations, such as Electronic Arts, Ericsson, Huawei, Intel, and Samsung, have established R&D units in Finland, recognizing the quality of the Finnish pool of ICT skills. The Finnish base of ICT knowledge benefits companies working at the forefront of developments in areas such as mobile technologies. The pool of talent is more dispersed than it was during the heyday of the Nokia cluster, but it constitutes fertile ground for new start-ups and growth companies (such as Finland's game industry, described in box 3.6). The ICT 2015 Working Group points out that the state's role is to construct an environment that facilitates the renewal and growth of all companies (MEE 2013, 10), while holding on to dynamic large companies.

Figure 3.5 Employment in the ICT Sector in Finland, by Subcategories, 1990–2012

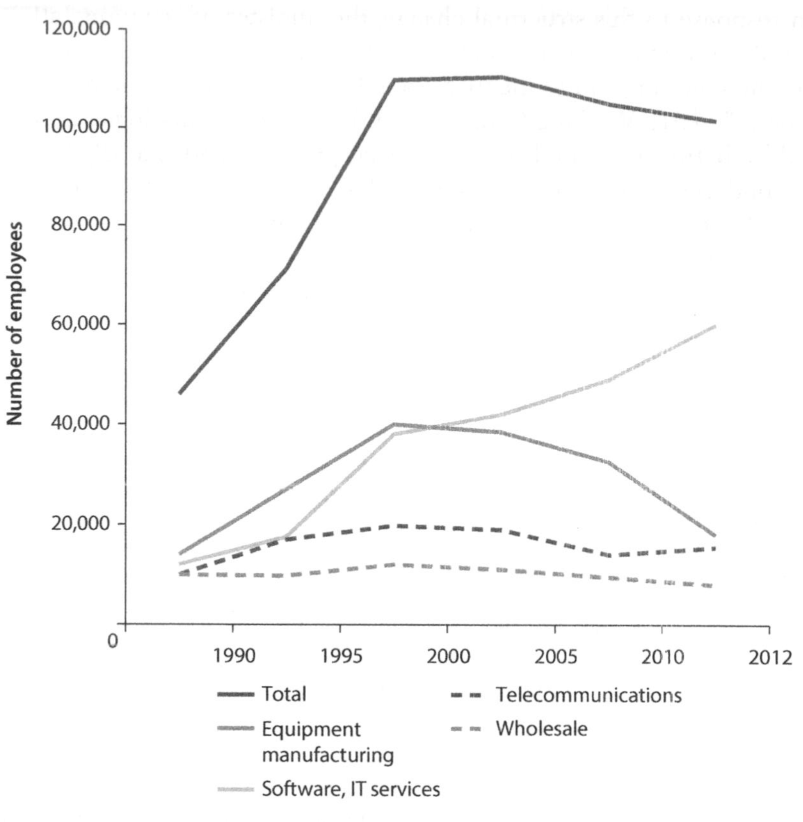

Sources: Based on Ali-Yrkkö *et al.* 2013; Statistics Finland data (https://www.tilastokeskus.fi/index_en.html).

Box 3.6 Game Industry and Information Security Cluster

The *Finnish game industry* (including mobile, console, personal computer, and Internet games) is growing rapidly, around 200 percent in 2012. Estimated turnover of the whole industry is €800 million (€250 million in 2012). Most of the companies are quite small, with only a few employing more than 50 employees. Among the most famous and successful Finnish companies are Rovio (Angry Birds) and Supercell (Clash of Clans). Both companies have used public funding (for example, Tekes funding) to develop their products and business. Supercell—bought by Japanese investors for around US$1.5 billion (approximately a third of Nokia's selling price) in November 2013—was part of the Vigo accelerator program (described in box 6.2 in chapter 6).

Another Finnish ICT industry with high annual growth rates is the *information security industry*. In 2012 dozens of Finnish companies formed the Finnish Information Security

box continues next page

Box 3.6 Game Industry and Information Security Cluster *(continued)*

Cluster (FISC). As of 2013, FISC encompasses some 50 companies (for example, F-Secure), which employ approximately 2,000 information security experts. Annual average growth of the cluster has been more than 20 percent in recent years, and growth is projected to continue despite the ongoing economic crisis. Globally, the cyber security market, currently approximately US$60 billion, is expected to double in five years to US$120 billion in 2017.

Both of these industries are still relatively small and recent. However, they are growing fast, with even higher future expectations. Both are also experiencing challenges related to the lack of available professionals—a challenge characterizing the latest ICT structural change. Both industries have emerged from the bottom up, but the government—through strategies and public funding of agencies—has had a role in creating enabling structures and policies to improve the preconditions of these industries. The ICT 2015 Working Group proposed the following measures to improve the operational preconditions of these industries: (1) increasing the amount and quality of training for the game industry to meet the need and (2) implementing pilot projects to integrate "gamification" and game interface forms into other industries and the public sector.

The measures promoting the information security industry include (1) increasing data security training and research in institutes of higher education and (2) forming a cyber-security center in Finland. The new center would also act as a partner for Finnish companies in developing new data security solutions.

For additional information, see ICT 2015 Working Group 2013; Neogames website (www.neogames.fi); FISC website (http://fisc.fi/).

Observations from the case:

- Economies will continue to evolve, moving toward higher productivity and higher added value. Innovation drives this change.
- Sometimes new industries, such as the Finnish software and game industry, spin out of existing clusters or emerge in new areas. At first, gaming was not considered a viable or promising industrial sector, but it has become one. Similar developments are taking place in all countries and industries. Some transitions are faster, some are slower.

Summary and Key Messages

As a small, knowledge-based economy, Finland has been increasingly subject to global influence and international competition. In addition to its strengths, Finland faces considerable challenges both domestically (worsening demographic dependency ratio, relatively high unemployment, slowdown in production) and internationally in efforts to maintain its position in world markets. Global competition has intensified significantly, and emerging economies are challenging Finland's role as a skills- and knowledge-driven economy. As production activities are increasingly located in countries with lower production costs, Finland is becoming increasingly reliant on exports with higher added value. The digitalization of services has opened up tremendous economic opportunities for producing knowledge-intensive services. New areas

Box 3.7 Key Messages

- All open economies are increasingly subject to global influence and international competition. This is particularly true for small, knowledge-based economies. The objective is not to avoid competition, but to improve and sustain competitiveness. Hence understanding global development trends and seeing changes as opportunities are important for policy planning. Countries should seek and be prepared for constant economic renewal.
- Improving the overall productivity of the economy and building its competitiveness and attractiveness for investors are a long-term process. In general, the relevant planning horizon should be a few decades rather than a few years, and there are no obvious shortcuts.
- Several characteristics are typical of this transformation (such as the increase in intangible investments and knowledge-based services) and can be used to indicate stages of change, progress, or development.
- Sometimes changes in technological paradigms offer opportunities for fast growth. ICT, in broad terms, has played an important role in Finland's transformation to a knowledge economy. During the 1990s, Finland was able to support the tremendous growth of the ICT sector and to use it to develop the knowledge economy. ICT still plays an important, but not an instrumental, role in the Finnish economy.

of the service sector, such as the game industry and the information security industry, are seen as future sources of growth. However, their potential remains to be seen.

Crises and structural transformations occur, affecting the economies of countries that are integrated into the global market economy. The fortunes of countries are determined by how they prepare for and respond to the challenges. What is important in such times of change is that national systems (research, innovation, education, economic policy) are prepared and ready for the upcoming transformation. A country should not emphasize a single sector of the economy without preparing alternative scenarios. A key concept in understanding challenges is forward planning (foresight), which is examined more closely in chapter 5.

Conditions that promote and support entrepreneurship are hard to create through direct state action, but as this book shows, the public sector can do much to create a desirable climate that supports multifaceted forms of entrepreneurship and encourages innovative companies to seek international growth. See box 3.7 for key messages of this chapter.

References

Ali-Yrkkö, J., M. Kalm, M. Pajarinen, P. Rouvinen, T. Seppälä, and A.-J. Tahvanainen. 2013. "Microsoft Acquires Nokia: Implications for the Two Companies and Finland." ETLA Brief 16, Research Institute of the Finnish Economy, Helsinki. http://pub.etla.fi/ETLA-Muistio-Brief-16.pdf.

Ali-Yrkkö, J., and P. Rouvinen. 2013. *Implications of Value Creation and Capture in Global Value Chains*. ETLA Report 16. Helsinki: Research Institute of the Finnish Economy. http://pub.etla.fi/ETLA-Raportit-Reports-16.pdf.

Autio, E., H. Rannikko, P. Kiuru, K. Luukkonen, R. Orenius, J. Handelberg, A. Bergenwall, and E. Berglund. 2013. *The Vigo Program Mid-Term Evaluation*. MEE Report 4/2013. Ministry of Employment and the Economy, Helsinki.

Finnish Broadcasting Company. 2012. "Nokian Bridge-ohjelma auttanut työttömiksi jääneitä [Nokia's Bridge Program Has Helped Staff Made Redundant]." Yle UUTISET, September 11. http://yle.fi/uutiset/nokian_bridge-ohjelma_auttanut_tyottomiksi_jaaneita/6289543.

Hernesniemi, H., ed. 2010. *Digitaalinen Suomi 2020 [Digital Finland 2020]*. Helsinki: Teknologiateollisuus ry. http://www.teknologiainfo.net/content/kirjat/pdf-tiedostot/Sahko_elektroniikka_ja_tietoteollisuus/digitaalinen_suomi-ekirja.pdf.

ICT 2015 Working Group. 2013. *21 Paths to a Frictionless Finland*. MEE 18/2013. Helsinki: Ministry of Employment and the Economy. http://www.tem.fi/files/36671/TEMjul_18_2013_web_15052013.pdf.

MEE (Ministry of Employment and the Economy). 2013. *21 Paths to a Friction-Free Finland*. MEE 4/2013. Helsinki: Edita Publishing. http://www.tem.fi/files/35440/TEMjul_4_2013_web.pdf.

MEE and Ministry of Education and Culture. 2009. *Evaluation of the Finnish National Innovation System*. Policy report. Helsinki: Taloustieto Oy. http://www.tem.fi/files/24926/InnoEvalFi_POLICY_Report_28_Oct_2009.pdf.

Napier, G., P. Rouvinen, D. Johansson, T. Finnbjörnsson, E. Solberg, and K. Pedersen. 2012. *The Nordic Growth Entrepreneurship Review, 2012*. Nordic Innovation Report 25:2012. Oslo: Nordic Innovation. http://www.nordicinnovation.org/Global/_Publications/Reports/2013/NGER_2012_noApp.pdf.

Nokia. 2011. *Nokia Sustainability Report, 2011*. http://i.nokia.com/blob/view/-/1961956/data/1/-/nokia-sustainability-report-2011-pdf.pdf.

Pajarinen, M., P. Rouvinen, and P. Ylä-Anttila. 2010. *Missä arvo syntyy? Suomi globaalissa kilpailussa*. ETLA Series B247. Helsinki: Taloustieto Oy.

———. 2012. *Uutta arvoa palveluista*. ETLA Series B256. Helsinki: Taloustieto Oy. http://www.etla.fi/wp-content/uploads/ETLA-B256.pdf. Summary in English: Pajarinen, M., P. Rouvinen, and P. Ylä-Anttila. 2013. "Services: A New Source of Value." ETLA Brief, Taloustieto Oy, Helsinki. http://pub.etla.fi/ETLA-Muistio-Brief-11.pdf.

Pohjola, M. 2010. "Miten tuottavuuden kasvun käy? [What Will Happen to Productivity Growth?]" In *Kriisin jälkeen*, edited by P. Rouvinen and P. Ylä-Anttila. Sitra 288. Helsinki: Yliopistopaino.

Szirmai, A., W. Naudé, and L. Alcorta. 2013. *Pathways to Industrialization in the Twenty-First Century*. Oxford: Oxford University Press.

CHAPTER 4

Education as Competitive Paradigm

Katri Haila

The role of education in Finland's knowledge economy has received positive attention, with educational achievement appearing consistently at the top of international performance rankings. Yet, due to increasing global competition, demographic challenges, and structural transformation, the Finnish education system needs to be improved.

This chapter presents the key elements behind Finland's educational success, highlighting the need to make systematic investments and take a long-term perspective, offer comprehensive basic education and effective guidance, as well as foster the ability to adjust to new challenges.

Reasoning Behind: Finnish Educational Success

A highly educated population is a crucial resource for building a knowledge economy. This, in turn, requires a comprehensive and efficient education system. It is widely acknowledged that a comprehensive and high-quality education system is a key building block behind Finland's economic success.

The Finnish education system is indeed an interesting and widely studied model. Total educational expenditure in Finland is at the same level as the average for the Organisation for Economic Co-operation and Development (Kyrö 2012 figures), and yet the Finnish education system ranks high in international comparisons. Recently, Finland took first place in a study comparing literacy rates, school attendance, and university graduation rates around the world (Economist Intelligence Unit 2012). In the 2000s, Finland emerged as the leading country in Program for International Student Assessment (PISA) reviews assessing the learning outcomes of students 15 years of age in mathematics, science, and reading literacy. However, the most recent results show that the reading and mathematical literacy of Finnish students has been declining (Hautamäki *et al.* 2013; Kupari *et al.* 2013). This decline implies a deeper ongoing cultural change affecting especially the younger generation and their attitudes toward formal education (Hautamäki *et al.* 2013). This further highlights the need to adjust the Finnish education system in the future.

According to the latest PISA results, Finland remains the highest in literacy and science among European countries. Finland's PISA success has been attributed primarily to the provision of uniform basic education, highly competent teachers, and autonomy for schools. Other factors include Finnish society's positive attitude toward education, attention accorded to individual support for learning and well-being in schools, and a very high-quality library system.

In addition to a high level of education for both women and men, the Finnish knowledge economy is based on equal opportunities in education, a lifelong learning policy, and flexibility of the education system to react to new labor needs. For example, gender differences in mathematics are minimal in Finland (Kupari *et al.* 2013). Most of these elements are common in other Nordic countries, but quite rare in other OECD countries. The following sections of this chapter discuss these elements in more detail.

Systematic Long-Term Investments

Finland has systematically and strongly invested in education since independence. Raising the level of education was a policy for the young nation from the very beginning, and investments in education have been a key driver of innovation since then. Education is widely seen as a key competitive paradigm.

Investments both in education and in research and development (R&D) were an important part of the recovery from economic crisis and restructuring of the economy in the early 1990s. Highly skilled technology experts were needed, for example, in the information and communication technology (ICT) sector and by Nokia. In the 1990s Finland's educational expenditure was at its highest and close to the highest in the OECD. In 1995, total educational expenditure accounted for 6.3 percent of gross domestic product (GDP), comparable to that of Canada, at 6.7 percent (Kyrö 2012). In 2008, total educational expenditure in Finland was at the same level as the OECD average, 5.9 percent of GDP, or approximately €10 million (Kyrö 2012; Statistics Finland; see also figure 2.2 in chapter 2).

General education, vocational education, and polytechnics are co-financed by the government and local authorities. All education providers, both municipal and private organizations, receive state subsidies. Benefits such as one meal a day, instruction materials, and transport to school increase the costs of education for the municipalities and the state (Kyrö 2012). The funding for basic education is based on the number of persons 6 to 15 years of age living in the municipality and special conditions of the municipality. In the funding of upper-secondary education and vocational education and training, the number of students reported by the school and the unit prices set by the Ministry of Education and Culture are taken into account. The government allocates funding for the polytechnics in the form of core funding, which is based on unit costs per student, project funding, and performance-based funding (Ministry of Education and Culture 2013).

According to the national education policy, Finland has focused investments on achieving a high level of competence (box 4.1). When compared internationally,

Box 4.1 History of the Finnish Education System in Brief

In the 1800s, Finland was an autonomous grand duchy in the Russian Empire. The official language of Finland at that time was Swedish. Before the establishment of the Finnish school system, the Lutheran Church organized traveling schools, which provided basic education in Finnish. The nationalist movement's goals included national public education taught in Finnish.

In 1861 Uno Cygnaeus, the father of Finnish comprehensive schools, proposed a plan and curriculum for basic primary education. He also started teacher education in Finnish language. The national school system of Finland, independent of the church, was set up in 1866. In 1869 the Board of Education was established under the Ministry of Education to inspect, monitor, and govern the school system. Finland became independent in 1917.

School inspections played an important role in quality assurance during development of the Finnish education system. They were implemented in the early 1900s and discontinued in the early 1990s. At present, quality assurance is achieved through legislative directives.

General compulsory education was prescribed by law in 1921. The first curriculum for compulsory basic education was accepted in 1925. The second curriculum reform was in 1946–52, and the third was in 1970. The comprehensive school, which consists of nine years of compulsory schooling, was created in the 1970s. The most recent basic education core curriculum is from 2004.

Vocational education began in the nineteenth century to meet the needs of the rapidly growing sectors of industry and construction.

Since the 1980s, state and local funding has provided information technology (IT) for schools. The state also has supported teacher training in the use of IT (Sinko and Lehtinen 1999).

Polytechnic education, a non-university sector of higher education, was founded in the 1990s. The first polytechnics were made permanent in 1996. At present, there are 25 polytechnics in the country.

The first *university* was founded in 1640. The University of Helsinki started out in Turku as a Swedish national university. In its second phase (1807–1917), the university was renamed the Imperial Alexander University of Finland and moved to Helsinki. The university formed part of a university network of the Russian Empire. Its third stage, as a university of the Finnish Republic, began with Finland's independence in 1917. The name was changed to the University of Helsinki in 1919. At present, there are 16 universities around the country.

educational expenditure is highest in Finland in lower-secondary and higher education. The higher education expenditure per university and polytechnic student is clearly above the OECD average (Kyrö 2012). The government provides some 70 percent of the budget of universities. Two universities are foundation universities, and the rest are public corporations. Every three years, each university and the Ministry of Education and Culture set operational and qualitative targets for the university as well as the resources required. The universities are expected to raise external funding from both national and international sources (Ministry of

Education and Culture 2013). Structural changes in the polytechnic sector will take place beginning in 2014. In the first phase, these changes will include amendments to legislation concerning the funding model, operating licenses, and educational responsibilities of the polytechnics.

Efficient Steering Combined with Local Autonomy

The basic right to education is established in the Finnish constitution. The legislative instruments contain provisions on the general aims, subjects to be taught, languages of instruction, learning outcome assessment, and rights and duties of pupils. The ideology is to steer by providing information, support, and funding. There are 48 Finnish acts and decrees concerning education (available in English at the Ministry of Education and Culture's website, www.minedu.fi). These national arrangements are influenced by policies and objectives established jointly in the European Union (EU), the Council of Europe, the OECD, and the United Nations and in Nordic cooperation.

The governance of education is implemented on the national, regional, and local levels. The government and the Ministry of Education and Culture are responsible for planning and implementing education policy at the national level. The lines of education are determined in a development plan for education and research, which is approved by the government. Nearly all publicly funded education is subordinate to, or supervised by, the Ministry of Education and Culture. In addition, the ministry prepares legislation and national budgetary proposals regarding education and science and drafts government resolutions on these topics. The ministry also steers the activities of polytechnics and universities by means of performance management. Polytechnics are municipal or private institutions, whereas all universities are either independent corporations under public law or foundations under the Foundations Act.

The regional state administrative agencies and the centers for economic development, transport, and the environment (ELY centers; see chapter 6) handle certain educational matters at the regional level. Local authorities—that is, municipalities—are responsible for providing basic education for children living in the municipality. General upper-secondary education is provided by local authorities or their consortia, registered organizations, and foundations. Vocational education and training may also be provided by the government and state companies (Ministry of Education and Culture 2013).

Local authorities—most commonly municipalities or joint municipalities—determine the allocation of funding, local curricula, and how much autonomy is passed to schools. The schools are responsible for the effectiveness and quality of education. In practice, teachers choose the methods of teaching, including materials. Furthermore, the schools organize their own administration and, in many cases, recruit staff for the school (Ministry of Education and Culture 2013).

The aim of education policy is to influence the direction of education by providing information, support, and funding instead of exercising control.

The objectives are laid down in legislation and national core curricula, but educational autonomy is high at all levels. The National Board of Education is responsible for providing the national core curriculum for basic and upper-secondary education. The core curriculum determines matters that are central to education and teaching, such as the goals. The local curricula are designed by the education providers, in most cases the local authority (see boxes 4.2 and 4.3).

Comprehensive Educational Structure

The main objective of Finnish education policy is to offer all citizens equal opportunities to receive education regardless of age, domicile, financial situation, sex, mother tongue, or geographic location. Basic education is completely free of charge, including instruction, school materials, school meals, health care, dental care, commuting, special-needs education, and remedial teaching (Finnish National

---

Box 4.2 Core and Local Curricula for Basic Education: Guaranteeing Equal Quality and Enabling Autonomy

The national core curriculum for basic (grades 1–9, 7–16 years of age) and upper-secondary education (including general upper-secondary education ending in a matriculation exam and vocational upper-secondary education) is determined by the National Board of Education—on the basis of government acts and decrees—and confirmed by the government. The curriculum includes the objectives and core content of different subjects as well as the principles of pupil assessment, special-needs education, pupil welfare, and educational guidance, a good learning environment, approaches to work, and the concept of learning. The current national core curriculum for basic education was confirmed in January 2004 and introduced in schools in August 2006.

Due to flexible time allocation, individual schools may focus on different subjects in different ways. However, all Finnish pupils in every part of the country receive the same education in grades 1–6 (7–13 years of age). This is also true in grades 7–9 (14–16 years of age), but in these grades there is more flexibility, and pupils (officially the parents) can choose more freely between subjects.

The core subjects taught to all pupils in the basic education syllabus are the mother tongue and literature (Finnish or Swedish), the other official language, one foreign language (mostly English, but also German, Russian, and French, among others, depending on the school), environmental studies, health education, religion or ethics, history, social studies, mathematics, physics, chemistry, biology, geography, physical education, music, art and crafts, and home economics. In addition, optional subjects can be determined by local authorities and schools. The core curriculum also includes the National Board of Education's recommendation for instruction in the native languages of immigrants. Within the framework of the national core curriculum, local education authorities and schools can determine their own curricula.

For additional information, see the National Board of Education website (www.oph.fi/english/education).

Box 4.3 Evaluating Education

In Finland, education providers have a statutory duty to evaluate their own activities and to participate in external evaluations. Evaluation data are used in developing the evaluation system, evaluation policy, and the core curricula and in teaching in the classroom.

Quality assurance focuses on self-evaluation of schools and education providers. The aim is to offer information, support, and funding to support quality assurance rather than to control it. The objectives laid down in legislation, the national core curriculum, and qualification requirements are the key documents for guidance. In addition, national evaluations of learning outcomes seek to determine how well the objectives have been reached. Educators receive their own results for development purposes. The matriculation examination is the only national assessment; it is taken by general upper-secondary school students.

Separate evaluation bodies are responsible for external evaluations. The evaluation of universities and polytechnics is the responsibility of the Finnish Higher Education Evaluation Council (FINHEEC), which conducts audits of universities and polytechnics. It seeks to support education providers (basic education, upper-secondary education, vocational education, adult education, and Swedish-speaking education) in matters concerning educational evaluation. Both FINHEEC and the Education Evaluation Council operate under the Ministry of Education and Culture. The National Board of Education produces national information on the quality and outcome of evaluations. For more information on evaluation practices in Finland, see chapter 7.

Board of Education 2013). Furthermore, there are no tuition fees at the post-compulsory level in general and vocational upper-secondary education, in polytechnics, or in universities.

The Finnish education system is composed of nine years of basic education (comprehensive school), preceded by one year of voluntary pre-primary education, upper-secondary education comprising vocational and general education, and higher education provided by universities and polytechnics (figure 4.1). All students are given the opportunity to progress from one level of education to the next, and this right is safeguarded by legislation. A student completing one level is always eligible for the next level of studies. The qualifications of each level are governed by a separate act of parliament. The higher education system comprises universities and polytechnics, in which the admissions requirement is a secondary-level general or vocational diploma. Universities, which are academic or artistic institutions, focus on research and on research-based education. Polytechnics offer work-related education in response to labor market needs and focus on regional development (Hanhijoki *et al.* 2012; Ministry of Education and Culture 2013). At the levels of general and vocational upper-secondary education, polytechnics, and universities, there are no tuition fees. At these levels of education, students pay for their textbooks, travel, and meals (Ministry of Education and Culture 2013).

Figure 4.1 Finnish Education System

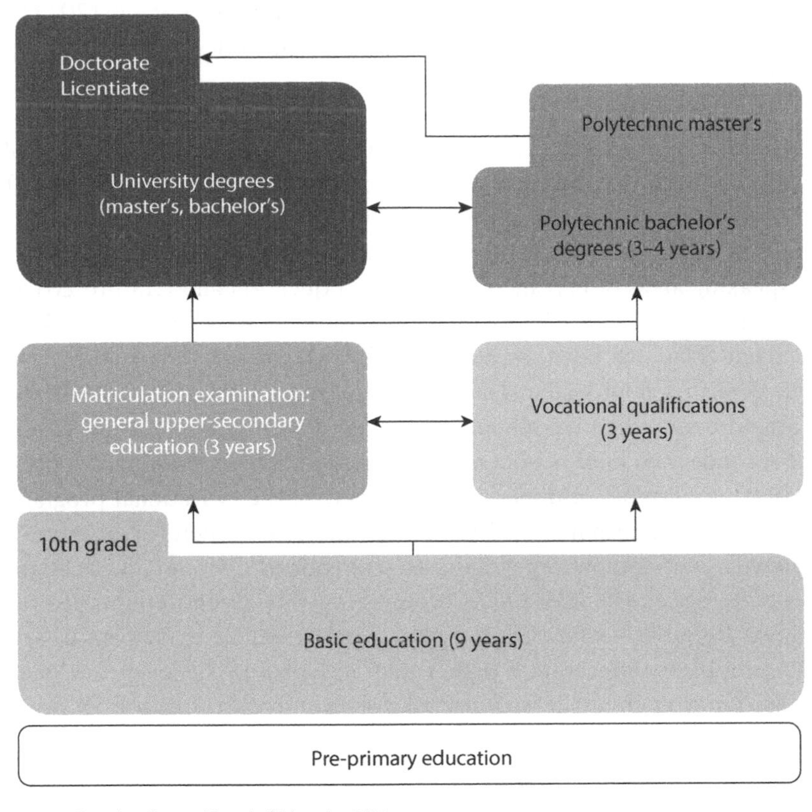

Source: Based on National Board of Education 2013.

The Finnish education system is regionally comprehensive. There are some 3,200 schools providing basic education, around 200 organizations providing vocational education and training, 25 polytechnics, and 16 universities (Ministry of Education and Culture 2013). In fact, one of the major characteristics of Finnish education is the uniform quality of education irrespective of the geographic location of the school. The school network is regionally extensive. For example, in basic education the number of pupils was 541,000 and the number of public schools was 2,719 in 2011. In 2007 the number of private schools for basic education was 59. There are plenty of small schools in Finland's sparsely populated areas. Almost all pupils attend their nearest local school. The average size of comprehensive schools was 189 pupils in 2011 (National Board of Education 2013). The average class size was less than 20 in lower-secondary schools (Kyrö 2012).

Socioeconomic background is relatively weakly correlated with student performance (Hautamäki *et al.* 2013). For example, the results of PISA 2009 showed that background is associated with reading performance in all countries, but differences are smaller in Finland than in most OECD countries. The link between socioeconomic background and performance is weakest in countries with the highest performance in reading—that is, Canada, Finland, and the Republic of Korea (Kyrö 2012). However, as Hautamäki *et al.* (2013) point out, mothers' educational level and children's attitudes toward learning are correlated.

Another characteristic of the Finnish education system is that it is very comprehensive with regard to demographic minorities. Finland has two official languages, Finnish and Swedish. The proportion of pupils in schools offering basic education in Swedish is approximately 6 percent (Statistics Finland). Local authorities are required to offer education in the Sami language in the Sami-speaking areas of Lapland (Ministry of Education and Culture 2013). The proportion of pupils in schools offering basic education in Sami is less than 0.1 percent (National Board of Education 2013).

The Finnish school system has no sex-specific school services. All boys and girls attend comprehensive school. The level of women's education is high. Of upper-secondary school students, 57 percent are women, accounting for 51 percent at all types of upper-secondary and further vocational programs and 55 percent at polytechnics. In 2009 approximately 92 percent of women had completed a post-compulsory qualification in Finland, compared with 88 percent of men. There are only three OECD countries—the Czech Republic, Korea, and the Slovak Republic—where the proportion of women 25 to 34 years of age with a post-compulsory education is higher than in Finland. The level of education is also high for women at the university level. Women account for 53 percent of university students (Kyrö 2012).

Educating Educators as a Key to Success?

Teachers in comprehensive schools have been university-educated since the early 1970s. The education of kindergarten teachers was transferred to universities in the mid-1990s. Today, according to Sahlberg (2010), excellent teachers are considered a key element in Finnish PISA success.

Teaching is a highly respected profession in Finnish society. A master's degree is required to teach basic education and general upper-secondary education. Vocational teachers are required to have an appropriate higher or postgraduate academic degree, teachers at polytechnics are required to have either a master's or a postgraduate degree, and university teachers are generally required to hold a doctoral or postgraduate degree. Different types of teaching posts have different qualifications, which were codified in the Teaching Qualifications Decree (986/1998) (National Board of Education 2013).

Teaching is a regulated profession in Finland, which means that specific qualifications and types of education are required to become a teacher (box 4.4). In principle, all preschool teachers have a university degree, and the entry to teacher training (in universities) is very competitive. Throughout their career, teachers are encouraged to develop their professional competence. At most levels of education, teachers are required to participate in in-service training every year as part of the agreement on salaries. In addition, in-service training is provided in

Box 4.4 Teacher Education in Finland

Teachers are certified either as class teachers (grades 1–6) or as subject teachers (grades 7–9 and upper secondary schools). This division was adopted in 1970 when the Finnish school system was redefined. Teachers certified as subject teachers may also work in vocational education and adult education.

Education for both class and subject teachers (as well as kindergarten teachers) is provided by university departments of teacher education. Seven Finnish-language universities and one Swedish-language university provide teacher education.

To obtain a degree, 300 European Credit Transfer and Accumulation System (ECTS) are needed for class and subject teachers (usually five years) and 180 ECTS are needed for kindergarten teachers (three years). This includes 60 ECTS of pedagogical studies and 20 ECTS of practical training for class and subject teachers and 25 ECTS for kindergarten teachers. Pedagogical studies combine theory and practice. Practical training is organized by universities together with so-called affiliated schools.

Subject teachers usually study a particular subject (such as history) in another university department e.g. department of history, and then apply for training as a subject teacher. In practice, this usually means completing the degree in the particular subject and then entering the teacher education department.

As with all university studies in Finland, teacher education is completely free-of-charge.

For additional information, see the National Board of Education website (http://www.oph.fi/english/education/teachers/teachers_in_general_education).

areas important for implementing education policy and reforms. In 2010 the Ministry of Education implemented a special national program (Osaava Program) for teachers' continuing education (Ministry of Education and Culture 2013).

New Needs Call for Adjustments

In the 1990s, Finland experienced a major structural change moving from an industrial economy to a knowledge economy and innovation-driven economic development (see chapter 3). The high educational level of the population and the quick response of the education system to the growing need to produce new engineers were among the key factors facilitating Finland's transformation (Dahlman 2007). Currently Finland is facing new challenges requiring the education system to adapt. According to the government's development plan (Ministry of Education and Culture 2012), a primary aim is to enhance the competitiveness of Finnish knowledge and competence. Moreover, Finland's success in global competition, the promotion of well-being in society as a whole, and the prevention of exclusion require that the entire population and workforce have a strong base of knowledge.

First, due to the demographic changes and worsening demographic dependency ratio, further development is needed to extend careers and to improve the match between the skills of individuals entering the labor market and those needed by businesses and public bodies.

Second, the structural transformation occurring in the Finnish electrical, electronics, and information technology (IT) services sector has had a significant effect on Finland's current and future labor market needs (Ylä-Anttila 2012). Technology is the most important industrial sector in Finland, directly employing 290,000 persons and having a total employment effect of 700,000, equaling a quarter of the Finnish workforce (Federation of Finnish Technology Industries 2013). Many high-skill jobs are disappearing from the ICT sector (that is, the Nokia cluster) due to diminishing production and employment in mobile telecom industry. At the same time, employment in IT services is increasing. In addition, new ICT-related jobs are being created in mechanical and electrical engineering integrating software, intelligence, and services in their products (Ylä-Anttila 2012).

These challenges require adjustments to both the structure of education through system-level reforms and the "educational profiles" of individuals through continuous reskilling and competence building.

At the system level, education policies strive to support the creation of new jobs in Finland and enable both individuals and businesses to adapt to the changes caused by globalization. One way of addressing this is by adjusting the intake numbers of universities and polytechnics. According to the Ministry of Education and Culture (2012), the entrance targets for 2016 will be cut back in the fields of culture, natural sciences, natural resources and the environment, tourism, catering, and domestic services. It is estimated that the need for education in culture is 3,000 entrants less than the current intake. Furthermore, cuts will be made in initial vocational and polytechnic education in tourism and initial vocational training in hotel management and catering, because the need for entrants in tourism, catering, and domestic services is 1,300 less than the current intake. Instead, the offer of education will be increased in the social services, health care, and sport sectors as well as in the field of humanities and education. More spots are needed in vocational automotive technology and logistics training and in health and social services education. Generally, the intake numbers in both secondary and higher education will increase more than the size of the age group. The aim is to increase the share of post-primary qualification holders 25 to 34 years of age to 92.5 percent by 2015 and to 95 percent by 2020.

At the level of the individual, the Finnish education system focuses on providing a learning pathway without dead ends. Adult education is provided at all levels of education, and it is planned to be as flexible as possible in order to enable adults to study while they work. Adult education is composed of education and training leading to a degree or a certificate, liberal education, and staff training. In vocational training, competence-based qualifications are specifically intended for adults. In higher education, polytechnics offer separate adult education programs. Furthermore, some universities have separate centers for continuing education.

Recently, Hanhijoki *et al.* (2012) estimated the entrance targets for 2016. The estimates are lower than the targets set by the Ministry of Education and

Culture for university education. In the future, the increasingly global labor market will call for closer international cooperation to develop models anticipating the need for education and skills. As an example, the need for employees with technical backgrounds, such as engineers, declined from the early 1990s to 2010, whereas the share of Nokia recruits with business related educational background increased.

In terms of education, qualification completion times should be accelerated, flexibility at transition points between different levels of education should be improved, educational overlaps should be reduced, and recognition of prior learning should be enhanced (Hanhijoki *et al.* 2012). Additionally, there is a growing discussion on the need to retain foreigners who are studying in Finland. Several initiatives and projects target these needs. In the recent national immigration strategy, these issues were strongly highlighted (Ministry of the Interior 2013). Furthermore, there are several mobility programs at the EU and the Nordic level. A key actor in coordinating these activities and supporting internationalization is the Center for International Mobility, which is under the Ministry of Education and Culture. National arrangements and decisions of the education system are informed and influenced by international policies and objectives jointly formulated in the EU (for example, the Copenhagen process, Bologna process), the OECD, and the United Nations as well as in Nordic cooperation.

In addition, business will increasingly be transacted in global networks comprising a wide range of actors. The sectors are networking to form close-knit clusters. It is important to anticipate the future needs of a network economy. For example, a project entitled Competence Needs of Learning Networks, financed by the European Social Fund, the Finnish National Board of Education, and the Confederation of Finnish Industries, aims to understand Finland's future competence needs. The success of learning networks depends on the synergy between specific areas of competence (Confederation of Finnish Industries 2013).

In the future, there will be a need to enhance entrepreneurship education at all levels. Recently, Nokia has been a good source of highly skilled labor for start-ups and small and medium enterprises (SMEs; Pajarinen and Rouvinen 2013). Economic growth is increasingly based on entrepreneurship, new companies, and SMEs (Ylä-Anttila 2012). SMEs have a significant role in Finnish business. Firms employing fewer than 250 people constitute 99.8 percent of all companies, and SMEs are responsible for 50 percent of the turnover of all Finnish enterprises (Statistics Finland, https://www.tilastokeskus.fi/index_en.html). The Ministry of Education has set development priorities by type of education to make entrepreneurship a more attractive career choice. Furthermore, measures have been taken to develop entrepreneurship education in teacher's initial training. At present, all vocational qualifications include entrepreneurship and business studies and on-the-job learning. More than 30 percent of entrepreneurs have a vocational qualification, and many have a university or polytechnic degree. In higher education, entrepreneurship education will be increasingly offered as an elective course available to all students.

Entrepreneurial training can be provided in various ways, such as a polytechnic master's program in SME business or cooperation between higher education and business. As an example, Aalto University has created new "factories" where students and researchers work together with companies and other communities (box 4.5). The education sector participates in the factories, where new knowledge produced by research is transferred to teaching. Furthermore, the Aalto Center for Entrepreneurship (ACE) works to create a culture of entrepreneurship (box 4.6). Also Demola (box 3.3 in chapter 3) is a good example of combining entrepreneurial activities and education.

Summary and Key Messages

Investments in education are the basis for the knowledge economy. Finland has systematically and strongly invested in education. Besides taking a "big picture" view of education, Finland has achieved educational success by supporting education through legislation and national policies, funding

---

Box 4.5 Aalto University: Adjusting to Needs at the Structural Level

Aalto University started operating in 2010. Three universities (Helsinki School of Economics, Helsinki University of Technology, and the University of Art and Design Helsinki) were combined to form this multidisciplinary, foundation-based university involved in the fields of technology, economics, art, and design.

Aalto University was established to strengthen the Finnish innovation system by integrating the study of science and technology, business and economics, as well as art and design. The mission of the university is to support Finland's success through high-quality research and teaching, to strengthen Finnish society, and to build competitiveness.

Capital for the university (a total of €700 million) was received from the government (€500 million) and Finnish industries and other financiers (€200 million). The new University Act (2010) increased the autonomy of Aalto University and improved the preconditions for its operations and basic research.

At present, Aalto University has six schools: School of Arts, Design, and Architecture, School of Business, School of Chemical Engineering, School of Electrical Engineering, School of Engineering, and School of Science. In reforming the curriculum, priority is being given to future skill needs, opportunities to study and work internationally, and learning-driven teaching methods. Digital resources will be used more in the future, which will make open-access teaching materials and courses possible. In 2012, Aalto University had 19,993 undergraduate and doctoral students, 5,330 staff members, and 366 professors. For additional information, see the Aalto University website (www.aalto.fi).

Observation from the case:

- Promoting multidisciplinary collaboration and cross-disciplinary innovations is essential in adjusting to new needs. Sometimes adjustments may also be needed at the structural level.

Box 4.6 Aalto Factories and the Center for Entrepreneurship: Adjusting to New Needs within Higher Education

In order to understand the scope of the major challenges facing society, Aalto University has developed a platform for multidisciplinary collaboration between Aalto students and researchers as well as the business world and the public sector. This platform includes four "factories": design, media, service, and health. The factories serve as multidisciplinary platforms combining the expertise of the university's various schools as well as that of companies and communities. Developing new teaching and learning approaches is one of their central goals. Research data generated by the factory projects are incorporated into teaching.

Aalto factories have generated a lot of interest both in Finland and internationally. Design factories have been started at Tongji University in China and Swinburne University of Technology in Australia. In 2012 international cooperation agreements were signed with the Catholic University of Chile in Santiago and the European Laboratory for Particle Physics in Geneva.

The Aalto Center for Entrepreneurship coordinates all activities related to technology transfer, intellectual property management, start-up companies, and the teaching and research of entrepreneurship at Aalto University. It aims to create business success within the Aalto community. ACE is an example of the wide range of proactive work being done to promote entrepreneurship and create new business. In 2012 it processed 215 innovation proposals, filed 17 patent applications, approved assistance for 10 new companies set up by Aalto researchers and students, and transferred 14 innovations to four companies.

For additional information, see the Aalto factory websites: Aalto design factory (www.aaltodesignfactory.fi), Aalto health factory (http://elec.aalto.fi/fi/research/health_factory/), Aalto media factory (http://mediafactory.aalto.fi), and Aalto service factory (www.servicefactory.aalto.fi). See also the ACE website (www.ace.aalto.fi).

Observation from the case:

- The Aalto factories and ACE are promising initiatives that promote interplay between education and businesses. These light networking and coordination models could be easily adapted in other contexts as well.

teacher education, and creating a comprehensive education system, including the following:

- *Competent teachers.* Teaching is an attractive profession in Finland. Only 10 percent of all applicants are accepted into teacher education. Teachers are highly educated and respected.
- *Equality in education.* All citizens are offered equal opportunities to receive an education regardless of age, domicile, financial situation, sex, or mother tongue. Education is provided free of charge at all levels from pre-primary to higher education. Women are highly educated, and there are no separate schools for males and females.
- *Comprehensive basic education.* Basic education includes school materials, school meals, health care, and dental care, all free of charge.

- *Extensive school network*. Finnish education is of uniform quality irrespective of the location of the school. The local authorities have a statutory duty to provide basic education for children living in the municipality. Most pupils attend the nearest school.
- *Focus on lifelong learning*. Finns may continue their studies at an upper level of education after the obligatory level. There are no dead ends in education.
- *High level of educational achievement*. Finland's population is highly educated, and the employment rate is especially high among highly educated people. In 2010 approximately 84 percent of persons with tertiary-level degrees were employed, compared with approximately 69 percent of the population 15 to 64 years of age. The employment rate of those with polytechnic and higher-level university degrees is at record levels. For example, in 2010 more than 90 percent of doctors were employed.
- *From control to autonomy*. Autonomy is high at all levels of education. School inspections, which ended in the 1990s, were important for the development of Finnish schools, but quality assurance is now based on objectives laid down in legislation, the national core curriculum, and qualification requirements. There are no school rankings. In Finland, educators have a statutory duty to evaluate their own activities and to participate in external evaluations.

In the future, actions will be needed to address the needs of the aging population, to enhance the efficiency of the education system, to speed up transition points, and to shorten study periods. The increasingly global labor market calls for closer international cooperation to develop models to anticipate future needs for education and skills. Moreover, better entrepreneurship education is needed at all levels. Box 4.7 presents the key messages from this chapter.

Box 4.7 Key Messages

- A strong educational base is the backbone of a knowledge economy.
- Finnish education policy emphasizes comprehensiveness and equality (regardless of age, domicile, financial situation, sex, or mother tongue). A knowledge economy needs a vast pool of educated professionals.
- Quick results should not be expected: improving the educational base requires systematic and long-term investments.
- Competent teachers are the starting point for a successful education system.
- A strong legal basis and effective steering—without weakening the autonomy of schools—are important in guaranteeing a high quality of education.
- The education needs of an economy and a society can change relatively rapidly: the education system should be flexible and able to adjust quickly. Opportunities for lifelong learning should be supported and promoted at all education levels.
- Promoting entrepreneurial elements in all areas of education and encouraging interplay between businesses and education are increasingly vital.

References

Confederation of Finnish Industries. 2013. "Welcome to the Confederation of Finnish Industries." Helsinki. http://www.ek.fi.

Dahlman, C. 2007. "Conclusions and Lessons from Finland's Knowledge Economy for Other Economies." In *Finland as a Knowledge Economy: Elements of Success and Lessons Learned*, edited by C. J. Dahlman, J. Routti, and P. Ylä-Anttila, 99–110. Washington, DC: World Bank.

Economist Intelligence Unit. 2012. *Learning Curve Report, 2012*. Pearson. http://thelearningcurve.pearson.com/.

Federation of Finnish Technology Industries. 2013. "The Federation of Finnish Technology Industries." Helsinki. http://www.teknologiateollisuus.fi/en/.

Hanhijoki, I., J. Katajisto, M. Kimari, and H. Savioja. 2012. *Education, Training, and Demand for Labour in Finland*. Publication 2012:16. Helsinki: Finnish National Board of Education.

Hautamäki, J., S. Kupiainen, J. Marjanen, M.-P. Vainikainen, and R. Hotulainen. 2013. *Learning to Learn at the End of Basic Education: Results in 2012 and Changes from 2001*. Research Report 347, Faculty of Behavioral Sciences, Department of Teacher Education, University of Helsinki, Helsinki.

Kupari, P., J. Välijärvi, L. Andersson, I. Arffman, K. Nissinen, E. Puhakka, and J. Vettenranta. 2013. "PISA12 ensituloksia: Opetus- ja kulttuuriministeriön julkaisuja 2013:20." http://www.minedu.fi.

Kyrö, M. 2012. *International Comparisons of Some Features of Finnish Education and Training System, 2011*. National Board of Education, Helsinki.

Ministry of Education and Culture. 2012. *Education and Research, 2011–2016: A Development Plan*. Report 2012:3, Ministry of Education and Culture, Helsinki.

———. 2013. "Ministry of Education and Culture." Helsinki. http://www.minedu.fi.

Ministry of the Interior. 2013. *Valtioneuvoston periaatepäätös maahanmuuton tulevaisuus 2020strategiasta*. Helsinki. http://www.intermin.fi/download/44618_Maahanmuuton_tulevaisuus_2020_.pdf?f9ad5860b446d088.

National Board of Education. 2013. "About FNBE." Finnish National Board of Education, Helsinki. http://www.oph.fi/english.

Pajarinen, M., and P. Rouvinen. 2013. *Nokia's Labor Inflows and Outflows in Finland: Observations from 1989 to 2010*. ETLA Report 10, Research Institute of the Finnish Economy, Helsinki.

Sahlberg, P. 2010. *The Secret to Finland's Success: Educating Teachers*. Center for Opportunity Policy in Education, Stanford University, Palo Alto, CA. http://edpolicy.stanford.edu/sites/default/files/publications/secret-finland%E2%80%99s-success-educating-teachers.pdf.

Sinko, M., and E. Lehtinen. 1999. "Bitit ja pedagogiikka: Atena Kustannus." Sitra, Helsinki.

Ylä-Anttila, P. 2012. "Sähkö-, elektroniikka- ja tietotekniikka-ala: Tuotantoketjut hajautuvat, osaamistarpeet muuttuvat." ETLA Discussion Paper 1273, Research Institute of the Finnish Economy, Helsinki.

References

Confederation of Indian Industries (CII). [illegible] Systems [illegible]
[illegible]

Dahlman, C. 2009. "Conclusions and Lessons from Indian [illegible] Experience." In [illegible] Knowledge Economy [illegible], [illegible] Kuznetsov, [illegible] and T. Yla-Anttila, [illegible] Washington, DC: World Bank.

[illegible]

CHAPTER 5

Governing the Knowledge Economy Ecosystem

Kimmo Halme, Kimmo Viljamaa, and Maria Merisalo

As a small country with relatively limited resources, Finland has an inherent need to pool scarce resources both across sectors and ministries and across the public and private sectors. This requires consensus and collaboration among all actors, from strategic-level agenda setting to hands-on governance. One of the key characteristics of Finland's approach to development of a knowledge economy has been its systemic, coordinated, and engaging approach to an education, research, and innovation policy agenda.

This chapter highlights the importance of a shared vision and collaborative policy planning process with significant stakeholder engagement. Furthermore, it touches on the potential pitfalls and lessons for developing countries facing challenges in establishing the joint mission as well as guiding its implementation.

Reasoning Behind: A Changing Ecosystem

New Topics and Challenges, New Kinds of Thinking

Over the past decade, a substantial reappraisal of research and innovation policy has taken place in Europe with impact also in Finland. Initially, the drive was the realization that efforts to underpin the technological base, though vital, were insufficient to provide an environment in which innovative firms could flourish and grow (Blind and Georghiou 2010). The starting point for this new policy was the Aho Group's (2006) report ordered by the Council of Europe. The group's chairman, Esko Aho, former prime minister of Finland, was invited to conduct the task in recognition of to Finland's technological competitiveness and investment in research and development (R&D) during the recession of the 1990s.

The Aho Group's report, "Creating an Innovative Europe," focuses on Europe's need to take a market-friendly approach to innovation. The report raised, for the first time at the European Union (EU) level, the issue of the need for strong innovation policy measures and drew urgent attention to policy, particularly on the demand side but also on the supply side. Important elements include actions to develop cross-sectoral cooperation and to create innovation-friendly lead markets as embodied in the Lead Market Initiative (see, for example, Dachs *et al.* 2011).

The next turning point in the EU's innovation policy took place during Finland's presidency, in 2006 (see, for example, EU 2006), when a *broad-based innovation policy* began to emerge (COM 2006). Broad-based innovation policy provides a balance between the supply and demand sides of innovative activity, includes non-technical innovations, and emphasizes wider societal considerations in addition to direct economic impacts. The approach embraces innovations in organizational processes and services in addition to innovations in traditional technological processes and goods products. Hence it seeks to broaden the concept of innovation. Here, the term "innovation" includes non-high-tech, non-scientific, and non-technological areas. The notion of innovation is not restricted to activities carried out by companies. Innovations originate in interactive, collaborative processes that involve significant input from the users of innovations, whether products or services (for example, Edquist, Luukkonen, and Sotarauta 2009; Blind and Georghiou 2010).

Broad-based innovation policy emphasizes the needs of customers. Products are developed by enhancing the users' and developers' collaborative development work. Innovations are viewed more from the commercial perspective (Edquist, Luukkonen, and Sotarauta 2009). In other words, the process identifies the needs of the markets and the customers, and the policy proposes that the end customer may have the best know-how to make new innovations. The emphasis on more broad-based innovation activity in Finland rests on the realization that the country's future cannot rely on a few leading industries.

New Thinking, New Kind of Policies

In today's more global, more competitive economic environment, the focus of innovation policy needs to be more demand based than sector based or technology oriented (Sabel and Saxenian 2008, 120). As the competitiveness in future is based on radical innovation the strategy of creating innovations through strong R & D inputs is no longer solely sufficient.

Policy makers have become increasingly aware of these "bottlenecks" in the system and have launched several structural reforms. These include, among others, structural development of universities and other higher education institutions, reform of government (sectoral) research, improved national infrastructure policy, and implementation of a revised researcher career system as well as a revised national innovation strategy. National funding for enterprise support has been decreased, with innovation support being a notable exception. These structural reforms have been accelerated by the increasing financial pressures in the public sector.

In general, the Finnish national agenda setting and governance structures have changed from a rather narrow technology-led vision toward a more broad-based vision that pays increasing attention to non-technological demand- and user-driven innovation as well as to education policy (STPC 2008). In other words, the knowledge economy ecosystem has been increasingly transformed from technology and knowledge to learning and the capability of continuous knowledge-based renewal. The Committee for the Future at the Finnish Parliament talks about the renewal of Finland based on learning and about a competence-driven economy. This approach rests on the notions that future competitiveness rests on the ability to absorb knowledge from elsewhere and to renew knowledge-based capabilities continuously.

The objective is to make the system more efficient and to remove bottlenecks. This approach calls for broad-based development of content, structure, and funding. At the same time, requires for more specialization while identifying promising new business areas with increasing emphasis on introducing new instruments and agendas (box 5.1). The following sections provide an account of experiences with how this new approach has been addressed in Finnish governance and guidance practices. Implications for hands-on implementation are discussed in chapter 6.

Box 5.1 Research and Innovation Policy Guidelines for 2011–15: Streamlining the Finnish Innovation System

The current policy agenda to continue developing the knowledge economy is summarized in the latest review by the Research and Innovation Council (RIC 2010). The review states that the strategy of Finland is to ensure sustainable and balanced social and economic development and that the key factors contributing to this strategy are (1) high educational levels (provided by efficient and high-quality education), (2) intensive development and exploitation of knowledge (with a clear emphasis on creating not only knowledge but also the ability to use it for the benefit of the economy and the society), (3) accumulation of know-how and intangible assets, and (4) multilateral cooperation with emphasis on international links. However, this agenda has not ruled out relatively significant changes in education, research, and innovation policies during recent years. The guidelines reflect recent changes in policy. In the field of education, research, and innovation policy, these include reform of the university and other higher education institutions, adoption of a national innovation strategy, reform of sectoral research, and adoption of a national infrastructure policy.

The guidelines also acknowledge that Finland has become one of the leading knowledge economies in the world, but that the "overall functionality of the innovation system" could be streamlined and improved (RIC 2010). The country's well-established national innovation system has become too complex and fragmented. At the same time, Finland

box continues next page

Box 5.1 Research and Innovation Policy Guidelines for 2011–15: Streamlining the Finnish Innovation System *(continued)*

is in a position of having to implement austerity measures, including cutting public spending. As a result, funding for economic development and R&D has been cut lately, although moderately. However, instead of general cuts, Finland's national policy seeks to concentrate funding further for the most important issues, such as providing the basic conditions for research and innovation as well as for responding to major societal challenges, such as climate change, energy, food security, and aging of the population.

As part of this "streamlining" process, the need for *specialization* is evident in several themes: (1) specialization in competitive business areas, (2) specialization in promising research as well as business areas, and (3) specialization in the form of attractive (regional) "poles of excellence." Streamlining is visible in public expenditure on R&D, which has decreased slightly in recent years relative to other public spending.

For further information, see RIC (2010).

A Shared Vision and a Strategy That Supports It

The Finnish case highlights the importance of shared vision, collaborative preparation, and stakeholder engagement. This section describes the evolution and current issues facing the Finnish strategy.

Key Concepts and Principles

The current mode of governance for developing a knowledge economy in Finland dates back to the early 1990s, when the foundations for the current innovation-driven policy and knowledge-based approach to growth were laid and innovation system thinking became a national agenda. The fundamental concept in the policy agenda has been the concept of a *national system of innovation*. First introduced in the 1990 review by the Science and Technology Policy Council (STPC) national system of innovation has been the backbone of innovation policy ever since. The approach was rapidly adopted to steer the development of science and technology policies in a more comprehensive (or *systemic*) way, highlighting the increasingly complex and interdependent links between the creation, circulation, and use of knowledge. The innovation system approach was complemented by an increasing focus on knowledge-based production and the knowledge intensity of the Finnish economy. This focus is evident in the long-term aim of increasing R&D expenditure in both the public and private sectors.

The systemic approach has been a distinctive feature of the policy agenda and reflects the work of the RIC (see box 5.4) in coordinating various activities in education, research, and innovation policies. There have been several updates to make innovation system "more dynamic," the approach still forms the basis of the Finnish agenda. The systemic view is also visible in the rapid increase in cooperation between research organizations and the private sector in the 1990s. This development has been facilitated by funding from Tekes (Funding Agency for Technology and Innovation), with Tekes technology programs becoming perhaps the dominant instruments.

Another important approach has been to focus resources on selected business or research areas. This occurred in the 1990s with the introduction of cluster policy and related instruments, such as cluster programs, the Center of Expertise Program, and, more recently, the strategic centers of science, technology, and innovation (SHOKs; see chapter 6 on implementation). Mechanisms to support excellence in tertiary education as well research were introduced to focus resources on the most promising or best performing fields. Internationalization and global networking have been on the national agenda (Lemola 2002), especially since the opening up of the national economy in the late 1980s.

The 1990s Finnish approach adopted the concept of information society (IS). The IS supported subsequent development of the knowledge economy by addressing many of the key issues related to knowledge-based development, such as information infrastructure, regulations, and learning environment. The role of infrastructure was especially significant (for example, the development of broadband networks). Inspired by research as well as international policy debate, the IS concept was adopted relatively quickly in the Finnish policy agenda, reflecting a broad consensus that it was important for Finland to be at the forefront of IS development. First, the IS strategy was introduced in 1995, and specific reports and memos were produced. Several policy documents were produced in 1998 and 2007, and several IS programs were established by consecutive governments.

Innovation policy and IS policy both contributed to the Finnish knowledge economy development in the 1990s. They were closer to one another in the 1990s, when they were both more technology driven, which to some extent was criticized (Oksanen 2006). In the 2000s, the policy fields differed somewhat. IS policy has evolved to focus more on society, paying more attention to needs of the citizens and engagement of them e.g. in innovation process addressing e.g. the development of digital services. Innovation policy has evolved to become more broad based, addressing the non-technological side of knowledge-based development as well. Compared with innovation policy, implementation of the IS policy agenda has been more fragmented. In innovation policy, there has been a relatively clear distinction between different actors in the government, as a result of the high-level agenda-setting support provided by the STPC and RIC. However, IS and science and technology policies are still connected at the policy level; for example, STPC has discussed IS-related issues in most of its reviews.

Perhaps the most significant contribution of IS policy was the development of shared understanding and commitment to knowledge-based development in the 1990s. Several strategies and programs launched in the 1990s clearly indicated this view of shared development. These strategies were drawn up to facilitate the transformation of Finland into an IS seen as a national project (STPC 1996).

New National Innovation Strategy

During the past decade, the Finnish national strategy has evolved further. Country has achieved top positions in international comparisons, and many targets, such as R&D intensity of the economy, were met. From this new position, policy could no longer be based on trying to catch up with the leading economies.

As a result, there has been discussion on the direction and approach that need to be taken to respond to the future. Finland's new position, together with the recent economic crisis, industrial restructuring (including information and communication technology [ICT]), and increasing difficulties in financing the welfare state, has posed new challenges for the national innovation strategy.

Against this background, the government (2007–10) announced that it would prepare a national innovation strategy for the coming years. The new strategy, published in 2008 (box 5.2), sought to achieve economic growth and improve the well-being of people and the environment. Based on this principle, the strategy set two main goals: (1) innovation-based development of productivity and (2) pioneering in innovation activity. These goals saw Finnish enterprises succeeding and growing on the international market due to their competitive

Box 5.2 National Innovation Strategy Process in Finland

The Ministry of Employment and the Economy (MEE), which was the Ministry of Trade and Industry until the end of 2007, was responsible for organizing the national innovation strategy. The strategy was prepared in an exceptionally open and collaborative manner, by engaging a broad range of experts, stakeholders, and citizens. During the fall of 2007, 11 innovation policy workshops were held, focusing on the key policy challenges. Nearly 800 experts were consulted (MEE 2008a; Edquist, Luukkonen, and Sotarauta 2009).

A steering group was established to guide preparation of the strategy, with Esko Aho, then president of the National Fund for Research and Development (Sitra), as its chair. At that time, Aho was a spokesman for innovation policy, having successfully led the Aho Group for the European Commission. The steering group presented its proposed national innovation strategy to the MEE in June 2008 (see MEE 2008a). Largely, but not solely, based on that suggestion, the Finnish government submitted its "innovation policy review" to parliament. The government review, a strategy document, raised issues that required attention and suggested changes in policy. It emphasized *broad-based innovation policy*, which had already been adopted as one of the overriding approaches in the government program (Edquist, Luukkonen, and Sotarauta 2009).

The strategy reviews innovation activity and the required development measures via four basic choices: (1) world without borders, (2) demand and user orientation, (3) innovative individuals and communities, and (4) a systemic approach (figure B5.2.1). Within each of these basic choices, two focal points were identified, each including one to four measures (MEE 2008a).

box continues next page

Box 5.2 National Innovation Strategy Process in Finland *(continued)*

Figure B5.2.1 Basic Choices and Focus Points of the Finnish National Innovation Strategy

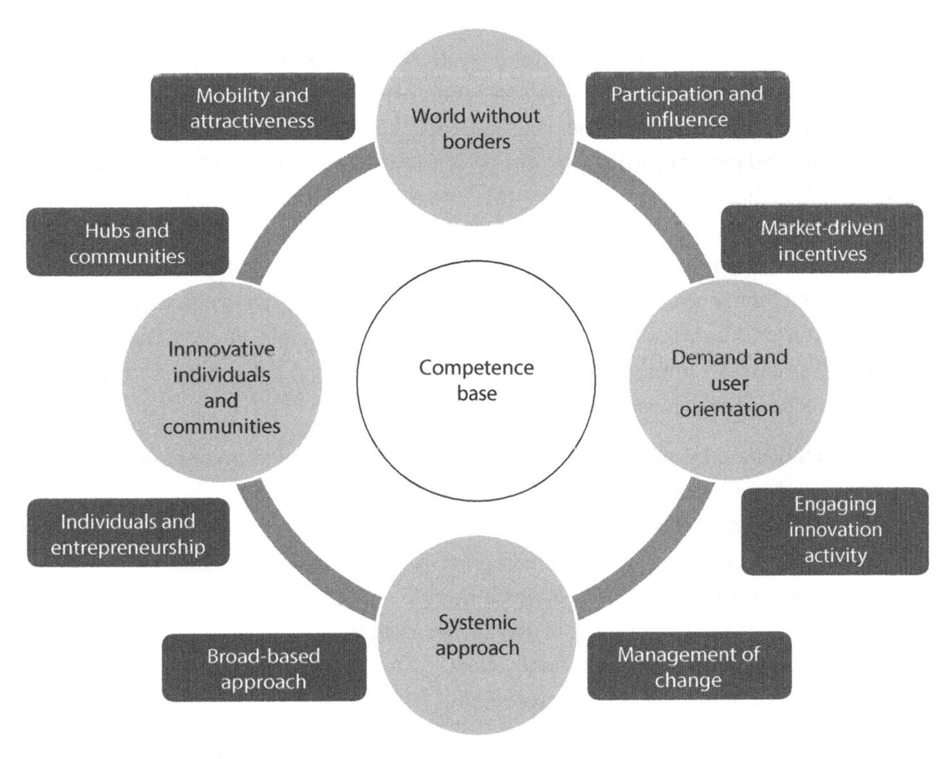

Source: Based on MEE 2008a.

Observation from the case:

- Whenever major revisions to policies and strategies are needed, it is important to engage all expertise and stakeholders in the process as widely and as early as possible. This will help to ensure that all relevant knowledge is applied and that strategic decisions have appropriate buy-in.

strength, which is a consequence of enhanced expertise and productivity. In addition, the strategy stated that the public sector needed to reform its service systems and operating methods by developing innovations.

The new strategy also focused on challenge-driven innovation policy: country must meet social challenges with a comprehensive, consistent innovation policy across administrative boundaries, paying close attention to both the technological and non-technological sectors of innovation activity. Furthermore, Finland must generate globally significant added value and attract both skillful experts and investments (MEE 2008a; box 5.3).

Box 5.3 Joint Action Plan and Policy Framework for Demand- and User-Driven Policy

As part of the implementation of Finland's national innovation strategy, the Ministry of Employment and the Economy outlined an action plan and policy framework for 2010–13, laying down the key elements of a demand- and user-driven innovation policy. The action plan was implemented jointly by various ministries along with a broad range of stakeholders, such as Tekes, the Technical Research Centre (VTT), the National Consumer Research Center, and Forum Virium Helsinki.

The action plan, prepared jointly with a broad group of stakeholders, consisted of seven themes, each identifying concrete actions to be taken. The themes were based on an analysis of demand- and user-driven innovation policy prepared by the MEE in 2009. This analysis of the policy framework comprised the first part of the plan. The second part focused on turning policy into action. The following were the seven themes:

1. Competitiveness by strengthening the base of knowledge and awareness of demand- and user-driven innovation
2. Innovation by bolstering demand
3. Renewal of the public sector as a source and target of pioneering actions
4. Incentives for enhancing grassroots initiatives
5. More impact from increased use of user-driven methods
6. Networks enhancing diffusion of innovations
7. Evaluating the impact of the action program.

For further information, see the MEE website on demand- and user-driven innovation (http://www.tem.fi/index.phtml?l=en&s=2382).

Observations from the case:

- Promoting new approaches to policy instruments as well as practices requires a dedicated effort in order to avoid fragmenting the new initiative.
- In addition to dividing tasks clearly between various actors, it is important to set clear targets and to dedicate resources to implementation.

Building Consensus and Engaging Stakeholders

Building consensus and engaging stakeholders as relevant actors operating and implementing initiatives within the knowledge economy ecosystem is crucial. In the fields of science, technology, and innovation, the core of consensus policies and shareholder engagement in Finland has often been attributed to the planning and coordination function of the Research and Innovation Council and its network of contacts across sector ministries (box 5.4).

The RIC acts as a high-level advisory body for the government and is responsible for the strategic development and coordination of Finnish education, research, and innovation policies. The RIC has traditionally been the platform

Box 5.4 Research and Innovation Council: Strategic Development and Coordination of Agenda Setting

The RIC, chaired by the prime minister, advises the Council of State and its ministries on important matters concerning research, development, and innovation (RDI). The council is responsible for the strategic development and coordination of Finnish science and technology policy as well as the national innovation system as a whole. Its key tasks include following national and international developments in RDI, addressing important matters related to the development of science, technology, and innovation policy, addressing matters related to the development and allocation of public research and innovation funding, and coordinating the government's science, technology, and innovation activities.

One of the council's main tasks is to publish a science and technology policy review every third year, which amounts to a national strategy and vision for the national innovation system. The review analyzes past developments and makes proposals for the future, with most of the recommendations being adopted by the ministries concerned. In practice, the council influences policy through its official statements, but also through the individual council members who meet to share and discuss ideas.

The RIC consists of three separate bodies: the council, the subcommittees, and the secretariat. The council is chaired by the prime minister. The membership consists of the minister of education and science, the minister of economy, the minister of finance, and a maximum of six other ministers appointed by the government. In addition, the membership includes 10 members well versed in science and technology. The council has a science policy subcommittee and a technology policy subcommittee charged with preparatory tasks. These are chaired by the minister of education and science and by the minister of economy, respectively. The council's secretariat consists of one full-time secretary general and two full-time chief planning officers.

The predecessor of the RIC—the STPC—had been established in 1987. In 2009 the council was given its current name to reflect the increasing significance of horizontal (broad-based) innovation policy in the development of society and an economy based on knowledge and know-how. For additional information, see the RIC website (http://www.minedu.fi/OPM/Tiede/tutkimus-_ja_innovaationeuvosto/?lang=en).

Observations from the case:

- Coordination of science, technology, and innovation, or the knowledge economy at-large, is a horizontal issue and relevant to most government sectors. In order to ensure proper assessment, planning, and coordination of knowledge economy–related policies, it is important to assign a cross-ministerial function, such as the RIC in Finland.
- Key success factors for the RIC are related to its high-level mandate (prime minister), collaboration in national budget planning, and broad representation of all relevant political, government, private sector, and expert stakeholders as well as interface with civil society.

and process for joint planning of policies, while implementation has been split between sector ministries. However, RIC reports and suggestions often remained at the generic (whole of government) level, and their implementation was not monitored systematically. Over the past years, the role, mandate, and functions of the RIC have been adjusted to the new situation—that is, responsibility for broader development than science and technology—and this is reflected in its name.

While the RIC proposes a general approach to education, research, and innovation policies, government programs set a more concrete agenda. At the start of a new term, each government formulates a program that sets key priorities for the next four years. Although these programs are often based on different, sometimes conflicting, goals (Tiili 2004), they have been relatively stable with regard to development of a knowledge economy. This relatively stable political agenda may be due to a wide consensus on the role of knowledge as a source of competitiveness and welfare in a small country such as Finland. It has even been argued that the development of a knowledge-based economy has been a national project (Schienstock 2007). The consistent national agenda is clearly visible in the latest government program (2011), which states, "Finland's success and enhanced welfare is dependent on broad-based knowledge, professional skills, and high levels of expertise .... Investments in education and research are part of a long-term growth policy. The Government will ensure sufficient funding for education, know-how, and research." The national project is visible in education policy, which became more oriented toward technology and expanded tertiary education in the 1990s (Raivola *et al.* 2001). As a result, the population of Finland is among the most educated in the world (OECD 2012).

A more practical example of how agenda setting has resulted in concrete policy actions is the establishment of the SHOKs (see more in chapter 6).

Horizontal Collaboration across Ministries

Horizontal collaboration is an important element of governing Finland's knowledge economy. There is a long history and a steady increase in the level of collaboration across sectors and ministries and in recent years, this collaboration has taken more concrete forms.

Broad horizontal coordination and consensus building are among typical characteristics and strong points of Finland's knowledge economy, with roots dating back several decades. Close social networking is typical, particularly among senior actors across ministries, large companies, academic leaders, trade unions, and intermediary bodies. This tradition has been particularly evident in science, technology, and innovation policy and in development of the knowledge economy at large. Most particularly, in times of economic crisis—during the severe economic crisis in the early 1990s—horizontal collaboration was intense (see Dahlman, Routti, and Ylä-Anttila 2007).

As the challenges to knowledge economy policy are increasingly systemic in nature, addressing of them requires broad-based collaboration involving several sector ministries. How is such collaboration best organized? Far too often sector ministries tend to divide their responsibilities, instead of truly collaborating and working jointly for a common solution. Although it is widely thought that cross-sectoral cooperation leads to good results, this type of cooperation is still relatively new in Finland. Typical challenges include lack of understanding, lack of ownership, lack of resources, and lack of coordination, posing new challenges for policy making (on agenda setting or electronic systems, for example). Box 5.5, on TINTO, briefly describes how horizontal collaboration between ministries is implemented at the strategic level, whereas box 5.6, on the Action Program on eServices and eDemocracy (SADe), describes a more hands-on collaboration between ministries.

Box 5.5 TINTO: Joint Implementation between Ministries

In 2011 the RIC asked the key ministries—the Ministry of Employment and the Economy and the Ministry of Education and Culture—to elaborate plans for implementing innovation policy and science policy. This was the first time that ministries were requested to report back to the RIC on how they were implementing policy recommendations. Because the implementation plans were to serve as input for the mid-term review of the national program, the plans could directly influence budgeting and political decisions. This significantly raised the stakes and interest.

The two ministries decided to join forces and to prepare a joint action plan for implementing research and innovation policy. They called the project TINTO, a Finnish acronym for RIC Action Plan. An external consultant facilitated the process. This was the first time that two ministries had prepared a joint action plan for the implementation of policies. They carried out the parallel, but mutually coordinated process with their respective stakeholders and internal staff. Toward the end, the two processes converged. A large stakeholder seminar was organized, in which the two policy views were synchronized. The preparation was largely consultative and open, with several workshops and hearings.

The TINTO process is perhaps the most concrete and latest example of joint policy planning and implementation between two ministries and their respective stakeholders. Similar developments do occur elsewhere in the government, but they typically are initiated by the central government and are of a political nature (that is, they are identified in the government program and executed by relevant ministries). One such process was the preparation of the *Government Report on the Future: Well-Being through Sustainable Growth* (Prime Minister's Office 2013), which was coordinated by the Prime Minister's Office (see box 5.8 for details).

Observations from the case:

- It is sometimes easier to design and define horizontal policies than to implement them through collaboration at the ministerial level. However, TINTO illustrates how a joint policy was put in practice by two ministries.
- It is important to plan how horizontal knowledge economy policies will be implemented by the relevant ministries and agencies.

Box 5.6 SADe: Cross-Sectoral Cooperation at the Program Level

The Action Program on eServices and eDemocracy develops comprehensive services for citizens, companies, authorities, and other stakeholders. The program is among the government's key projects and the first comprehensive and national e-service development program in Finnish public administration. It aims to develop customer-focused and interoperable services to enhance quality and cost-efficiency in the public sector. The program has a strong customer orientation; its purpose is to meet customers' needs in different situations and at different stages of their lives, regardless of administrative sector and organizational boundaries.

The project is coordinated by the Ministry of Finance and implemented by dozens of actors, including state authorities (including six ministries), municipalities, joint municipal authorities, companies, and private organizations. The program began in 2009 and runs until the end of 2015. It comprises eight projects, which emphasize cost-efficiency, cross-sector collaboration, customer focus, quality, and innovativeness.

SADe is linked to measures of state and municipal administration, such as the effectiveness and productivity program, the municipal productivity program, customer strategy project, and public sector customer service development project. In implementing services, the program uses common interfaces and services as well as best practices and collaborates with other development projects. This work is based on shared operating models related to linguistic equality of the two official languages, open-source code, information security, accessibility, environmental impact of information and communication technology (ICT), and interaction with users and markets.

For more information, see SADe's website (http://www.vm.fi/vm/en/05_projects/03_sade/index.jsp).

Observations from the case:

- Development of e-governance can boost the quality and efficiency of public services as well as facilitate the development of new private services.
- SADe provides an example of how e-government can be organized in a comprehensive way, with a strong customer orientation.

Governance within Policy Sectors

Policies related to the knowledge economy have become increasingly overlapping and interdependent, requiring not only horizontal collaboration across ministries but also increasingly effective and deeper governance among actors within one sector. In 2008 a working group was established to prepare the merger of three ministries: the former Ministry of Trade and Industry, the Ministry of Employment, and some units of the Ministry of the Interior were merged to become the Ministry of Employment and the Economy. This "super ministry" has much better resources to coordinate innovation policy than its predecessors (Edquist, Luukkonen, and Sotarauta 2009).

The MEE and the Ministry of Education and Culture share responsibility for funding public sector RDI activity, whereas the MEE is in charge of funding innovation activity. Innovation funding accounts for one quarter (€823 million) of the MEE's €3.3 billion budget. The Ministry of Education and Culture is responsible for funding education, science, and research and, by means of regulation, guides the activities of universities and other higher education institutions (MEE 2013).

The MEE has various tasks and responsibilities. For example, it invests in environmental and energy technologies in order to achieve international goals related to the climate and to develop business growth related to the energy and climate sector; to improve cooperation with other administrations for a better matching of labor supply and demand. It also coordinates business development services, funding for innovative companies, and skills development support services; and management of new employment and economic policy solutions, labor market flexibility, and worker safety issues in order to address unemployment.

The MEE group comprises more than 20 organizations and employs some 10,700 people. Government agencies, institutions, and organizations within the MEE's branch of government are key actors in implementing innovation policy. They can be divided into four groups by level of guidance (box 5.7). The objective is for the MEE to focus on actual guidance instead of creating different practices for all actors as well to facilitate cooperation among the

---

Box 5.7 Steering Model of the MEE Group

Steering and coordinating the more than 20 organizations within the Ministry of Employment and the Economy group require strong cooperation across organizational boundaries as well as effective steering mechanisms. To achieve this, the newly established ministry conducted a project to develop steering processes within the MEE group (see Figure B5.7.1). A private consultancy company was contracted to facilitate the work.

The objectives of the project were to build a steering model for steering as well as to identify and develop specific approaches, tools, and leadership practices to support the model. Special attention was paid to achieving comprehensiveness (to include all key issues and processes), practicality (to be practical rather than theoretical), and value added and to ensuring that the model would function on both the strategic and the operational levels. The role of the MEE focuses on determining strategies, setting objectives, and monitoring their implementation with indicators. The organizations are responsible for planning their own strategy, for planning and managing operational functions, and for reporting to the ministry.

In practice, the model has seven core phases:

1. Defining the MEE group strategy
2. Defining the strategies for policy areas
3. Coordinating the steering of agencies and institutions

box continues next page

Box 5.7 Steering Model of the MEE Group *(continued)*

4. Defining the strategies of individual agencies and institutions
5. Negotiating performance agreements and the setting of objectives between individual agencies and the MEE
6. Managing the operations of agencies and institutions
7. Monitoring, reporting, and evaluation.

Figure B5.7.1 Steering Model of the MEE Group

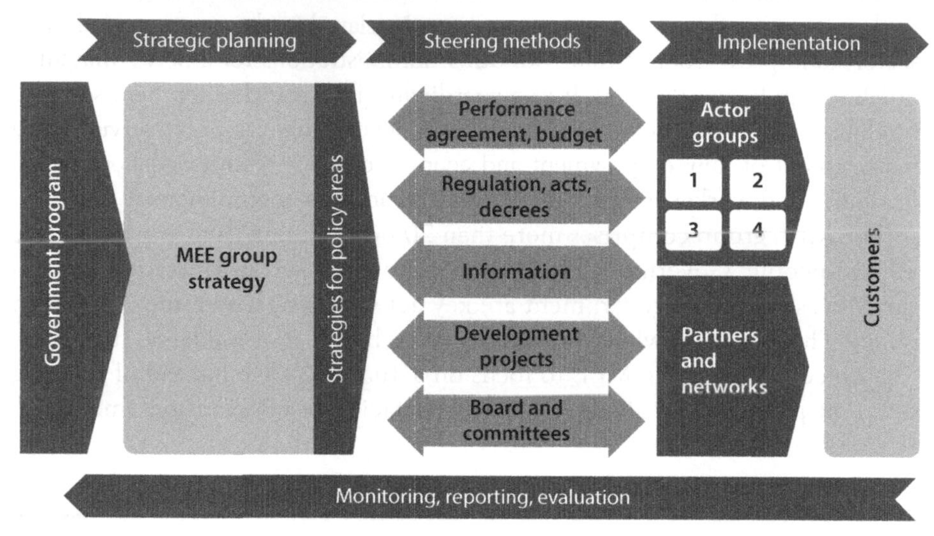

Source: MEE 2008b.

Observation from the case:

- Effective governance of ministries and their agencies is of instrumental importance to the successful implementation of policy. The MEE governance model took a strong strategic approach to the overall coordination and management of agencies.

actors and build know-how on guidance among responsible staff (MEE 2008b). The actors and the groups are presented in table 5.1.

Looking Ahead

Along with strategy, drafting, coordination, and horizontal activities, an integral part of the governance and agenda setting of the knowledge economy ecosystem is adopting a forward-planning (foresight) approach to produce producing information as well as engaging and building consensus among different actors.

The Finnish system has integrated forward planning to the national agenda-setting. Although extensive, the foresight system is rather fragmented. At the level of national policy, there is a dedicated, established organization that

Table 5.1 Actors of the MEE Group, by Type and Scope of Activity

	Scope of activity	
Type of activity	*Wide*	*Specialized*
Development and business	*Group 1:* ELY centers, Tekes, Finnvera plc, Finpro, Industry Investment, Technical Research Center (VTT), and Geological Survey of Finland	*Group 2:* Foundation for Finnish Inventions, Finnish Standards Association, the Finnish Tourist Board, and other foundations and institutions
Authoritative activities	*Group 3:* National Board of Patents and Registration, Center for Metrology and Accreditation, Finnish Safety and Chemical Agency (Tukes), and National Consumer Research Center	*Group 4:* Finnish Competition and Consumer Authority, Energy Market Authority, and National Emergency Supply Agency

integrates forward planning in the policy-making process (see Eerola and Holst Jørgensen 2008). This process is based on a dialogue between the government's foresight report prepared every four years (once during each electoral cycle) and submitted to parliament. The report typically takes a 15-year perspective on the policy goals of growth and well-being and presents the government's vision of the future with regard to selected issues and policies. The report is discussed and evaluated in the parliamentary Committee for the Future, which in turn responds by providing its own report.

The Committee for the Future coordinates various forward-looking exercises and studies and provides information on related issues to other committees. The committee, established in 1992 as a result of a citizen's initiative, has become important institution for providing information for parliament as well as the ministries. The committee is also responsible on behalf of parliament for appraising the effects of scientific research and technology on society.

In addition foresight is used at other levels of government. Various organizations carry out their own projections including, among others, the Ministry of Education and Culture, Tekes, Sitra, the Academy of Finland, and regional administrative bodies, such as the ELY centers. A long-term perspective is especially important in education, labor, and innovation policies. For example, the National Board of Education maintains a national service, ENSTI, with the aim of coordinating projections, especially in the fields of education and labor policies. The Academy of Finland and Tekes have also carried out foresight projects during recent years separately as well as collectively (for example, the Finnsight 2015 process in 2005). All in all, these efforts provide feedback on future development paths and the expected degree of need for key skills and technologies.

An important step in organizing the Finnish model of agenda setting and foresight was the establishment of Sitra, an independent body with the task of promoting stable and balanced development, economic growth, and international competitiveness and cooperation in Finland (see box 5.9).

Box 5.8 Government Foresight Activity

In Finland each sitting government has the obligation to submit a foresight report to the parliamentary Committee for the Future on the government's view of the future during the next 10 to 20 years. The report focuses on a defined set of strategically significant issues that will affect the government's policies over the period of the report and presents the government's view on the chosen issues and associated policies and focuses on a theme of significance for the country. For 2012–13 the main theme was sustainability and welfare. Previous themes have included climate and energy policy (2009) and population, immigration policy, and aging (2004).

The Prime Minister's Office is responsible for drawing up the foresight report and, after its completion, for promoting its implementation. In practice, the Prime Minister's Office owns the process, while a sectoral ministry organizes the content (the MEE for 2012–13). In the current instance the Prime Minister's Office and the responsible sectoral ministry are implementing the process together with Tekes, the Academy of Finland, and the government think tank, Sitra. In practice, the foresight report has been based on an exercise drawn up by an expert group of senior officials and other subject matter experts commissioned by the responsible sectoral ministry.

The most recent process adopted a new approach that opened foresight to wider participation. It started with future analysis, which is based on meta-analysis of national and international policy analyses, foresight reports and strategies, as well as a survey of experts and the general public. Based on the aggregation of these data, six subthemes were chosen and ratified by the working group of ministers. The subthemes were developed further through an iterative set of workshops where an invited expert panel of academics and industry participants discussed each of the themes and forged a vision for the future, mapped the necessary competencies to attain the vision, and proposed policy experiments. This process invited private citizens, experts, and officials to participate through a web portal and several stakeholder workshops. Forward planning provided a basis for the *Government Report on the Future* prepared by the working group of ministers. For additional information, see the Prime Minister's Office website (http://vnk.fi/hankkeet/tulevaisuusselonteko358587/en.jsp).

Observations from the case:

- Anticipating the future with professional foresight and systematic analysis of available policy options is an essential element of good governance, particularly in times of change.
- Approaches to developing foresight vary, but the Finnish model illustrates the value of involving a broad array of stakeholders and civil society to ensure awareness, engagement, and commitment to policy choices. In this respect, the foresight process may be more valuable for policy makers than the actual outcome it produces.

Box 5.9 Sitra: An Independent "Agent of Change"

Sitra was established in 1967 as an independent development fund. By law, its duty is to promote stable and balanced development in Finland, the qualitative and quantitative growth of its economy, and international competitiveness and cooperation. Compared with other funding and development organizations, Sitra has an independent position under parliament; it is not responsible for implementing policy. Sitra's operations are funded with endowment capital and returns from corporate funding operations. Sitra's annual budget comes to about €40 million.

One of Sitra's primary tasks has been to assist Finnish decision makers and the public at-large in making informed decisions on how to improve the Finnish economy and society in the context of a changing world. This has been carried out through various development initiatives and studies. Sitra has been seen as an "agent of change," with an independent mandate to develop, pilot, and incubate new policies and measures. Another role has been to act as an intermediary between parliament, ministries, and industry by offering a forum for discussions.

In 2005 Sitra adopted a program-based approach. This model concentrated on development areas around selected core themes, relating to both the economy and the society. Recently the focus has been revised further. At the end of 2012, Sitra stopped using the program-based approach and adopted instead three themes derived from its strategy: sustainable lifestyles and smart use of natural resources, renewable leadership and well-being services, bottlenecks and new opportunities for economic growth.

In addition to studies and development initiatives, Sitra also operates through investment and business development operations (development projects and investments in funds and companies). Through these, Sitra aims to promote the growth and international operations of Finnish companies and to use the expertise and networks of international funds.

In recent years, Sitra's role as a think tank has been strengthened with aim to influence to influence the agenda of major decision makers and participating in open interaction in various policy fields. For additional information, see Sitra's website (http://www.sitra.fi/en) and Vihko *et al.* (2002).

Observation from the case:

- A clear advantage of Sitra over dedicated think tanks and foresight organizations is the fact that Sitra has its own funding for development activities and a relatively independent position.

Summary and Key Messages

The main approach to the Finnish policy agenda has changed little in recent years. There is a broad consensus that the success of the country depends on the ability to create and use new information, to build high-quality technological and business competence, and to understand markets. Consequently, Finland has chosen to invest in developing knowledge and know-how. Moreover, the development of education, research, technology, and innovation has been a "national project." One of the key strengths of the policy agenda has been the persistence of a long-term policy from government to government.

In addition to strong R&D- and ICT-oriented activities, which dominated the strategy earlier, a more horizontal approach has been taken for innovation activities covering all of society. In this approach, the key to building a successful knowledge economy is combining material, intellectual, and social capital.

From the agenda-setting perspective, achieving a wide consensus in support of the national strategy of making Finland a knowledge economy has been important. This has remained consistently for the past two decades, and the basic approach has been relatively stable as successive governments have assumed power. Despite significant budget cuts in recent years, the relative importance of education, research, and innovation policies has remained stable.

Secondly, the long-term perspective is visible in how the government, parliament, and different agencies use foresight processes to support policy making. Foresight is used to guide not only individual policies but also the broad national agenda. This is a definite strength of the Finnish approach.

Thirdly, the strong coordination of education, research, and innovation policy at the national, strategic level, especially through a high-level coordination body—the Research and Innovation Council—has significantly enhanced the development of Finland's knowledge economy.

Another aspect is the emphasis on integrating education policy into the national strategy. Education has been a high priority in terms of both the high-level educational attainment of the population as well as the high-quality basic education that is available for everybody. Box 5.10 presents the key messages of this chapter.

Box 5.10 Key Messages

- The Finnish approach to governing the knowledge economy emphasizes the importance of having a shared vision of the future and a collaborative policy-planning process, as well as stakeholder engagement in all parts of the process. This approach is likely to enhance the consistency, stability, and predictability of policies, too.
- Finland is a small country, and the scarcity of available resources further highlights the importance of having a broad consensus, collaborative preparation, and stakeholder engagement on a strategic level. Also the adoption of a long-term perspective and the integration of education policy in the national strategy are crucial.
- An implicit challenge is the question of whether an approach based on strong consensus allows sufficient "out-of-the-box" thinking—hence the emergence of radical changes and innovations and, equally, radical decision making when such is needed. Bold political decisions are typically made during times of crisis, when decisions based on consensus are not sufficient.
- Putting a broad-based strategy into practice requires systemic and engaging practices and processes for coordinating across ministries as well as within individual policy sectors.

References

Aho Group. 2006. "Creating an Innovative Europe." Report of the Independent Expert Group on R&D and Innovation appointed following the Hampton Court Summit and chaired by Mr. Esko Aho, Luxembourg. http://ec.europa.eu/invest-in-research/action/2006_ahogroup_en.htm.

Blind, K., and L. Georghiou. 2010. "Drivers and Impediments for Innovation in Europe." *Intereconomics* 45 (5): 264–86.

COM (Commission to the Council). 2006. "Putting Knowledge into Practice: A Broad-Based Innovation Strategy for the EU." Communication from the Commission to the Council, the European Parliament, the European Economic and Social Committee, and the Committee of the Regions, Brussels, Belgium. http://eur-lex.europa.eu/LexUriServ/LexUriServ.do?uri=COM:2006:0502:FIN:en:PDF.

Dachs, B., I. Wanzenböck, M. Weber, J. Hyvänen, and H. Toivanen. 2011. *Lead Markets*. Task 4 Horizontal Report 3, European Commission, Consortium Europe, INNOVA Sectoral Innovation Watch, Brussels, Belgium. http://ec.europa.eu/enterprise/policies/innovation/files/proinno/lead-markets-report_en.pdf.

Dahlman, C., J. Routti, and P. Ylä-Anttila. 2007. *Finland as a Knowledge Economy: Elements of Success and Lessons Learned*. Washington, DC: World Bank.

Edquist, C., T. Luukkonen, and M. Sotarauta. 2009. "Broad-Based Innovation Policy." In *Evaluation of the Finnish National Innovation System: Full Report*, 11–70. Helsinki: Taloustieto Oy. http://www.tem.fi/files/24929/InnoEvalFi_FULL_Report_28_Oct_2009.pdf.

Eerola, A., and B. Holst Jørgensen. 2008. "Foresight in Nordic Countries." In *The Handbook of Technology Foresight*, edited by L. Georghiou, J. Harper, M. Keenan, I. Miles, and R. Popper. PRIME Series on Research and Innovation Policy. Cheltenham: Edward Elgar.

EU (European Union). 2006. "Finland's Presidency of the EU: Results." EU2006.fi, Prime Minister's Office, Helsinki. http://www.eu2006.fi/news_and_documents/other_documents/vko52/en_gb/1166173795584/_files/76535077126275317/default/results_presidency_221206_en.pdf.

Lemola, T. 2002. "Convergence of National Science and Technology Policies: The Case of Finland." *Research Policy* 31 (8–9): 1481–90.

MEE (Ministry of Employment and the Economy). 2008a. "Finland's National Innovation Strategy." Helsinki. http://ec.europa.eu/invest-in-research/pdf/download_en/finland_national_innovation_strategy.pdf.

———. 2008b. "Työ- ja elinkeinoministeriö: Kehityshanke hallinnonalan konserniohjauksen mallintamiseksi ja toteuttamiseksi. [MEE Group Steering Model, Development Project Report]." Helsinki. http://www.tem.fi/files/29824/Konserniohjausmalli.pdf.

———. 2013. "Innovation Policy Implementation." MEE, Helsinki. http://www.tem.fi/index.phtml?l=en&s=4947.

OECD (Organisation for Economic Co-operation and Development). 2012. *Education at a Glance 2012: OECD Indicators*. Paris: OECD Publishing. http://www.uis.unesco.org/Education/Documents/oecd-eag-2012-en.pdf.

Oksanen, J. 2006. "Information Society Governance and Its Links to Innovation Policy in Finland." In *Governance of Innovation Systems*, vol. 3: *Case Studies in Cross-Sectoral Policy*, edited by OECD. Paris: OECD Publishing.

Prime Minister's Office. 2013. *Government Report on the Future: Well-Being through Sustainable Growth*. Helsinki: Prime Minister's Office. http://vnk.fi/julkaisut/listaus/julkaisu/fi.jsp?oid=398205.

Raivola, R., K. Kekkonen, P. Tulkki, and A. Lyytinen. 2001. *Producing Competencies for Learning Economy*. Sitra Report 9. Helsinki: Edita Prima. http://www.sitra.fi/julkaisut/raportti9.pdf.

RIC (Research and Innovation Council). 2010. *Research and Innovation Policy Guidelines for 2011–2015*. Kopijyvä. http://www.minedu.fi/export/sites/default/OPM/Tiede/tutkimus-_ja_innovaationeuvosto/julkaisut/liitteet/Review2011-2015.pdf.

Sabel, C., and A. Saxenian. 2008. *A Fugitive Success: Finland's Economic Future*. Sitra Report 80. Helsinki: Edita Prima. http://www.sitra.fi/julkaisut/raportti80.pdf.

Schienstock, G. 2007. "From Path Dependency to Path Creation: Finland on Its Way to the Knowledge-Based Economy." *Current Sociology* 55 (1): 92–109.

STPC (Science and Technology Policy Council). 1996. *Finland: A Knowledge-Based Society*. Helsinki: STPC.

———. 2008. *Review 2008*. Helsinki: STPC.

Tiili, M. 2004. "Strategic Political Leadership: A New Challenge for Finnish Ministers." Paper prepared for the European Group for Public Administration annual conference, "Four Months After Administering the New Europe." Ljubljana, September 1–4.

Vihko, R., M. Castells, L. Georghiou, S. Jalkanen, F. Meyer-Krahmer, P. Vuokko, and M. Gröhn. 2002. "Evaluation of Sitra, 2002 [in Finnish]." Sitra, Helsinki. http://www.sitra.fi/julkaisu/2011/evaluation-sitra-2002.

CHAPTER 6

Implementing Innovation Policy

Kaisa Lähteenmäki-Smith

Putting knowledge economy policies efficiently into practice across different sectors require an effective organizational structure and appropriate policy instruments. In Finland, the policy-making role of ministries has been separated from the "professional implementing role" of agencies and their specific instruments.

This chapter first discusses the characteristics of the Finnish model of implementation and then describes how the implementation is done by key actors and initiatives. By presenting the Finnish experiences, the chapter provides examples of how to combine centralized funding with regional elements and how to enable cross-border innovation.

Reasoning Behind: Implementing Innovation Policy in the Finnish Context

Finnish innovation policy has recently developed into one of the core elements of public policy, whereby growth, welfare, employment, and competitiveness are promoted. The government has delegated the implementation of innovation policy to a network of expert organizations at the national and regional levels, ranging from universities to other research, development, and innovation (RDI) organizations. These actors and institutions form the basis for the implementation of Finnish innovation policies and strategies (for governing the system, see chapter 5; for an overview, see chapter 2).

The Finnish model for implementing innovation policy is marked by decentralization and a high degree of regional involvement, as analyzed, for instance, in the international evaluation of the Finnish innovation system (Veugelers *et al.* 2009, 42–43). Close connections between industrial policy and science and technology policy have been typical of the Finnish policy portfolio as well.

Despite increasing centralization around a few growth centers, the Finnish university network has remained highly regionalized and dense, as is the implementation structure, with regional centers, regional councils, and the Funding Agency for Technology and Innovation (Tekes). Regional authorities and state agencies at the regional level have been significant in providing support for implementation. Various policy instruments and programs have been promoted and implemented locally and regionally and are being implemented in urban centers across the country (for example, through the Center of Expertise Program, discussed later in this chapter).

A link between research and development (R&D) and societal problem solving is clearly emerging, as public research is increasingly expected to contribute to addressing of societal problems. The public research organizations, in particular, are connected to ministries through performance guidance and expected to support policy-relevant research and societal objectives. The most important societal objective is to promote scientific knowledge (48 percent of public funding); other goals are to promote production and technology (19 percent) and to provide public policy and services (28 percent) (Statistics Finland, https://www.tilastokeskus.fi/index_en.html).

The overall strength of the system is contrasted with difficulties in adopting the latest technologies, where Finland only ranks 25, according to the World Economic Forum (WEF 2013, 11). Improving this aspect of innovation could create important synergies and consolidate the country's position as one of the world's leading innovation economies. One of the objectives of introducing the strategic centers for science, technology, and innovation (SHOKs), discussed later in this chapter, was to bridge the gap between inputs and outputs: in international comparisons, Finland has consistently high levels of education and input for publicly supported innovation, but relatively low levels of output.

Turning new ideas to competitive advantage is required if industries are to revitalize, and this renewal is required to create employment and improve welfare. Many of the traditional truths no longer apply, and policy implementation is under more pressure to achieve innovation and sustainable growth. Some of the drivers of change and potential ways of responding to them have been addressed recently in numerous working programs, task forces, and policy papers (for example, Alahuhta 2012; Eloranta 2012; MEE 2013). As outlined in Känkänen, Lindroos, and Myllylä (2013, 62).

> As the business environment becomes more complex, it is becoming more difficult to implement industrial policy. Traditional national clusters are making way for global value chains, and the national accounts are not always able to keep up with this trend. The interests of businesses and the national economy are diverging. Essential components of economic growth, namely the amount of work input and development in the productivity of labor, will nonetheless remain the key factors of economic growth.

For instance, according to a task force working in the information and communication technology (ICT) sector, a policy enabling appropriate change and flexibility would entail four key elements: infrastructure, expertise, financing, and working practices and operative cultures (ICT 2015 Working Group 2013). These are valid points for other sectors as well because infrastructure clearly is needed to enable effective and coordinated services for both businesses and the public sector. Expertise has to be sustained and promoted in a way that allows companies to maintain an advantage vis-à-vis their competitors. Financing needs to be sufficient and appropriate at different stages of the lifecycle of companies as well as supportive of risk taking. Changing the work practices and cooperative culture is perhaps the most demanding goal, as it relates to intangible cultural factors that are not easily changed through policy in the short or medium term. These aspects are all drivers of effective policy implementation in the innovation sector.

Implementing the Knowledge Economy at the National Level

Finnish policy implementation has been striving to find and maintain a good balance between science, research, and innovation policies and on the other hand, their funding and implementation in the following areas:

1. Private financing vs. public funding
2. Competitive vs. basic funding of research organizations
3. Top-down (strategically targeted) vs. bottom-up (free, academically peer-reviewed) funding
4. Centralized (national) vs. decentralized (regional or provincial) funding.

The overall objective has been to maintain the 4 percent budget level allocated for public RDI (as a percentage of gross domestic product). In 2012 public funding for RDI was around €2 billion (table 6.1). Although the budget share allocated to RDI has declined in recent years, it remains relatively high in international comparison. Universities' share of this budget is approximately 29 percent (€576 million in 2013). Tekes's funding for technology development is approximately €542 million (27 percent). The third largest share of funding is allocated to public research institutes (15 percent, or approximately €304 million).

Although Finnish innovation policy is built on a model of decentralized implementation, financial resources are relatively centralized. Tekes (technology and innovation funding) and the Academy of Finland (scientific research funding) are

Table 6.1 R&D Funding in 2013, by Type of Institution

Type of institution	*Amount of R&D funding (€ millions)*	*Share of all R&D funding (%)*
Total public R&D funding	2,001.6	100.0
Universities	575.6	28.8
Tekes	542.3	27.1
Academy of Finland	329.3	16.5
Research institutes	303.7	15.2
Other	219.7	11.0
University hospitals	31.0	1.5

Source: Statistics Finland 2013.

the main organizations funding R&D and the main organizations implementing the Finnish government's selected policy choices in the innovation and business development fields. Other implementing agencies are listed at the end of the report (see also figure B2.1.1 in chapter 2 for an overview of the Finnish innovation system).

Finland has a long tradition of sector research—that is, public sector research organizations and institutes under the auspices of particular ministries that provide research and expertise to support their decision making. There have been nearly 20 such research institutes, although some of them have been merged recently or are currently undergoing major reforms. Organizations have been under increasing pressure to ensure more evidence-based decision making and to provide effective and cost-efficient support for the ministries. The largest institutes include the Technical Research Centre (VTT), under the auspices and guidance of the Ministry of Employment and the Economy (MEE), the National Institute for Health and Welfare, under the guidance of the Ministry of Social Affairs and Health, as well as the Finnish Environmental Institute, under the Ministry of Environment. For other institutes, see the list of actors at the end of this book.

In 2013 a government resolution was passed calling for comprehensive reform of state research institutes and research funding (for more information, see the Prime Minister's Office website, www.vnk.fi/tula). The reform sought to meet the challenges and knowledge needs of society and the government by strengthening multidisciplinary, high-level research of social significance. It also sought to organize research institutes into larger and more effective entities and to provide a new funding model for research and analysis that will directly serve the knowledge needs of the government, in both the shorter and longer terms. For instance, an instrument will be established for funding strategic research that supports the knowledge needs of the government and its ministries in the longer term (three to six years). Under the auspices of the Academy of Finland, an additional €70 million will be available for strategic research funding in 2017, administered by a new independent body, the Strategic Research Council. Research and analysis activities supporting more short-term (one to three years) societal decision making by the government and its ministries will also be strengthened. This will be accomplished by accumulating funding in stages from the budget-funded research appropriations of state research institutes and placing them at the disposal of the government and its ministries. This will be carried out in stages between 2014 and 2016, making an initial €5 million available in 2014, €7.5 million in 2015, and €12.5 million in 2016 in non-earmarked funds for research, assessment, and analysis activities meeting the immediate information needs of the government and its ministries. For the purposes of identifying knowledge needs and coordinating efforts in this respect, each ministry is drafting a brief research plan, which is coordinated by the Prime Minister's Office.

Programs have been the main tool for implementing Finnish innovation policy in recent decades. They have proved to be a well-suited instrument for implementing targeted policy action in a decentralized system. However, implementation has been shifting from a purely program-based to a thematic model. Tekes also has been moving in this direction (box 6.1). Another trend in Finland, as elsewhere in the European Union (EU), is a move toward addressing societal challenges as an organizational principle for policy planning and implementation (box 6.2). A recent example of this shift in orientation is the new Innovative Cities (INKA) program, discussed later in this chapter.

Box 6.1 Tekes: Public Incentives for Technology and Innovation

The Finnish Funding Agency for Technology and Innovation, founded in 1983 to boost the development of Finnish industry following the economic recession of the 1970s, is a publicly funded nonprofit agency under the Ministry of Employment and the Economy.

Approximately 20 programs are in operation, undertaking diverse activities, ranging from forward planning (foresight) to funding and expert services, and providing a platform and network for collaboration across the Finnish community and beyond. Tekes has six areas of focus:

- Natural resources and sustainable economy
- Intelligent environment
- Vitality of people
- Business in global value networks
- Value creation based on service solutions and intangible assets
- Renewal of services and production by digital means.

In 2012 Tekes supported companies and research organizations with €570 million in funds. Of this total, €350 million was allocated to company projects, with 68 percent targeting small and medium enterprises, a strategic area of Tekes. On average, Tekes has an estimated impact factor of 21: on average €1 from Tekes to companies provides €21 in annual turnover.

Tekes is a central actor within the Finnish innovation system. It finances some 1,500 business R&D projects and almost 600 public research projects every year. Since the 1990s, Tekes funding has doubled, totaling €610 million in 2011 (€429 million in 2005). Some 75 percent of the funding is allocated from the government budget. The number of Tekes employees has increased from 20 (1983) to more than 400 in Finland and abroad (2013).

Tekes's main objectives are to strengthen the knowledge base, to support innovative growth companies, to increase regional vitality, to increase international innovation activities to help industries to improve productivity, and to boost societal well-being through innovative activities. In recent years, Tekes has increasingly pushed for a broad-based view of innovation, emphasizing the significance of service-related design, business, and social innovations alongside more "traditional" forms of innovation. Besides funding activities, Tekes provides expert services to companies, for example, in finalizing business plans. Tekes also promotes the development of new research areas by implementing technology programs involving a specific field.

box continues next page

Box 6.1 Tekes: Public Incentives for Technology and Innovation *(continued)*

Tekes finances industrial R&D projects as well as projects in universities and research institutes, focusing especially on innovative and high-risk projects. Tekes funding may be a low-interest loan or a grant, depending on the stage of the innovation and the nature of the proposed project. In recent years, a major share of Tekes funding has been allocated to SHOKs. For additional information, see the Tekes website (www.tekes.fi).

Observations from the case:

- The availability of a full set of research, development, and innovation (RDI) funding instruments and government subsidies are a key catalyst for research, innovation, and renewal of the economy.
- Organizing RDI funding into an agency separate from the ministry and policy making emphasizes the professional role of the agency in funding decisions, administration, and monitoring of grants.

Box 6.2 Vigo Business Accelerator: Fostering Renewal through Entrepreneurship

The Vigo business accelerator program was launched in 2009 to bridge the gap between early-stage technology firms and international venture funding. The program is aimed at young, innovative, and growth-oriented companies, especially start-ups aiming to compete in global markets.

At Vigo's core are the Vigo accelerators: independent companies led by serial entrepreneurs. They offer start-up capital funding, expert and mentoring advice, and guidance for the selected business ideas selected by the program. At the moment, 10 accelerators are in operation. They invest time and money in the target companies and take a strategic and an operational role in them.

The private financiers of Vigo consist of capital investors, angel investors, funds, and business incubators. The public funding of Vigo comes from financial instruments under Tekes and Finnvera. As a sign of Vigo's success, Vigo portfolio companies have raised more than €100 million since the program began. Supercell, one of the Finnish game industry's recent successes, took part in one of the accelerators, Lifeline Ventures, which focuses on health technology (medtech, biotech, e-health), games, and the internet.

A steering group set up by the MEE guides implementation and development of Vigo. Profict Partners is in charge of implementation, having been commissioned by the MEE. For additional information, see the Vigo website (www.vigo.fi).

Observations from the case:

- It is important to engage experienced entrepreneurs as business angels and mentors for new start-ups.
- Besides providing private equity, experienced entrepreneurs are an important source of proven business experience and role models for new entrepreneurs.

Implementing a Knowledge Economy at the Regional and Provincial Levels

When assessing implementation, it is significant that the Finnish innovation policy is implemented largely in a decentralized policy system, where the centrally agreed policy goals and objectives are operationalized. The decentralization of implementation makes it possible for geographically vast or diverse countries to take into account regional characteristics and to coordinate and promote the development of regional expertise. Moreover, sector research institutes, referred to above, traditionally have decentralized units, cooperating closely with universities across the country.

The guidelines for regional innovation policy are based on the government's framework for national regional development. Within this framework, the MEE and the Ministry of Education and Culture are responsible for preparing the appropriate policy measures.

Regional innovation policy aims to "support the use of expertise outside regional centers and to see that the whole country can make use of the increasing amount of funding allocated to technology and expertise." This policy has been implemented through the Center of Expertise Program (see box 6.3). Other initiatives within the regional innovation policy framework include strengthening the regional activities of universities and polytechnics (see the MEE website, http://www.tem.fi/en/regional_development).

Other key organizations in Finnish regional implementation of the knowledge economy are the 15 centers for economic development, transport, and the environment (ELY centers), which are responsible for the regional implementation and development tasks of the central government. Their portfolio includes responsibility for promoting regional competitiveness, well-being, and sustainable development and for curbing climate change. The organizations'

Box 6.3 Competitiveness through Regional Expertise Networks

The centers of expertise have been the main instrument of Finnish regional innovation policy since their introduction in the 1990s. Their main objectives are to use high-level expertise as a resource for business activities, the creation of new jobs, and regional development.

Originally organized around a regional, decentralized network of more than 20 centers, during 2007–13 the Center of Expertise Program (OSKE) implemented 13 national competence clusters, each of which comprises four to seven regional centers of expertise. Each cluster is intended to form its own network of public-private partnerships, managed with a view toward fulfilling shared objectives in turning research into business. Each cluster has an appointed program director to coordinate the cluster's national and international operations. On the national level, the program is coordinated by a multidisciplinary committee appointed by the government. The total estimated budget of the centers for 2009–12 was €62.8 million (mostly from Tekes). During 2007–13, 3,000 jobs were created,

box continues next page

Box 6.3 Competitiveness through Regional Expertise Networks *(continued)*

almost 581 companies were established, and more than 44,000 individuals received training. For additional information, see the (OSKE) website (www.oske.net/en).

After the positive experiences of the centers of expertise and in light of recent economic and societal developments and upcoming challenges (related to globalization, demographic change, and urbanization), the centers of expertise have been developed in an evidence-based fashion, taking into consideration the findings and recommendations of external evaluations (five in all). The most recent evaluation, in 2010, was followed by further development of the concept: in 2013 OSKE was replaced by the Innovative Cities (Innovatiiviset Kaupungit, INKA) program, built more firmly around and concentrated in urban centers and seeking to use more effectively the purchasing power, service structure, and international networks of Finland's main urban centers. To foster growth, INKA is also implementing large development projects (housing, traffic) in these urban regions in cooperation with the government. These large (infrastructure-related) development projects can be used as test laboratories to create new markets for Finnish know-how. In 2014, the situation is that the Ministry of Employment and the Economy has approved five national themes for the program and named the urban regions responsible for leading the work in them. The themes are bioeconomy, sustainable energy solutions, future health care, and smart cities and industrial regeneration. Government funding for the program is 10 million euros with additional 10 million euros coming from the urban regions. Also EU Structural Funds are allocated for program implementation. The themes and regions will be reviewed in 2017.

The Center of Excellence program (STET) is a scientific research "counterpart" to the centers of expertise. The centers of excellence in research strive to raise the quality of Finnish research by allocating funding to "cutting-edge" research units in their respective fields. Centers of excellence in research are selected—after a two-stage process and on the basis of international peer review—and funded by the Academy of Finland with additional funds from Tekes, host organizations, and business companies. In the 2012–17 program there are 15 centers of excellence in research. Total funding for 2008–12 was a slightly more than €56 million.

The STET is particularly important in a country that has a relatively fragmented university structure. In Finland geographically dispersed universities provide good opportunities for accessing universities for research collaboration or education purposes, but university research groups have tended to remain small from the point of view of international competitiveness. For additional information, see the Center of Excellence website (http://www.aka.fi/en-GB/A/Centers-of-Excellence-/).

Observations from the case:

- The Center of Expertise, the Center of Excellence, and the INKA programs all aim to spread and use regional expertise and thus may contain valuable elements for geographically vast or diverse countries.
- The INKA concept, built around networks of urban centers and their potential to boost innovation through innovative solutions for public services, public procurement, as well as various types of locally based innovation pilots and demonstrations, could prove to be an interesting benchmark for other countries, so it is worth paying close attention to its development.

duties range from financing and development services for enterprises, employment-based aid and labor market training, as well as agricultural and fishery issues and road maintenance. ELY centers were established as part of the reform of the state regional authorities in 2010, with the aim of providing a more effective and efficient model for regional governance and ensuring further efficiency in personnel resources. However, these goals have not yet been met, and the role of ELY centers still needs clarifying. Coordinating sector responsibilities has been especially challenging, given the range of responsibilities of ELY centers. In the innovation field, Tekes has regional experts in each center, ensuring implementation and flow of information across the country.

The regional implementation network is supplemented by a variety of regional and provincial innovation actors, usually private companies owned by municipalities or their consortia. As a tool for coordinating this network, the MEE set up the innovation network concept in 2005. Key activities include trainings, seminars, data sharing, pilot projects, and networking.

Cross-Sectoral Implementation: The SHOKs

The Finnish strategic centers for science, technology, and innovation are one of the newest and biggest instruments of Finnish innovation policy. They aim to combine applied and blue-sky research and to reconcile excellence (traditionally the key criteria for the Academy of Finland and other academic research funding organizations) with relevance (traditionally the key criteria for companies and their funding instruments). SHOKs have been evaluated recently, providing a suitable case for assessing the successes and challenges of policy implementation and providing lessons of broader interest to other countries seeking to tackle similar challenges and limitations in their innovation policy.

The SHOKs were established in 2006 as public-private partnerships to speed up innovation processes and to renew the Finnish industry clusters by creating new competencies and radical innovations at the system level. SHOKs demonstrate many of the characteristics of the coordination and management mechanisms, roles and responsibilities inside the institutional environment, as well as the interplay between the spatial dimensions (global and international industries, cross-sectoral but location-specific innovation ecosystems, in addition to national implementation and policies for regional and local environments).

The SHOKs and associated research programs are funded mainly by Tekes. The intellectual property rights are shared between the collaborators in SHOK research programs, but they may be retained by industry partners in SHOK industrial R&D projects. The Academy of Finland funds (basic) research associated with the objectives of SHOKs, and its Center of Excellence program supports SHOKs because individual centers funded by the academy are associated with them.

The budget for the SHOKs for 2007–12 was approximately €800 million. Tekes, the main funding organization, has been committing a considerable share of SHOK funding (approximately 50 percent), nearly 40 percent comes from the companies, and the rest comes from universities and research organizations. The SHOKs may also apply for funding through EU research programs, although such funding has remained largely underused.

In October 2013 six SHOKs were in operation:

- CLEEN Ltd. (in the area of environment and energy)
- FIMECC Ltd. (in the metal industry)
- SalWe Ltd. (in health and well-being)
- DIGILE (formerly known as TIVIT Ltd., in the ICT and digital services sector; see box 6.4)
- RYM Ltd. (in the area of built environments)
- Finnish Bioeconomy Cluster FIBIC Ltd. (in biotechnology).

Box 6.4 The DIGILE SHOK

DIGILE SHOK (formerly known as TIVIT) seeks to create new ICT-based ecosystems to support opportunities for global growth of new business for DIGILE's owners and partners, consisting of 40 companies, universities, or public organizations. In practice, DIGILE organizes research programs for selected research areas in collaboration with stakeholders. In October 2013, six research programs were planned or ongoing:

- *Device and interoperability ecosystem,* focusing on new intelligent devices and spaces
- *Cloud software,* focusing on the value chain of Internet services, sustainable development, user experience, and information security
- *Next media,* focusing on media's new revenue models
- *Internet of things,* focusing on establishing a competitive ecosystem, creating business enablers, improving Finland's global visibility, and affecting the evolution and standardization of technology
- *Data to intelligence,* focusing on the development of intelligent tools and methods of managing, refining, and using data
- *Digital services,* focusing on creating and developing new digital services.

DIGILE has its own FORGE Service Lab, a development laboratory for digital services. It is located in Kajaani, some 550 kilometers north of Helsinki. It is designed to be a cloud service and a forum for gathering open-source thinking. The laboratory also supports the growth of other branches of industry as well as the efforts of public administration to provide better services.

Like all SHOKs, DIGILE is a public limited company. The managing board is responsible for the normal operations of the corporation but also for the content of its research programs. Operational management is carried out by the chief executive officer and the director of technology. Program managers (coming from companies) are responsible for implementing each program. In total, DIGILE has nine employees (of which five are administrative and four are research staff).

box continues next page

Box 6.4 The DIGILE SHOK *(continued)*

In 2010 the joint budget of the research programs was €50 million. The funds are allocated in each research program based on applications. All participants sign a consortium agreement. After the agreement, the program applies to Tekes for public funding.

The name DIGILE, a combination of "digital" and "agile," was adopted in August 2013 to highlight the role of digitalization in all businesses and services. For additional information (including a detailed description of the model and results), see the DIGILE website (www.digile.fi).

SHOK operations apply new methods for cooperation, co-creation, and interaction. International cooperation is also important. Furthermore, testing and piloting creative research environments and ecosystems constitute an essential part of the SHOKs' operations. In the SHOKs, companies and research units are intended to work in close cooperation, carrying out research that has been jointly defined in the strategic research agenda of each center. The research aims to meet the needs of Finnish industry and society within a period of 5 to 10 years. In engaging in new path-breaking research areas and seeking to promote new collaborative knowledge, the commitment and patience of those providing the funding and infrastructure are naturally an important prerequisite for commitment of the parties involved.

One element of such long-term commitment is involvement of the government in the process. While the MEE has set up a national strategic steering group, chaired by the permanent secretary of MEE, the main strategic guidance at the level of individual SHOKs is set out in the strategic research agenda, drafted as a result of dialogue among SHOK shareholders. Despite the top-down approach to creating the program, individual SHOKs are independent corporations and free to choose their activities within the thematic area. They are virtual centers of excellence and usually employ a few people who organize the collaboration and administer the SHOK. The individual projects first are approved by the SHOK board or council and then apply for research grants. In practice, the SHOKs are self-governing and are relatively free to work within the framework.

The SHOKs demonstrate many of the key features of the policy styles and governance characteristics underlying Finnish innovation policy. They provide a platform for cooperation for innovative, ambitious companies and research institutions (universities, research institutes). They have been seeking to promote and accelerate innovation processes. These processes achieve competitive advantages by coming up with and using new ideas, processes, and products that involve new economic, business-related, social, technological, or organizational characteristics. The way in which SHOKs have been defined also emphasizes the cross-sectoral nature of the clusters, in terms of both industrial branches and the academic disciplines involved. This type of cluster instrument is promoted first and foremost as a means of crossing the traditional industrial boundaries and being cross- or multidisciplinary in nature.

The Rationale and Need to Set Up SHOKs

The SHOK concept was introduced as a means to support the parallel objectives of industrial renewal and academic excellence. It illustrates how Finnish innovation policy has been developed to respond to identified gaps and failures across time. It was intended to provide a science-based solution to industry-driven problems and, as such, constituted a novel policy experiment. Traditionally, the two processes have been kept largely apart and promoted through separate policy measures.

New instruments are often introduced in response to regular evaluations of policies. In the case of SHOKs, this evaluative assessment came from a broad-based working group assessing the challenges of globalization for Finland and the possible means of responding to them through the Finnish portfolio of innovation policy. The starting points included the realization that, as a small country, Finland has to be very careful in choosing its areas of focus and investments, quality has to meet the highest international standards in order to be able to compete for the best talent, and in the long term the activities should result in both high-class expertise and innovation, which can also lead to commercial applications.

This new instrument emerged incrementally: the origins of the SHOK concept were connected to the gradual development of more diverse program-based policy instruments in the innovation sector. The idea of establishing SHOKs goes back to 2004 to a report drafted by the Prime Minister's Office (2004). The report emphasized that reaching (or in some cases maintaining) a high international standard in education, scientific excellence, and relevance of research and teaching would require the creation of sufficiently large concentrations of expertise to form a critical mass. Among the concerns raised in the report were the outdated nature of the concept of linearly applied innovation and the need to base the new framework regulation and key definitions on a modern concept of the networked and highly interactive nature of R&D; innovation was seen as a broader concept that includes more than just R&D in the traditional sense (see chapter 5).

The ideal goal, as suggested in the report, was to create a few clusters of high-quality competence inside of Finland (box 6.5). This initial proposal was followed by another report in 2004 that recommended that Finland create more internationally visible and attractive, high-quality research units, R&D clusters, and programs. The next step in the process was to pass a resolution on the structural development of the public research system, which was adopted by the Finnish government in April 2005. Here, the government required the Science and Technology Policy Council to take the lead in drawing up a national strategy for creating and reinforcing internationally competitive science and technology clusters and centers of excellence. This was addressed in June 2006 in a report on the development potential of strategic centers of excellence (as they were called in the report) and national infrastructures. Work was thus launched to establish SHOKs in areas of expertise that were considered crucial for the future of the business sector and Finnish society at-large.

Box 6.5 SHOK Selection Criteria

SHOKs are intended to operate in nationally important strategic areas, that is, areas where there is a "national interest" in maintaining research, development, and innovation (RDI) as well as industrial activity and in supporting specialization in higher education and research with the potential to be globally cutting edge. The industrial areas selected for the SHOK clusters cover almost all key industrial areas. The SHOKs have five selection criteria.

First, they must be highly significant in terms of their potential impact on society and the national economy, and they must involve significant investments in research and development.

Second, they need to achieve sufficient critical mass with regard to their personnel and financial resources. The total financial volume of center activities must reach an annual level of €50 million to €100 million.

Third, the centers need to be constructed around applications central to the future of the sector in question. An application-driven approach implies that the RDI activities carried out by the center should combine various types of expertise and sources of innovation, crossing many types of borders.

Fourth, the core expertise for the centers should come from Finland, with each center having the potential to be among the best in the world. The centers need to have international credibility and visibility and be able to attract the most qualified experts and best companies.

Fifth, the centers need to be based on the strong commitment of the main companies, universities, research institutes, funders, and ministries in the field in question.

The Results and Experience So Far

The SHOKs were evaluated during 2012–13. The evaluation concluded that they have succeeded in creating strategic agendas for their respective industries and have vitalized a new depth of research collaboration between stakeholders. Moreover, the stakeholders are committed and generally satisfied with the operation of the SHOKs, and some catalytic effects on innovation environments have been achieved. The actual impact, however, is harder to assess, as the SHOKs have been operating for a relatively short time compared to the span of the research agendas.

In many respects, high expectations have not been met, largely due to the difficulties of guiding new ways of working and thinking. Concerns remain over the functionality of the SHOK concept as a whole as well as its ability to provide value added. This is mainly because some of the objectives are mutually exclusive and contradictory. More selective approaches and choices are needed. While companies have been successfully integrated into their operations, the academic community has been less central. One way of achieving better integration would be to include the Academy of Finland in funding the instrument. This would be essential to achieving the goals of excellence and relevance, which have been well promoted.

The operational model in which independent companies coordinate the efforts, the MEE provides national-level guidance, and the national-level SHOK steering group provides governance (it is still seeking a role and exact function within the governance structure) is not without problems. Although the autonomy and legal status of SHOKs, which reflects the voice of shareholders seeking to maximize profit, needs to be respected, the high level of public funding requires public accountability; the guidance model and governance bodies need to pay attention to this external dimension as well.

The SHOK concept enables internationally competitive research, based on the collaborative efforts and shared interests of industry and the academic community. There are, however, several challenges in defining and achieving these shared interests.

- One key challenge lies in the temporal dimension: while the companies are expected to achieve results for their shareholders in the short term, academic research is often concerned with the long term.
- Another challenge pertains to openness. On the one hand, companies want to create new knowledge that they can use within their own organization. They weigh this need against the knowledge and value added of their competition (Do they achieve more or better results faster than their main competitors?) and are therefore more closed in nature. (They do not share innovations until they have been fully capitalized.) On the other hand, the academic community is concerned with open competition and assessment by peers.
- Another difference pertains to the market and instrumental nature of the innovations achieved. Companies necessarily seek to introduce innovations and products that have demand and potential value on the market (in the short term), while the academic community is seldom concerned with the market perspective and is more likely to promote innovation that is not directly marketable and that has more inherent value in itself.
- Differences also exist between blue-sky research and applied research, which is a potential tension between industrial and academic interests.

To conclude, policy instruments such as SHOKs are central in implementing policy and in seeking to coordinate and cross-fertilize the sectors, disciplines, and research areas, providing a welcome boost for new ideas, solutions, and practices. Network-based program instruments rely on industry collaboration, and in many cases the success factors have relied on the ability to use these networks in policy implementation. The SHOK concept has been a flagship in recent years. All in all, it has emerged as a novel take on the old industry–public sector partnership and has shifted some strategic influence to the newly established SHOK companies and their networks. However, the model has been unable to address the underlying tension between industry-driven relevance and academia-driven excellence.

Summary and Key Messages

Finnish innovation policy is built on a model of decentralized implementation, although the financial resources are relatively centralized (in particular, through Tekes). For a geographically diverse country, this model of centralized financing is probably the most feasible and ensures a strategic overview.

While the concentration of resources is important in light of their increasing scarcity, and efficiency and effectiveness are important assessment criteria, the diversity and multiple sources of innovation are clearly valued in Finland. Multiple funding modes and sources are likely to contribute to the diversity and viability of the research and innovation community; for this reason, implementation should not be streamlined excessively. Tekes and the Academy of Finland have different strategies, and rightly so, but to ensure the best use of all sources of innovation and expertise, dialogue and close collaboration between them are essential.

The dualism between industrial and academic interests has been dealt with largely through the distribution of responsibility between Tekes and the Academy of Finland, as exemplified by the centers of excellence, or the SHOKs, for instance. If academic and industrial interests are to be reconciled, it should be through the implementation of programs and projects; in this area, SHOKs have been the first test case, where the two sources of financing and the two strategies could meet. This is still very much a work in progress, but providing sufficient financial incentives, as well as opening the relevant governance structures to both parties are means of achieving this. The Research and Innovation Council can play a key role here.

The degree of Finnish government intervention is traditionally high, though not without debate. Main issues have involved the nature of intervention and the extent to which government should restrict itself to dealing with market failure or indeed involve itself in a more proactive role, even picking winners. SHOKs are illustrative in this regard: the structure is clearly more encompassing than selective, enabling the ability of committed actors and organizations within the RDI system, from companies to research organizations, to determine success.

The overlapping roles of expert organizations and public authorities have continued to be a source of lively debate. While the Finnish system is far from perfect, the Finnish experiences provide ample lessons learned with regard to the need for transparency, for clear roles and responsibilities, as well as for striking a balance between implementation (this chapter), planning and guidance (chapter 5), as well as monitoring and evaluation (chapter 7). Box 6.6 presents the key messages from this chapter.

Box 6.6 Key Messages

- An essential element of Finnish policy implementation has been in finding and keeping a good balance between science, research, and innovation funding and policy implementation with respect to the following: (1) private financing vs. public funding, (2) competitive vs. basic funding of research organizations, (3) top-down (strategic) vs. bottom-up (free) funding, as well as (4) centralized (national) vs. decentralized (regional or provincial) funding and implementation.
- In Finland, policy making related to the knowledge economy has been separated from policy implementation. The latter function has been given to implementation agencies, with sufficient professional experience and a set of instruments. Such a clear distinction between roles and responsibilities has proven to be an effective way to implement policy and ensure that all aspects and policy objectives are pursued.
- The Finnish SHOKs provide an interesting example of an attempt to combine the objectives of organizing large-scale public-private partnerships with strong industrial leadership, strong strategic prioritization with high scientific ambitions, as well as development of long-term competence with medium-term industrial renewal.

References

Alahuhta, M. 2012. "Team Finland: Taloudellisten ulkosuhteiden verkosto [A Network of External Economic Relations]." Ministry for Foreign Affairs, Helsinki.

Eloranta, J. 2012. "Investointeja Suomeen: Ehdotus strategiaksi ja toimintaohjelmaksi Suomen houkuttelevuuden lisäämiseksi yritysten investointikohteena [Investments in Finland: A Proposal for a Strategy and Action Plan to Improve the Attractiveness of Finland for Foreign Investors]." Ministry of Employment and the Economy, Helsinki.

Känkänen, J., P. Lindroos, and M. Myllylä. 2013. *Elinkeino-ja teollisuuspoliittinen linjaus*. Publication 5/2013. Helsinki: Ministry of Employment and the Economy.

MEE (Ministry of Employment and the Economy). 2013. *21 Paths to a Friction-Free Finland* [in Finnish]. MEE Publication 4/2013. Helsinki: Edita Publishing. http://www.tem.fi/files/35440/TEMjul_4_2013_web.pdf.

Prime Minister's Office. 2004. *Strengthening Competence and Openness: Finland in the Global Economy*. Interim report, Helsinki.

Statistics Finland. 2013. "Valtio rahoittaa t&k-toimintaa 2 miljardilla eurolla vuonna 2013." http://tilastokeskus.fi/til/tkker/2013/tkker_2013_2013-02-27_tie_001_fi.html.

Veugelers, R., K. Aizinger, D. Breznitz, C. Edquist, G. Murray, G. Ottaviano, A. Hyytinen, A. Kangasharju, M. Ketokivi, T. Luukkonen, M. Maliranta, M. Maula, P. Okko, P. Rouvinen, M. Sotarauta, T. Tanayama, O. Toivanen, P. Ylä-Anttila. 2009. *Evaluation of the Finnish National Innovation System: Full Report.* Helsinki: Taloustieto, Helsinki University. http://www.tem.fi/files/24929/InnoEvalFi_FULL_Report_28_Oct_2009.pdf.

WEF (World Economic Forum). 2013. *The Global Competitiveness Report, 2012–2013*. Geneva: WEF.

CHAPTER 7

Monitoring and Evaluating Investments

Kalle A. Piirainen

For policy making to be effective, policies have to be well focused and implemented efficiently. In practice, improving the effectiveness of policies is realized largely through systematic monitoring and evaluation and the willingness of policy-makers to learn and understand from their own and others' experiences and to adapt policies accordingly. Moreover, monitoring and evaluation are crucial for transparency and legitimacy of the whole system.

In general, Finnish knowledge economy policies have been considered rather effective, and there has been a culture of systematic assessments to learn from experience and improve performance. This chapter discusses some of the key elements behind this tradition and draws lessons for developing countries looking to improve the transparency and effectiveness of public investments.

Reasoning Behind: Monitoring and Evaluation as Mechanisms for Policy Learning

Policy learning, monitoring, and evaluation are all about learning from past experience, improving knowledge economy policies, and assessing the effectiveness of public investment. While many decisions related to the development of a knowledge economy are political—that is, based on value judgments—requiring monitoring and evaluating the success of policies enable drawing conclusions on how well the actions that were taken solved the issues targeted. Thus monitoring and evaluation are intended to produce relevant and timely knowledge for policy making and enable learning from past experiences.

Evaluation Practices in Finland

In Finland, policy evaluations started in the 1970s in the wake of the new public management movement, with evaluations of government institutions and programs conducted by government-appointed committees comprising government officials, civil servants, and representatives of interest groups.

Influence the Organisation for Economic Co-operation and Development (OECD) led to evaluations become more commonplace, and to the appointment of (independent) investigators. The new public management movement started to gain momentum at the turn of the 1980s and in the 1990s, as the use of outside experts became more prevalent, contributing to building a professional evaluation culture. During the 1990s, Finland started to lean toward Europe, entering the European Union (EU) in 1995. The influence of the EU and the European Commission in the late 1990s contributed to the development of program evaluation and the practice of commissioning evaluations from independent professional contractors. During the first decade of the new millennium, evaluation practices matured in the sense that evaluations became more frequent, organized, and professional.

The Research and Innovation Council (RIC), formerly the Science and Technology Policy Council (STPC), has laid out recommendations for evaluations. According to the RIC statement, the responsibility for developing evaluation, impact assessment, and forward planning (foresight) concerns all actors in the innovation system, but applies in particular to public funding organizations or policy agencies. The recommended actions include acquiring knowledge on the technical aspects of evaluation and foresight as well as networking between organizations to reinforce the overall picture of the innovation system and develop consistent incentives for private and public actors alike. One particular action in this respect is the development of indicators for analyzing the impact of public research, development, and innovation (RDI) incentives. Moreover, the knowledge base that is developed through evaluation and foresight should be adequate and linked with decision making. The RIC acknowledges that the main challenges in policy learning stem from unsystematic evaluation and foresight, use of different methods and standards by different organizations, complexity of the causal chain from intervention to societal impacts, especially in evaluating investments in basic research, lack of a big picture in policy making, and unclear responsibilities, producing suboptimal results (STPC 2007a, 2007b).

Dimensions and Levels of Evaluation

An important basis for policy learning comes from statistics that establish a baseline for monitoring economic progress as well as improvements in RDI. These data include statistics on gross domestic product, value added, productivity, RDI spending by the public and private sectors (government budget appropriations or outlays for R&D and business expenditure in R&D), fraction of RDI personnel or science and engineering majors in the workforce, investments in capital and RDI, number of patents and inventions disclosed, amount of paid subsidies, as well as science metrics, such as number of publications, impacts, or citations, and education statistics, including average years of schooling and share of engineers and science majors in the population. These data are collected and administered mainly by Statistics Finland, which is a centralized national statistics and census bureau.

Complementing the economic indicators, which can be used to monitor development of the economy and the impact of policies, evaluations provide detailed data and judgment on specific policy instruments within the general policy mix. Accordingly, the Finnish innovation system and policy mix, including individual policy instruments, are evaluated periodically. Table 7.1 illustrates the levels of evaluation with examples of recent evaluations. Finnish practice differs from that of many other countries on the systemic and institutional levels. Finland employs institutional evaluations, in particular, more often than many other countries. These evaluations carry historical significance in the Finnish context, as discussed above. In Finland, the program sponsor commissions the evaluation although is not a recommended practice given the fundamental conflict of interest.

Evidence-Based Policy Making

Policy learning is associated with fact-based or evidence-based policy making (James and Lodge 2003; Parsons 2003). Evidence-based policy making is most common in the health care sector, where it is also called

Table 7.1 Evaluation at Different Levels of the Finnish Knowledge Economy

Level	*Examples*
System	Evaluations are often attached to a policy-making cycle; for example, the evaluation of the Finnish national innovation system (Veugelers *et al.* 2009) was attached to the national innovation strategy (Aho *et al.* 2008), with the aim of evaluating how well the strategy was implemented. The evaluation was commissioned by the Ministry of Employment and the Economy, which is in charge of developing the innovation system. System evaluations may also be periodic, such as the semiannual state of scientific research in Finland review, conducted by the Academy of Finland, which is in charge of implementing science policy on behalf of the Ministry of Education and Culture and international review panels (see, for example, Treudhardt and Nuutinen 2012).
Institution	Institutional evaluations are attached to the implementation of policy—for example, the Ministry of Employment and the Economy (MEE) commissions evaluations of institutions and policy agencies within the MEE group and large programs executed by the group roughly every five years. For example, see the evaluation of Tekes (Van Der Veen *et al.* 2012) and the evaluation of the strategic centers of science, technology, and innovation (Lähteenmäki-Smith *et al.* 2013). Institutions and agencies also commission evaluations of themselves. Tekes periodically conducts an impact assessment that informs itself and MEE on the impact of its activities on the macroeconomic level and complements the evaluation of the outcome of individual programs.
Program	Institutions and implementing agencies commonly evaluate their program activity. For example, Tekes evaluates the individual programs it implements during each program (mid-term) and afterward (ex post) (see, for example, Raivio *et al.* 2012). These evaluations are technically summative and commonly focus on the activities and implementation of the program as well as the outcomes.
Project	The implementing agencies or project management themselves may commission evaluations for large or high-profile projects, such as the evaluation of the Finnish national foresight project (Piirainen and Halme 2013). Sometimes these project (self-) evaluations are mandated by funding terms and conditions, as is the case of European Union structural funds, including the European Regional Development Fund and European Social Fund.

evidence-based clinical practice and evidence-based medicine (see, for example, Muir Gray 2004). The qualitative difference between evidence-based policy making and lesson drawing or policy transfer is that the moniker "evidence-based" implies that the policy and instrument design are based on careful consideration of fact and evidence, often scientifically verified, and that the effects, impacts, and externalities of the policy can be better foreseen and controlled based on relevant scientific evidence. In fact, evidence-based policy making is similar to successful lesson drawing or policy transfer (Dolowitz and Marsh 2000). Furthermore, evidence-based policy making does not preclude democratic public discussion about the goals of policy and associated value judgments. In the Finnish context, the 2007 RIC statement highlighted the need to develop evaluation and foresight practices to support policy making. Evidence-based policy making is advocated even more strongly in the report of the Working Group on Developing Evaluation and Impact Assessment (Prime Minister's Office 2011), which concluded that a wealth of information, evaluation results, and research is available to policy making, but the information and evidence are not used systematically and do not meet the needs of policy making. The working group recommended a model resembling the idealized EU policy-making model discussed in the next section.

The call for evidence was made some years ago and, due to budgetary pressures and economic stagnation in Finland as well as other European welfare states, public spending will come under even closer scrutiny in the future. Finland responded to the recent economic downturn by cutting budgets for everything except spending on RDI and education, but in light of recent public debates around, for example, evaluation of the strategic centers for science, technology, and innovation (SHOKs), the legitimacy of public RDI spending may come into question (see, for example, the 2013 discussion in *Helsingin Sanomat*, the largest newspaper in Finland). This call to examine the return on public investment may indeed drive evidence-based policy making.

Two more recent trends in Finnish policy making are policy experimentation and participatory policy making. Both of these trends are evident in the process and content of the Finnish national project related to the government's foresight report (see box 5.8 in chapter 5). The foresight process was built to enable broad-based participation through a Delphi survey, an edited web portal, and a series of regional workshops that fed into the mainline process. Further, the results of the foresight theme "administration as an enabler" suggest that public administration will be more transparent and open in the future. Policy experiments are also associated with the national foresight process and advocated by the parliamentary Committee for the Future (Berg 2013). Policy experiments are undertaken to test the principle or intervention logic of a policy instrument by implementing it on a small scale to gather evidence on outcomes and impacts, a process that enables fact- or evidence-based decision making on whether the instrument should be implemented nationwide with a large budget.

Basic Setup for Learning by Evaluating

Figure 7.1 presents a framework for policy making and learning that approximates the Finnish system. Issues are chosen through a political process, typically in parliament, and the corresponding policies, instruments, and interventions are designed to solve those issues, typically through ministries or policy agencies. These policies are then accepted in the political process and implemented. Monitoring, evaluation, and learning come into play during or after implementation of the intervention, as data and evidence on the progress, outcome, and impact of the policy are collected and used to inform further decision making.

Evaluation means determining the worth, significance, or condition of something usually by careful appraisal or study. For programs and policies, evaluation means a systematic appraisal of the merit, worth, and significance of an intervention, using criteria related to objectives. Monitoring is an associated and parallel activity, which means recording data and evidence on the progress of an intervention. In policy learning or evaluation, monitoring means recording data in the form of specific indicators that measure how well the policy intervention fulfills its goals. Figure 7.2 illustrates the basic logic of evaluation: the outcomes and impacts are studied and measured against the objectives. Key concepts of evaluation, discussed at length below, are intervention, evaluation criteria, and intervention logic.

Intervention is deliberate action taken to solve a defined problem through a set of activities. An intervention can be a policy, instrument, program, or individual project that has goals and logic.

Figure 7.1 An Idealized Policy-Making Process Modeled after the European Commission

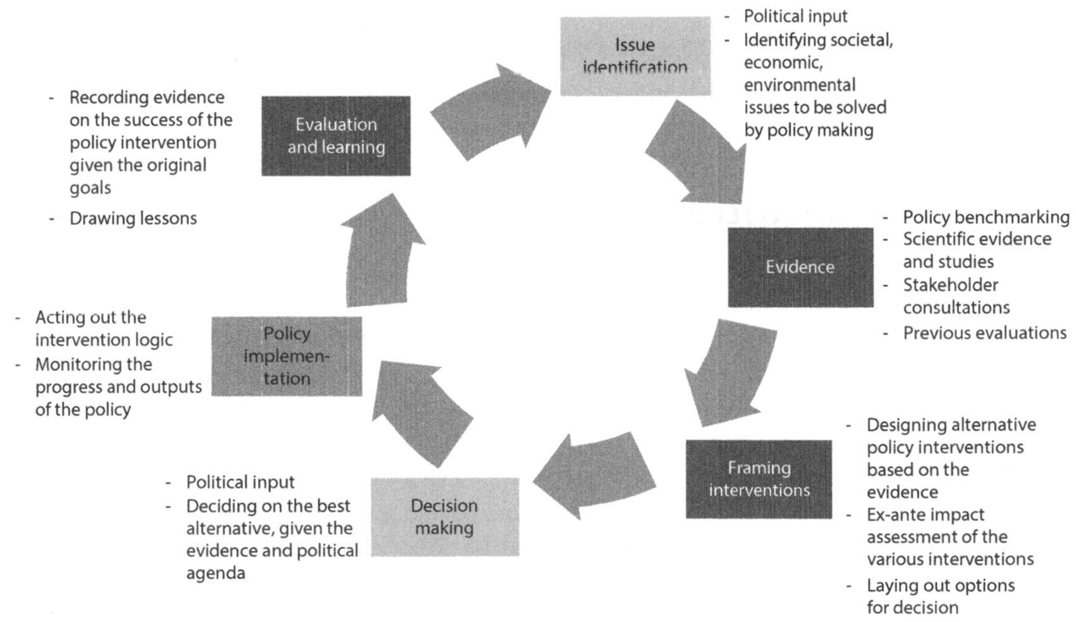

Issue identification
- Political input
- Identifying societal, economic, environmental issues to be solved by policy making

Evidence
- Policy benchmarking
- Scientific evidence and studies
- Stakeholder consultations
- Previous evaluations

Framing interventions
- Designing alternative policy interventions based on the evidence
- Ex-ante impact assessment of the various interventions
- Laying out options for decision

Decision making
- Political input
- Deciding on the best alternative, given the evidence and political agenda

Policy implementation
- Acting out the intervention logic
- Monitoring the progress and outputs of the policy

Evaluation and learning
- Recording evidence on the success of the policy intervention given the original goals
- Drawing lessons

Source: Adapted from http://ec.europa.eu/digital-agenda/en/how-does-policy-making-30-differ-current-practices.

Figure 7.2 Basic Logic of Ex Post Evaluation on a Project Level

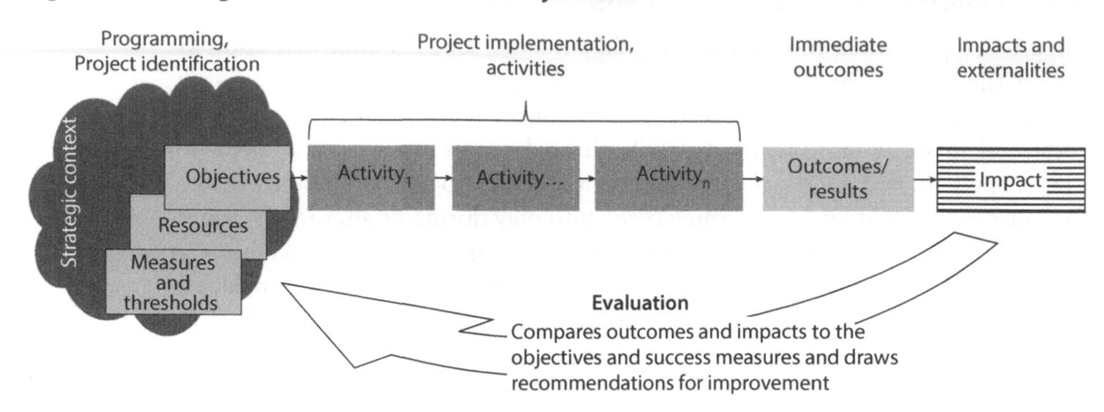

Another key concept is theory of change or intervention logic, which is the logical backbone of the policy, instrument, program, or project to be evaluated (Mason and Barnes 2007; Vogel 2012). Intervention logic explains how inputs are transformed into outcomes and impacts as a result of a set of activities. The term "theory of change" implies that the intervention logic should be based on relevant research and other evidence on the problem to be solved, which explains how the intended activities should contribute to attaining the goals of the intervention. Evaluation criteria are also called measures or indicators and are used to measure the outcomes and impacts of the intervention. The success of the intervention is thus based on the level of achievement as measured by these indicators, ideally by comparing the observed levels to predefined thresholds that define when an intervention can be considered successful.

Evaluation also enables learning from the past. First, it means that evaluation questions and measures have to be policy relevant, and second, it means that policy (instrument) and program design should explicitly correspond to the (political) objectives being sought (figure 7.3).

System-Level Evaluations

During 2008 and 2009, an international evaluation of the Finnish research and innovation system was carried out by a large international panel led by Professor Reinhilde Veugelers (Veugelers *et al.* 2009). The evaluation examined the Finnish innovation system as a whole and suggested solutions and recommendations that addressed the entire system and its operation rather than individual functions or organizations. The specific aim of the evaluation was to get an independent view of the system. The tasks included identifying current and future challenges and assessing how well the system recognized and was able to face them. The mission also identified systemic, institutional, or policy adjustments.

To a large extent, the international evaluation was initiated in response to the national innovation strategy published in 2008 (see Aho *et al.* 2008); its goal was to see how Finland's "traditional innovation system" implemented and responded

Figure 7.3 Relationship between Politics, Policy, and Evaluation

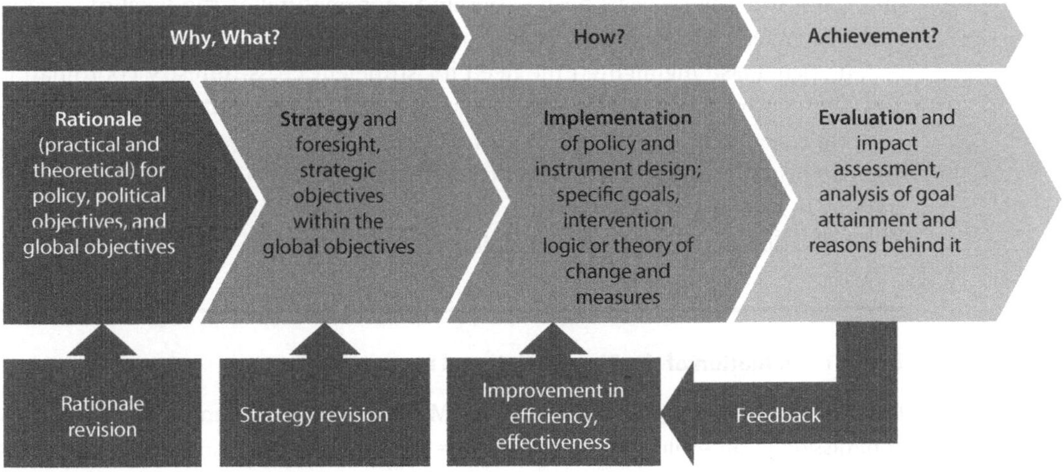

Why, What?
How?
Achievement?
Rationale (practical and theoretical) for policy, political objectives, and global objectives
Strategy and foresight, strategic objectives within the global objectives
Implementation of policy and instrument design; specific goals, intervention logic or theory of change and measures
Evaluation and impact assessment, analysis of goal attainment and reasons behind it
Rationale revision
Strategy revision
Improvement in efficiency, effectiveness
Feedback

Source: Loikkanen and Kutinlahti 2005.

to the new strategy. After all, the Finnish research and innovation system had remained largely unchanged since the establishment of Tekes (the Funding Agency for Technology and Innovation) in the beginning of 1980s. The system had been performing well for two decades, but in general discussions it was perceived that Finland had entered a new era of innovation and that policies, organizations, and instruments to support innovation should change accordingly.

Toward the end of the 2000s, the Finnish research and innovation system was highly ranked in several international comparisons, and its performance was considered high. Finland still ranks high on the EU Innovation Scoreboard, but, according to various science, research, and innovation indicators, its rating has begun to drop, raising concerns among policy makers. The situation called for a thorough and critical assessment of Finland's research and innovation system and its performance (for background on the national innovation strategy and evaluation of the innovation system, see Schienstock and Hämäläinen 2001; Georghiou *et al.* 2003.)

The evaluation found that the Finnish research and innovation system was in need of radical reform. The new strategy, the university reform, and several adjustments in the research and funding system were changing the direction of Finnish innovation and research policy.

Overall, the research and innovation system needed to be geared toward meeting future needs. This meant making it simpler and eliminating redundancy. According to the evaluators, Finnish organizations were anticipating reform, and thus the prospects for implementing change were good. At the same time, in order to ensure proper implementation of the reform, particular attention had to be paid to the cooperation and roles of the various ministries, especially the Ministry of Education, the Ministry of Employment and the Economy (MEE), and the Ministry of Finance. Cross-sectoral collaboration in the field of research and innovation had always been easier and more natural at the level of government agencies and research organizations than at the level of ministries.

The panel also highlighted the need for sufficient cross-ministry coordination and decision making. Problems were encountered, for example, in the reform of sectoral research (box 7.1). Reform of the government research institutions had been attempted several times, with little progress. (As of mid-2013, the discussion on how to restructure sectoral research is still ongoing.) To address such problems, the evaluation panel suggested changing the mandate of the RIC (see chapter 5).

Box 7.1 Evaluation of the Finnish National Innovation System

In 2008 the Ministry of Education and the Ministry of Employment and the Economy commissioned an evaluation comparing the Finnish national innovation system with systems in other countries.

The evaluation was undertaken within the context of a series of policy changes and structural reforms of the Finnish innovation system during the 2000s. These reforms included the development of higher education institutions, adoption of the national innovation strategy, creation of the SHOKs (see chapter 6), and reform of sectoral research.

The objectives of the evaluation were "to look into the current and future challenges and consider whether or not they are sufficiently acknowledged and addressed ... [and] to point out needs for institutional and policy adjustments and reforms, as well as to draw conclusions on policy governance and steering." The evaluation focused on the system as whole rather than on individual actors. Special attention was paid to whether public bodies and policies "assist both public and private individuals and organizations in generating and utilizing novel ideas" (Veugelers *et al.* 2009).

The evaluation was conducted by an independent panel with the support of Etlatieto Oy (a subsidiary of the Research Institute of the Finnish Economy (ETLA). The panel consisted of international and Finnish panelists from research institutions and universities. In collaboration with the two ministries, it settled on six main points, based on the basic choices identified in the national innovation strategy (see chapter 5). After that, the panel was organized into six subpanels according to the main points. Each subpanel was led by an international expert working with two Finnish experts (one academic scholar and one ETLA researcher). This was an important part of the evaluation structure as it provided an independent view, an element of international benchmarking, and national expertise. After the subpanels concluded their work, the larger panel drafted overall conclusions and recommendations.

The main evaluation was supported by dozens of separate studies. Primary methods were interviews of more than 100 key actors and experts and an electronic survey of individual actors. The work of the evaluating team was steered by a sounding board (consisting of nine representatives from five ministries), which also had a key role in defending the integrity of the panel. The work was supported by a research and support team of 18 members. The total budget for the evaluation was approximately €469,000, making it by far the biggest evaluation project in this field in Finland.

box continues next page

Box 7.1 Evaluation of the Finnish National Innovation System *(continued)*

The results of the evaluation were presented in a policy report and a full report, the former serving as a summary especially for policy makers. A similar arrangement with an international panel and a support team was adopted in the evaluation of SHOKs (for more information, see Lähteenmäki-Smith *et al.* 2013).

Observations from the case:

- The evaluation of the Finnish national innovation system was an extensive system-level evaluation, which also had significant implications for future (system-level) policy choices.
- The engagement of broad expertise and shareholders through the organization of the evaluation (panels, sounding board, support team) offers an example of good practice for similar types of evaluations.

Institution- and Program-Level Evaluations

At the operational level, Tekes, the largest implementer of policy by volume of funding and number of programs, provides a good example of evaluation practice. Tekes's foresight activities are discussed in chapter 5; here we focus on using evaluations to learn from the past. Programs are generally evaluated at three points: at a mid-term review, at the end of the program, and in some cases a few years afterward (Tekes 2011). Tekes's interim evaluations are either commissioned from contractors or (historically) conducted as self-evaluations by program management. The audience for evaluations consists of participating projects, program management, and the board. Interim evaluations are intended to support management and to redirect actions and suggest other adaptive measures, as needed.

Tekes offers a toolkit of evaluation instruments, including a survey platform, and these can be complemented with outside evaluations and case studies. The interim evaluation of the Tuli Program (Kuusisto *et al.* 2004), for example, used a questionnaire and case studies to measure perceived success and suitability of the program and to study how well the program management worked. In the interim evaluation of the Center of Expertise Program implemented by the Ministry of Education and the Economy (Pelkonen *et al.* 2010), the key areas of evaluation were the program's fit with national innovation strategy, the operations and productivity of competence clusters, and the operations and productivity of regional centers of expertise.

The final evaluations of Tekes programs are usually commissioned by the Tekes Strategic Intelligence Evaluation Unit to (independent) contractors, who design the study in collaboration with program management. The procedure is competitive, and the bidders can choose their own methods for answering the evaluation questions. The aims of the evaluations are to gain insight into the relevance of program activities and projects, effectiveness, participant satisfaction, and outputs—that is, the evaluations are technically summative. The mode of evaluation is often participant oriented, and the process is seen as developmental, not descriptive or judgmental. Thus the methods are often qualitative in nature, including document analysis, interviews, expert evaluations, and perception surveys, complemented by program monitoring statistics.

However, evaluation reports do not, as a rule, evaluate the impact of the program in quantitative terms, for example, using financial statistics or numbers and impacts of publications. One reason for this is conceivably the time span that it takes for a program to have a tangible impact and the difficulty in separating the effect of an individual program from the mix of constantly evolving programs, actions, policies, and other trends. However, the OSKE evaluation, for example, proposed a framework for evaluation based on a theory of change describing how the program is supposed to affect the national innovation system. The evaluation used data from policy documents, previous evaluations, and program documents and collected accounting data and statistics about the project as well as field data, such as interviews, workshops, and satisfaction surveys.

In addition to the evaluation of individual Tekes instruments, Tekes periodically commissions overall impact assessments. These assessments examine the economic impacts of Tekes activities over a longer period. Box 7.2 describes the design of the latest Tekes impact assessment, which was commissioned by Tekes Strategic Intelligence. A steering group was established to guide the evaluation and establish a dialogue between the evaluation team, Tekes management, and

Box 7.2 Tekes Impact Assessment

The Ministry of Employment and the Economy and Tekes agreed to monitor the impact and achievement of Tekes and its objectives primarily through impact analyses and studies of individual target areas: (1) productivity and renewal of industries, (2) capabilities, and (3) welfare. The purpose of the study was to analyze whether and how Tekes had reached its objectives. The main research question for the assessment was, *how have Tekes activities succeeded in improving the productivity and renewal of industries in Finland?*

The detailed model of impact and main objectives formed the basis of the conceptual framework of the analysis. The study had four tasks: (1) a literature review to elaborate and operationalize the impact model and to analyze the impact of public research, development, and innovation (RDI) subsidies in different contexts; (2) an econometric analysis of the impact of subsidies on productivity employing total factor productivity modeling and a conditional difference-in-differences estimation; (3) analysis of Tekes's impact on specific target groups, with additional qualitative case studies on how the subsidies affect firm development; and (4) analysis of the results vis-à-vis Tekes strategy. For additional information, see Viljamaa *et al.* (2013).

Observation from the case:

- Rigorous and systematic monitoring and assessment of the effectiveness RDI funding are essential for improving the effectiveness of the investments as well as promoting the legitimacy and transparency of the system.

key stakeholders. The steering group comprised the Tekes director general, the director of strategy, the head of the Innovation Unit at MEE, a senior adviser responsible for Tekes, and a leading researcher in the field of economics and innovation policy. The impact assessment was linked directly to planning Tekes activities, reporting Tekes's performance, and negotiating budgets and targets with the ministry through the steering group.

Learning from Others and Transferring Good Practices

Policy learning envelops terms such as "policy transfer," "lesson drawing," and "evaluations." Policy transfer is defined as copying and implementing policies, including institutional structures, legislation, and policy heuristics or interventions, from other contexts, often from other countries, or other sectors (Dolowitz and Marsh 2000). Policy transfer can be coercive (forced) or voluntary. Another distinction can be drawn between the "soft" transfer of broad policy ideas and bottom-up approaches or the "hard" transfer of practices, heuristics, and instruments, typically through top-down activity (Stone 1999). Lesson drawing means seeking benchmarking information and evidence as well as best practices from different contexts.

In the Finnish context, the dominant mode of policy learning is soft transfer, in the form of lesson drawing or benchmarking, which is commonly executed in planning and implementing new policy interventions. The usual benchmarks are other small, open, and knowledge- and services-intensive economies, such as Denmark, the Netherlands, and Sweden.

The design of the SHOKs (see chapter 6) is another example of lesson drawing, following the traditional Finnish model. A working group or committee was appointed to prepare a proposal for organizing the SHOKs. It conducted a study based on site visits and literature analyzing the objectives for the SHOKs and benchmarking several models for organizing strategic RDI initiatives and clusters (Karlqvist, Mähönen, and Sarkio 2006).

Another example of benchmarking on a national level is the Regenerative Innovation Policy Study, commissioned by MEE and Sitra, which was related to the larger process of formulating an action plan for RDI policy. The study analyzed instruments from different European countries with the aim of regenerating or renewing industry. The goal was to find policy patterns and ideas for new instruments. The study fed into the process of formulating the RDI policy action plan in the MEE and the Ministry of Education and Culture, which formulated a proposal for the RIC that was presented to the government (for more on the RIC, see box 5.4 in chapter 5).

One of the most formal learning channels found in the area of innovation policy is Vision ERA Net (a European Research Area Network, 2005–2009), a European collaborative network of innovation policy agencies funded by the EU Sixth Framework Programme for Research and Technological Development. An example with similar characteristics is the GLOVAL project (2009–12), which was funded by the EU Seventh Framework Programme for Research and

Innovation and sought to identify and share good practices and seek solutions to common problems across European countries. The project contributed to a better understanding of the implications of global value chains for national RDI policy. It conducted a survey of different policies and how they addressed global value chains, contributing to best practices for addressing value chains in policy design.

Important basic information for benchmarking comes from international reviews from the OECD, such as its Program for International Student Assessment (PISA) and Country Reviews, and the EU Community Innovation Survey/Innovation Union Scoreboard. During recent years, the balance has shifted somewhat from the OECD to the EU. This is due to the fact that ministries participate in the EU policy-making process and act as venues for the exchange of ideas and discussion. It is also fairly common for officials who participate in policy making and programming to seek benchmarks and lessons from other knowledge economies. It is relatively common for an adviser working in a ministry, particularly in the MEE or the Ministry of Education and Culture, to take leave and visit the OECD, the European Commission, or the World Bank Group and then return to the ministry. These "exchanges" are an informal way of drawing lessons through learning by doing.

However useful, policy learning also has documented pitfalls. In the case of direct policy transfer, it can lead to implementation failure if it is uninformed, incomplete, or inappropriate (Dolowitz and Marsh 2000; James and Lodge 2003). Copying a foreign instrument from one cultural and economic context and implementing it in another without understanding why it works in the native context can be misguided if the recipient innovation system works differently than the host system. Thus if lessons are not drawn from elaborations of intervention logic, impact analysis, and recognized environmental or contextual mediators—that is, from an understanding of the mechanism embedded in implementation of the instrument—the transfer may produce quite different results than expected. This challenge is especially relevant when transferring policies between countries with very different cultures, policy mixes, and stages of economic development.

Institutional Devices for Learning

Feedback and flexibility are important for policy learning and reactivity, as conditions change and more information is gathered. One way to improve reactivity is to *install feedback and learning loops to institutional and program structures*. In the Finnish context, the main institutional learning processes are associated with budget negotiations and the strategy processes of agencies, as is the case with Tekes. Budget negotiations provide the financial framework and political guidance for agencies, while strategy processes shape the vision and long-term goals and forge the strategy to attain them within the boundary conditions. At their best, strategy processes take stock of past performance and lessons, while looking toward future goals with an open mind.

Other structural elements that can facilitate learning are policy-making processes and the fundamentals of the implementation structure. Traditionally, policy making follows the basic cycle from identifying issues to be addressed by a policy intervention, studying the evidence and consulting with stakeholders, identifying possible interventions, and analyzing their implementation (for example, figure 7.1). The STPC (2007b) recommends using both evaluations of previous policies and foresight when identifying issues and designing interventions. In short, *policy making should encompass learning from the past as well as from the future* (for foresight activities, see figure 7.4; also see chapter 5).

A third lesson recognized at the level of both policy making and program implementation is the need for clear responsibilities, a chain of command, and a monitoring system (STPC 2007b; Lähteenmäki-Smith *et al.* 2013). In fact, experience has shown that successful learning from the past is built into policy making and the design of instruments and programming. Developing a joint understanding of the goals, approach, and intervention logic provides solid ground for implementation. Policies should have an "owner," separate from the implementer, who has a direct interest in following their progress. The owner should be empowered to monitor the progress of the intervention and take corrective action, including allocating resources within the agreed budget.

Figure 7.4 Evaluation and Foresight in Policy Making

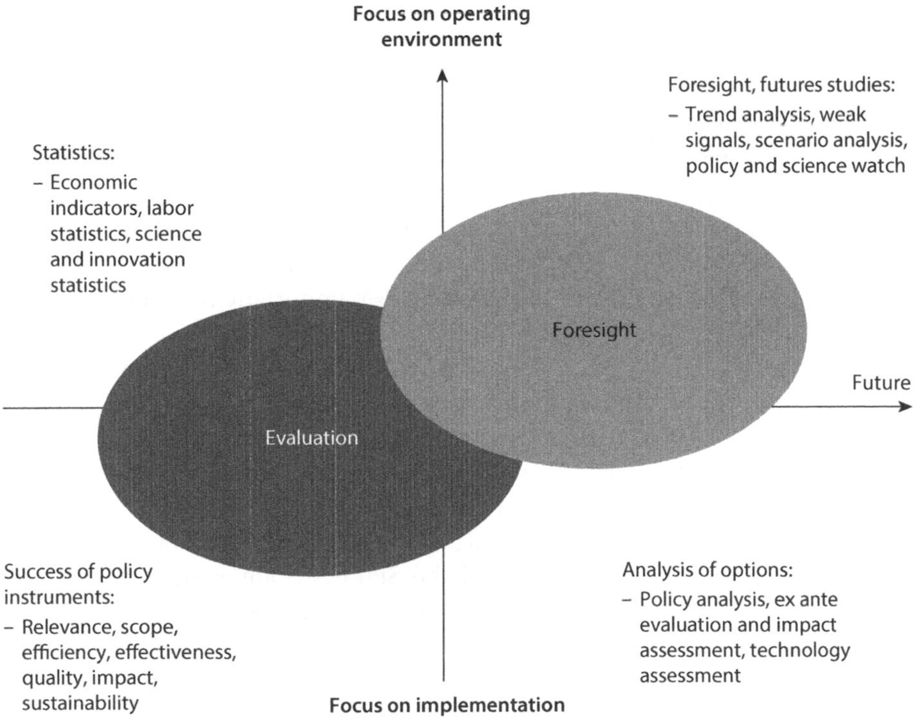

Source: STPC 2007b.

Ownership should be backed by mutually defined and accepted realistic goals, well-defined measures and indicators, and target levels. Implementation should follow a clearly defined intervention logic or theory of change, and the relevant indicators should be monitored and recorded from before to after implementation to enable longitudinal impact assessment. However, this does not mean that instruments or programs should be completely rigid in the face of a change in conditions or information. Adjustments can be made, but they should be purposeful and documented in the intervention logic.

Summary and Key Messages

Policy evaluation and learning are well instituted in the Finnish innovation system. Evaluations are frequent and relatively systematic, and all levels of the system are evaluated periodically. Nevertheless, there is ongoing discussion about the culture and practices of evaluation and how government spending should be monitored and evaluated, as exhibited by the STPC (2007b) and, more recently, by the Prime Minister's Office (2011). The working group concluded that challenges affecting the use of evaluations are fragmented knowledge, unsystematic practices, unusable information, as well as selective interpretation of the evidence (Lehtola 2011). Another is public and political discussion. Compared to health care and welfare policies, innovation and knowledge economy policies attract less public and political debate, and relatively large issues may be ignored.

Another, more insidious, pitfall concerns other modes of policy learning besides direct transfer. There are documented instances where "policy informs evidence" and not the other way around (Smith, Ebrahim, and Frankel 2001; Marston and Watts 2003). In this case, preconceived notions of the root causes of the problem to be addressed and what action should be taken as well as the escalation of commitment to a "favorite" course of action may lead to cherry picking evidence or interpreting data in favor of the preconceived idea (for example, Lehtola 2011). Failing to take all of the evidence into account may produce a suboptimal, inefficient solution or create negative externalities. Thus when drawing lessons, it is important to isolate evidence from political or other agendas.

At the more practical level, the main technical challenges in Finnish evaluation practice are that public entities often commission evaluations of themselves or their own programs, and that evaluation is commonly based on perceptional data. The relative methodological weakness can be also attributed to the programming phase, as many instruments or interventions do not have clear intervention logic from the start or well-defined measurable indicators. For example, the recent evaluation of the SHOKs (Lähteenmäki-Smith *et al.* 2013) and the impact assessment of Tekes (Viljamaa *et al.* 2013) found that evaluation was hampered by lack of clear intervention logic, well-defined performance indicators, clear thresholds or targets for performance, and systematic collection of performance data. Lack of predefined indicators attached to the underlying logic of the intervention and systematic collection of monitoring data make it difficult to collect data for evaluation. Consequently, rigorous impact assessment becomes more costly and time-consuming than is acceptable for most purposes and occasions. Although the applicability of this standard view of the literature on results-based management has been questioned in areas where "innovation"—resulting in unexpected outcomes—is important, these outcomes, technically called externalities, can also be included in evaluation. Further, assumed positive externalities should not be used to defend vague objectives, slovenly programming, or dilapidated implementation.

Often ignored in methodological discussions is that only evaluations that are genuinely insightful and critical can contribute to learning from experience. Critical evaluations thrive in an open and constructive culture, where people can give and receive constructive criticism trusting that it will not be taken as a personal offense and where risk taking and occasional failures are "allowed." If the environment is hostile, evaluations tend to take the form of vapid description of the object of evaluation and gleeful recounts of the successful aspects of the activities.

To summarize, this chapter has described policy learning and evaluation practices in the Finnish innovation system. Policy learning is part of Finnish policy making at different levels, from the institutional to the individual. Perhaps the most important way of learning is to conduct periodic evaluations of different institutions and programs.

While Finnish policy-learning practice may not be theoretically or technically perfect, the system and practices have developed over time. By taking a big-picture perspective and developing national statistics, assessment of the innovation system lays important groundwork for developing more intricate monitoring and evaluation systems. Moreover, developing an open evaluation culture takes time. In the Finnish case, evaluations started slowly in the 1970s, became common practice in the 1980s and 1990s and were institutionalized beginning in 2010. Involving the key stakeholders in evaluations through, for example, a steering group or a participative evaluation strategy may constitute a good start.

Finnish policy making learns largely by drawing lessons from experience. As discussed, lesson drawing in Finland happens both at the institutional level and through direct benchmarking. Benchmarking forms part of the design of many interventions; for example, preparation of the SHOKs program included a rather comprehensive benchmarking of similar centers of excellence around the world, to find best practices for implementation. Benchmarking, or lesson drawing, during the design of policy interventions has also become important. The significance of interacting with international organizations at the ministerial and individual levels is harder to assess, but Finland is active in EU policy preparation, in the OECD, as well as at the United Nations, and various officials commonly visit one of these organizations during their career.

There are two final, overarching lessons (see box 7.3 for key messages). First, impartial evaluations of institutions, policies, instruments, and programs are potentially valuable, as they offer feedback on actions. Further, evaluations potentially improve the transparency of government, if they are impartial,

Box 7.3 Key Messages

- Monitoring and evaluation of progress toward a knowledge economy and investments are important for policy learning. They enhance transparency, effectiveness of public investments, and good governance.
- In Finland, all areas of public expenditure are the subject of systematic monitoring and evaluation.
- Investing in building an open evaluation culture pays in the long run: evaluations make little contribution to learning from experience if they are not genuinely insightful and openly critical.
- Systematic data collection and monitoring are instrumental. Comprehensive and reliable basic data are the foundation of all evaluations.
- Building policy learning into structures is essential (for example, steering documents, key performance indicators, international benchmarking visits).
- When drawing lessons, the evidence and political agendas should be separated: policy learning, lesson drawing, and evaluation aim to gather evidence about how best to achieve the political objectives and implement the political agenda.
- Evaluation and monitoring should be planned carefully in *advance,* before the start of programs or other initiatives. Lack of clear goals and indicators attached to the underlying logic of the intervention, backed by systematic collection of monitoring data, makes evaluation and impact assessment costly and inefficient and does not support program implementation or corrective actions.

candid, and published afterward. Second, building the opportunities for evaluation into structures can support policy learning. For example, evaluation can be built into the governance of institutions and agencies, visits to international organizations can be planned into officials' career paths, and joining international organizations and committees can open up paths for inserting new ideas and feedback into policy making.

References

Aho, E., A. Brunila, J.-T. Erikson, P. Harjunen, R. Heikinheimo, S. Karjalainen, T. Kekkonen, P. Neittaanmäki, E. Ormala, P. Peltonen, K. Pöysti, M. Strengell, A. Stenros, J. Teperi, and H. Toivanen. 2008. "Kansallinen innovaatiostrategia [National Innovation Strategy]." Helsinki. http://www.tem.fi/files/19704/Kansallinen_innovaatiostrategia_12062008.pdf.

Berg, A. 2013. "Kokeilun Paikka! Suomi matkalla kohti kokeiluyhteiskuntaa [Time to Experiment! Finland on the Journey towards an Experimentation Society]." Parliament's Committee for the Future, Helsinki.

Dolowitz, D. P., and D. Marsh. 2000. "Learning from Abroad: The Role of Policy Transfer in Contemporary Policy Making." *Governance: An International Journal of Policy and Administration* 13 (1): 5–24.

Georghiou, L., K. Smith, O. Toivanen, and P. Ylä-Anttila. 2003. *Evaluation of the Finnish Innovation Support System*. Publication 5/2003. Helsinki: Ministry of Trade and Industry. http://julkaisurekisteri.ktm.fi/ktm_jur/ktmjur.nsf/all/172616819C0174EC C2256D2B003CA685/$file/ju5teoeng.pdf.

James, O., and M. Lodge. 2003. "The Limitations of 'Policy Transfer' and 'Lesson Drawing' for Public Policy Research." *Political Studies Review* 1 (2): 179–93.

Karlqvist, H., J. Mähönen, and J. Sarkio. 2006. *Osaamiskeskittymien hallintomallit [Governance Models for Centers of Expertise]*. Report to the steering group for centers of science, technology, and innovation, 2.3.2006.

Kuusisto, J., S. Kotala, R. Kulmala, A. Viljamaa, and S. Vinni. 2004. *TULI-ohjelman väliarviointi*. Teknologiaohjelman raportti 8/2004. Helsinki: Tekes.

Lähteenmäki-Smith, K., K. Halme, T. Lemola, K. Piirainen, K. Viljamaa, K. Haila, A. Kotiranta, M. Hjelt, T. Raivio, W. Polt, M. Dinges, M. Ploder, S. Meyer, T. Luukkonen, and L. Georghiou. 2013. *Licence to SHOK? External Evaluation of the Strategic Centers for Science, Technology, and Innovation*. MEE Publication 1/2013. Helsinki: Ministry of Employment and the Economy.

Lehtola, J. 2011. *Politiikkatoimien vaikuttavuusarvioinnin kehittäminen: Huomioita pilottihankkeista [Developing Evaluation and Impact Assessment: Observations from Pilot Projects]*. Publication 2/2011. Helsinki: Prime Minister's Office.

Loikkanen, T., and P. Kutinlahti. 2005. "Towards Systemic Future-Oriented Innovation Policy Studies: Perspectives of Finnish Knowledge-Based Economy." Paper presented at the conference "Innovation Systems in the Knowledge-Based Society," LABEIN Tecnalia, Bilbao, September 22–23.

Marston, G., and R. Watts. 2003. "Tampering with the Evidence: A Critical Appraisal of Evidence-Based Policy Making." *Drawing Board: An Australian Review of Public Affairs* 3 (3): 143–63.

Mason, P., and M. Barnes. 2007. "Constructing Theories of Change: Methods and Sources." *Evaluation* 13 (2): 151–70.

Muir Gray, J. A. 2004. "Evidence-Based Policy Making Is about Taking Decisions Based on Evidence and the Needs and Values of the Population." *British Medical Journal* 329 (7473): 988–89.

Parsons, W. 2003. "From Muddling Through to Muddling Up: Evidence-Based Policy Making and the Modernisation of British Government." *Public Policy and Administration* 17 (3): 43–60.

Pelkonen, A., J. Konttinen, J. Oksanen, V. Valovirta, J. Leväsluoto, and P. Boekholt. 2010. *Osaamisklusterit alueiden voimien yhdistäjänä: Osaamiskeskusohjelman (2007–2013) väliarviointi [Competence Clusters as Channels to the Regions' Strengths: Interim Evaluation of the Center of Expertise Program (2007–2013)]*. Publication 44/2010. Helsinki: Ministry of Employment and the Economy. http://www.tem.fi/files/27402 /TEM_44_2010_netti.pdf.

Piirainen, K. A., and K. Halme. 2013. *Tulevaisuusselonteon ennakointihankkeen arviointi: Loppuraportti [Evaluation of Government Foresight Project: Final Report]*. Helsinki: Valtioneuvoston kanslia, Sitra, Suomen Akatemia, and Tekes. http://vnk.fi/hankkeet /tulevaisuusselonteko/pdf/TUSE_arviointiraportti.pdf.

Prime Minister's Office. 2011. *Poliittisen päätöksenteon tietopohjan parantaminen: tavoitteet todeksi; Politiikkatoimien vaikuttavuusarvioinnin kehittämistyöryhmän raportti [Improving the Evidence Base for Political Decision Making: Goals to Reality; Report of the*

Working Group on Developing Evaluation and Impact Assessment]. Publication 8/2011. Helsinki: Prime Minister's Office.

Raivio, T., J. Lunabba, E. Ryynänen, J. Timonen, M. Antikainen, and S. Lanér. 2012. *Software, Mobile Solutions, and Games Industry: Evaluation of Tekes-Related Programs*. Program Report 2/2012. Helsinki: Tekes. http://www.tekes.fi/u/Software_mobile_solutions.pdf.

Schienstock, G., and T. Hämäläinen. 2001. *Transformation of the Finnish Innovation System: A Network Approach*. Sitra Report Series 7. Helsinki: Hakapaino Oy. http://www.sitra.fi/julkaisut/raportti7.pdf.

Smith, G. D., S. Ebrahim, and S. Frankel. 2001. "How Policy Informs the Evidence." *British Medical Journal* 322 (7280): 184–85.

Stone, D. 1999. "Learning Lessons and Transferring Policy across Time, Space, and Disciplines." *Politics* 19 (1): 51–59.

STPC (Science and Technology Policy Council). 2007a. "Tiede- ja teknologianeuvoston kannanotto vaikuttavuuden arvioinnin ja ennakoinnin kehittämisestä" [Council Statement on Development of Evaluation, Impact Assessment, and Foresight]. Background memorandum for the Council Statement on Development of Evaluation and Foresight, August 24.

———. 2007b. "Vaikuttavuuden arviointi ja ennakointi [Evaluation, Impact Assessment, and Foresight]." Background memorandum for the Council Statement on Development of Evaluation and Foresight, August 17.

Tekes (Funding Agency for Technology and Innovation). 2011. "Tekes: Programs; How Programs Are Evaluated? [in Finnish]." Tekes, Helsinki. http://www.tekes.fi/fi/community/Miten_arvioidaan/519/Miten_arvioidaan/1392.

Treudhardt, L., and L. Nuutinen, eds. 2012. *The State of Scientific Research in Finland, 2012*. Publication 7/12. Helsinki: Academy of Finland.

Van der Veen, G., E. Arnold, P. Boekholt, J. Deutuen, A. Horveth, P. Stern, and J. Stroyan. 2012. *Evaluation of Tekes: Final Report*. Publication 22/2012. Helsinki: Ministry of Employment and the Economy. http://www.tem.fi/files/33176/TEMjul_22_2012_web.pdf.

Veugelers, R., K. Aizinger, D. Breznitz, C. Edquist, G. Murray, G. Ottaviano, A. Hyytinen, A. Kangasharju, M. Ketokivi, T. Luukkonen, M. Maliranta, M. Maula, P. Okko, P. Rouvinen, M. Sotarauta, T. Tanayama, O. Toivanen, P. Ylä-Anttila. 2009. *Evaluation of the Finnish National Innovation System: Full Report*. Helsinki: Taloustieto, Helsinki University. http://www.tem.fi/files/24929/InnoEvalFi_FULL_Report_28_Oct_2009.pdf.

Viljamaa, K., K. Piirainen, A. Kotiranta, H. Karhunen, and J. Huovari. 2013. "Impact of Tekes Activities on Productivity and Renewal." Tekes, Helsinki. http://www.tekes.fi/Global/Nyt/Uutiset/Productivity%20and%20renewal%202013.pdf.

Vogel, I. 2012. "ESPA Guide to Working with Theory of Change for Research Projects." LTS International and ITAD, Edinburgh.

CHAPTER 8

Knowledge Economy and Globalization

Hannes Toivanen

Over the last decade, business, technology, and innovation have become globalized, leading to development of a global knowledge economy. This development is changing the roles traditionally played by advanced economies as well as by the emerging and developing economies. However, not all innovation comes from the advanced economies, nor are emerging and developing economies merely a source of resources. They are a true partner for collaboration and knowledge sharing.

This chapter discusses the new globalization and explores how it has been addressed by the Finnish innovation system. It highlights the need for new forms of collaboration both nationally and internationally.

Reasoning Behind: The New Globalization of Innovation

The early 2000s brought about sweeping changes in the global economic system, encapsulated in the concentration of high economic growth in developing countries and in plateaus and grinding financial problems in developed countries; inevitably, relationships between the two groups of countries began to change. Deep transformations in the nature, focus, dynamics, and geography of innovation processes, networks, and systems constitute key elements in this ongoing global transition, prompting incumbent innovation leaders, such as Finland, to reconsider their strategies and approaches to developing countries.

Two phenomena are motivating both developing countries and innovation leaders to forge new types of innovation cooperation. First is the recognition that *innovation plays an important role in development* and that a framework is emerging to guide how innovation systems can support broad-based development in the least-developed countries. While innovation has always been important for development, the adoption of a systemic approach to innovation is new (Lundvall *et al.* 2009). Second, *the emergence of a completely new type of pro-poor business model has recast the approach to low-income countries and people, who are now seen to have increasingly important global market potential.* Here, too, a pro-poor framework has been established to understand how innovation and business models can and should address the needs of the poor (Prahalad 2010). Combined, these represent a departure from national internationalization strategies focused on off-shoring manufacturing or forging high-tech innovation networks. As such, they entail political, organizational, strategic, and practical challenges, particularly for traditional innovation leaders.

The term "new globalization" as used here recognizes the increasing importance of emerging and developing countries in international affairs, economy, culture, and innovation. It stands in contrast to the globalization that followed the end of the cold war and was characterized, among other things, by off-shoring of manufacturing from developed countries to the developing world and by financial deregulation and integration. That globalization was often perceived as a projection of developed countries' global dominance.

Although it is difficult to pinpoint a single cause, the new globalization is essentially about the developing world being transformed from an object of globalization to a main actor. This proactive and increasingly important role of the developing countries and emerging economies themselves is transforming the processes of globalization and prompting many developed countries to revisit their globalization strategies and approaches.

The rise of the BRICS (Brazil, the Russian Federation, India, China, and South Africa), as well as other developing countries, is accompanied by a range of phenomena that have broad impact on both developing and developed countries as well as on their interactions. Of these, the relocation of global economic growth poles, the emergence of low-income market (or base-of-the-pyramid, BOP) business models, and innovation, as well as a deeper appreciation of the role of innovation in development, are critical in reframing the relationships between developing- and developed-country innovation systems.

Shift in the Sources of Global Economic Growth

There is little doubt that the global economic system is moving toward multipolar organization, as developing countries and emerging economies become the central sources of economic growth, and many of the rich countries are embroiled in a mix of economic stagnation and financial deficits. Demonstrating this transition, the World Bank (2011) argued, "By 2025, six major emerging economies—Brazil, China, India, Indonesia, the Republic of Korea, and Russia—will collectively account for more than half of all global growth." Similarly, in its recent analysis of the medium- and long-range outlook for global economic growth, the Organisation for Economic Co-operation and Development (OECD 2012) concluded, "Growth of the present non-OECD economies will continue to outpace that of the present OECD countries, driven primarily by catch-up in multi-factor productivity, but the difference will likely narrow substantially over coming decades."

At the heart of this transformation is the improved performance across the developing world, not only in the BRICS. Indeed, the United Nations' *Human Development Report 2013: The Rise of the South* concluded that between 1990 and 2012, all but two of the 132 countries tracked "improved their human development status" and that "progress was particularly rapid in more than 40 countries of the South, whose increases in Human Development Index (HDI) value were significantly larger than predicted for countries that were at a similar level of HDI value in 1990" (United Nations 2013, 12).

Although this unfolding transition is reconfiguring much of the global system, of particular interest here is the future of developing countries. Creation of a multipolar economic world system will give rise to two specific trends. On the one hand, it could fuel knowledge spillovers between emerging economies and developing countries that could benefit agriculture and manufacturing in the latter. On the other hand, it implies tighter global integration, increasing the risks and challenges for developing countries that face difficulties in fostering workable global networks (World Bank 2011, 9–10). Yet integration into global systems has benefited developing countries. Analyzing why the global South has performed better in reducing poverty than ever before, the *Human Development Report 2013* concluded, "Almost all countries with substantial improvement in HDI value over the past two decades have also become more integrated with the world economy" (United Nations 2013, 74).

In this context, developing countries need to forge smart globalization strategies—that is, tighter integration into global networks that selectively support competitive advantages inherent in them. In this regard, developing countries have acquired another competitive advantage over the last decade: fast-growing, low-income markets for products and services.

With the poor less poor and some achieving modest middle-class status for the first time, developing-country populations constitute one of the fastest-growing markets in the world. However, they have such special needs and structural circumstances that a whole new category of business and innovation has emerged in response. Thus when it comes to innovation, the co-creation processes between innovation actors from developing and developed countries provide some of the greatest potential opportunities for global networks, disregarding traditional one-way traffic of North-South cooperation.

Policies for Internationalization

Although the public and private sectors that participate in the innovation system are closely interlinked, they extend internationally according to very different logic and principles. Since the early 2000s, Finish policy makers have sought to devise policies and instruments to address these differences. Since 2000 the Science and Technology Policy Council (STPC), renamed the Research and Innovation Council (RIC) in 2009, has addressed internationalization as one of the key themes in its regular reviews and outlooks for Finnish innovation policy. In its 2003 review, the council identified the challenge of internationalization as twofold: "On the one hand, the Finnish system must be *able to compete*, … and, on the other hand, Finnish players must be *able to enter and make* use of the opening markets [italics in original]" (STPC 2003, 15). Furthermore, the council argued that the innovation system is at the core of the overall internationalization of Finland, calling for public policies to accelerate Finland's globalization and for incentives to encourage the international activities of the private sector.

While Finnish internationalization efforts in the 1990s and early 2000s sought to integrate with Europe's emerging research system and to strengthen links with U.S. innovation hubs, the focus shifted in the early 2000s, when the notions of "globalization" and "emerging economies" gained currency in public policy. An important impetus for the shift was a series of studies on globalization and its implications for Finland's competitiveness by the Prime Minister's Office (2004).

These studies documented how globalization was fundamentally altering the foundation of the Finnish economy. This included how the rise of emerging economies was changing global markets and demand as well as how globalization was altering the business and earnings logic of traditional Finnish export industries. The studies concluded that innovation and innovation policy should be placed at the center of Finnish globalization efforts, particularly in relation to the emerging economies. The efforts of Finnish information and communication technology (ICT) and machinery and equipment companies to enter the Asian, in particular Chinese, markets and to create an active research and development (R&D) base there intensified these conclusions (Ali-Yrkkö and Palmberg 2006).

The STPC reiterated the theme in subsequent policy reviews and recommendations. Its review in 2006 called for an enhanced presence in the emerging markets, particularly in China, Russia, India, and the new European Union (EU) member states, and pointed out that several activities along these lines had already been launched, such as the Finnish Innovation Center in China and the Asia Action Plan of the Ministry of Education (STPC 2006, 31). In subsequent years, the STPC continued to expand and intensify its international strategy and has placed more focus on the emerging economies.

The RIC's guidance for research and innovation policies in 2011–15 called for a national strategy in internationalization and identified the key change driving globalization as the rise of Brazil, China, India, as well as other African, Asian, and South American economies. The council called for reinforcing efforts to network and connect with innovation centers in the emerging economies (RIC 2010, 15). Indeed, whereas developing countries and emerging economies have traditionally played a relatively marginal role in the international dimension of the Finnish innovation system, recent years have seen a definitive shift in interest and possible activities. Several ministries, agencies, universities, as well as companies have actively explored the significance of these regions for Finland.

For practical implementation of Finland's internationalization strategy, which involves geographic orientation, choice of instruments, and cross-ministry coordination, these high-level policy reviews and guidance have played a critical role. The Prime Minister's Office, as well as the RIC, chaired by the prime minister, has worked to consolidate policy views into a broader framework of action for Finnish globalization efforts. At the heart of this framework has been the distinction between public and private sector globalization, and policies have explicitly sought to activate and enable the internationalization of companies. This division of labor, or objectives, has also been evident in the work of ministries and agencies, as they have devised practical instruments and programs in support of Finnish internationalization.

New Globalization, New Forms of Collaboration

The new globalization has entered the sphere of development policies, which has affected its underlying objectives and operational models. This section looks at the opportunities and challenges of globalization for Finnish innovation and development policies and describes the recent activities that have been undertaken.

"Discovering" the Emerging Economies and Developing Countries

The rise of developing countries and emerging economies in the globalization strategy of the Finnish innovation system has sparked several organizational and strategic changes that are still unfolding. This reflects in part the recognized role of developing countries and emerging economies as the key sources of global economic growth in the postcrisis world, but also the maturation of R&D-related relations between them and Finland. The 2009 evaluation of the Finnish innovation system argued that the "rapidly changing geography towards developing countries" should motivate Finland to move beyond its historical internationalization strategy and reach emerging economies and developing countries more effectively (Aiginger, Okko, and Ylä-Anttila 2009, 131).

However, given that the Finnish internationalization strategy and organizations for its implementation were built for very different purposes, there are also challenges. While large Finnish companies have actively forged global innovation networks, particularly in China and the rest of Asia, Finland is a latecomer. Indeed, compared with the international research collaboration networks of Africa or Brazil, Finland's interactions are still weak, despite recent efforts (Toivanen and Ponomariov 2011). From the perspective of innovation policy and system development, Finland is only now beginning to forge substantial relations with the developing countries and emerging economies.

The international dimension of Finland's innovation system has always reflected its internal phase of development as well as the broader international context. For this reason, it has passed through successive, overlapping phases. Access to the major European R&D programs and organizations since the mid-1980s marked the beginning of Finland's internationalization and continues today. Access in 1985 to Eureka, the European Economic Community's industrial R&D cooperation program, followed soon by the European framework agreement on research cooperation as well as membership in the European Laboratory for Particle Physics, marked a definite orientation toward the innovation system emerging in Europe, a development strongly reinforced by Finland's 1992 entry into the EU.

Whereas these developments integrated Finland into the European research and innovation system and laid the foundations for the national system, subsequent choices and strategies have approached the internationalization of science, technology, and innovation (STI) in a more instrumental and utilitarian way. With the big questions solved, policy makers and industry leaders have evaluated international activities with the objective of improving the national innovation system, the country's economic competitiveness, and the ambition to forge a stronger role in the global innovation landscape, including improved relations with the developing countries and emerging economies.

New Forms of Collaboration within the Finnish Innovation System

Since about 2010, Finland has sought to reposition its innovation system better in regard the global growth markets in emerging economies and developing countries. Although an umbrella framework for internationalization exists, various Finnish actors and organizations of the public innovation system forge their strategies and activities independently. Many of the sectoral ministries set up specialized internationalization agencies, units, or task forces a relatively long time ago, creating some legacy issues as the nature of Finnish internationalization has changed. Thus a wide variety of activities reflect the interests and capabilities of different organizations. Consequently, there is a relatively high degree of specialization, and some organizations have placed much more emphasis on emerging economies and developing countries than others.

Naturally, the Ministry for Foreign Affairs, the Ministry of Education and Culture, as well as the Ministry of Employment and the Economy (MEE) share responsibility for internationalizing the Finnish innovation system. Key government agencies that fund and create the enabling infrastructure for internationalization include Tekes (the Funding Agency for Technology and Innovation), the Academy of Finland, Finpro (the national trade, internationalization, and investment development organization), the Technical Research Centre (VTT), and the National Fund for Research and Development (Sitra). In addition, other public actors are involved: universities, polytechnics, regional development associations, and the strategic centers for excellence in STI (SHOKs).

Recently, these ministries and agencies have recognized the need to facilitate the internationalization of small and medium companies, as well as the converging interests in higher education, research, innovation, and trade. Indeed, so many organizations are implementing international activities in emerging economies and developing countries that several government task forces and initiatives have been established to improve coordination and cooperation over the last couple of years. Of these initiatives, perhaps the most significant is Team Finland, a network established jointly by the MEE, the Ministry for Foreign Affairs, and the Ministry of Education and Culture to promote external economic relations, internationalization of companies, and so forth (described in box 8.1). While still to be formed, it will function as a broad umbrella to coordinate different types of activities, including the globalization of innovation in developing countries.

Bottom-of-the-Pyramid Markets

The concept of "bottom of the pyramid," coined by C. K. Prahalad in his seminal book, *The Bottom of the Pyramid,* is premised on the observation that some

Box 8.1 Team Finland and FinNode

Team Finland brings together publicly funded activities. It has four main objectives: to support internationalization of businesses, to influence the external environment, to promote foreign direct investment in Finland, and to promote Finland's country brand.

Projects are carried out in cooperation between state and private actors. State actors consist of three ministries—the Ministry of Employment and the Economy, the Ministry for Foreign Affairs, and the Ministry of Education and Culture—and their publicly funded bodies in Finland and abroad. Abroad, more than 70 teams represent the Team Finland network. Publicly funded actors make up the core of the network, but cooperation with enterprises and universities is seen as highly important.

An important instrument for globalizing the Finnish innovation system has been the build-up of the FinNode Innovation Center network (recently reorganized under the name of Team Finland Future Watch, administered by Tekes), a direct outcome of the globalization studies conducted by the Prime Minister's Office. The FinNode network is charged with opening up markets and innovation systems for Finnish actors, attracting foreigners to Finland, and disseminating information about the Finnish innovation system.

Founded by the key innovation government organizations—Tekes, Finpro, the VTT, Sitra, and the Academy of Finland—the network was launched in 2005 with the inauguration of its first center in Shanghai, China. The network also includes centers in India, Japan, the Republic of Korea, the Russian Federation, and the United States. Besides its official funding organizations, the network relies on extensive domestic and global stakeholders, including the Confederation of Finnish Industries, the strategic centers for science and technology, universities, polytechnics, regional development companies, and professional associations.

The network seeks to bypass possible organizational legacy issues by spearheading new approaches to internationalization. Each center has a highly specialized focus on innovation and small and medium companies, working with research communities and innovative companies in particular. While the network has been regarded as something of a success and its expansion, say into Brazil, has been discussed, recent economic pressures have prevented this.

FinNode India in New Delhi aims to bridge Indian and Finnish innovation communities, including universities, research institutes, large firms, start-ups, co-creation hubs, final users, and consumers. Its main areas of focus are clean technology (renewable energy and clean water), education and learning, health care and well-being, as well as bottom-of-the-pyramid markets. The center caters to almost 100 Finnish firms active in India as well as to Indian firms interested in working in Finland. Finnish-Indian research cooperation is relatively modest, but an important part of the center's activities and focus. For additional information, see the Team Finland Future Watch website (http://www.tekes.fi/ohjelmat-ja-palvelut/kasva-ja-kansainvalisty/team-finland-future-watch/).

4 to 5 billion global poor are "unserved or underserved by the large organized private sector" (Prahalad 2010, 6). The BOP business model framework that has ensued seeks to improve the livelihoods of this consumer group by activating the profit motive of the private sector; as Prahalad put it, "Our goal should be to build capacity for people to escape poverty and deprivation through self-sustaining market-based systems" (Prahalad 2010, 8).

The BOP, in combination with developments such as microfinance, caused a sea change in the approach to poverty alleviation and low-income markets in the early 2000s. Whereas the private sector and "tied interests" were the traditional sore spot of development cooperation and global poverty alleviation efforts, the BOP helped to reinvent the role and meaning of the private sector as something that works more efficiently than government and, perhaps more important, addresses the issue of aid dependency. This, of course, requires a completely different approach and business model from the private sector too.

The BOP has reinforced the global "discovery" of low-income markets and their global importance. Going beyond corporate social responsibility and donor-funded demonstration programs, successful BOP companies and notable cases, such as M-Pesa (Foster and Heeks 2013) and Tata's Nano car (Wells 2013), have demonstrated the market's global business potential (for other success cases, see Hart 2010; Prahalad 2010). After these and other successes, companies from everywhere should be seeking ways to develop and introduce technologies, products, and services to the BOP market.

Despite its attractiveness, there are several barriers to entry into BOP markets. First, the global BOP sector is huge and diverse, and no single definition can do it justice. As Prahalad (2010) noted, "For those who want to engage in this opportunity, there is no single universal definition of the bottom of the pyramid that can be useful." BOP markets are highly diverse and differentiated in their local aspects, undermining attempts to scale up business models across countries. Another key barrier is insufficient market information about different BOP markets and their key constituents.

While other barriers exist, such as regulation, finance, and infrastructure, the diversity of global BOP markets and need to understand them more deeply are of particular importance in the context of the networks comprising developing and developed countries (Ramani, Sadre, and Geert 2012). Successful BOP cases typically involve sensitivity to local culture and social institutions, often realized through intermediaries who channel user and consumer feedback to developers and who introduce and spread the new services and products in user communities through social mediation, training, or other forms of capacity building. For example, Ramani, Sadre, and Geert (2012) describe the case of comprehensive pre- and post-delivery training and capacity practices followed by Indian sanitation entrepreneurs as they diffuse the Sulabh and Ecosan latrines in the Indian BOP markets.

Successful development of technologies, products, and services for the BOP market necessitates a solid understanding of the structural conditions of developing-country markets as well as the diverse social and cultural factors shaping the uptake of new innovations.

Most recently, the Ministry for Foreign Affairs and the MEE have launched a joint task force development group to explore the possibilities to foster inclusive innovation and business cooperation between Finnish and developing-country organizations as well as to improve coordination between other Finnish initiatives (box 8.2). The task force group broadly engages relevant stakeholders in developing funding and other services, including actors in the field, public agencies, enterprises, nongovernmental organizations (NGOs), research institutions, and universities. The results of this work were published in December 2013. The group proposed setting up a new program and fund for supporting innovation and business in developing countries.

Box 8.2 Advancing BOP Business

One particularly potent area in the new globalization has been the base-of-the-pyramid business model, which is particularly suited to small and medium enterprises (SMEs). It fosters the activities of a new population of firms, as large companies have been responsible for much of Finland's globalization (Halme and Lehtonen 2012).

In particular, Tekes has been funding research exploring the possibilities of BOP business, developing-country, and co-creation models. A series of research projects has explored the nature of BOP markets, structural shifts in the global innovation landscape, and the nature of developing- and emerging-country innovation systems, often carried out by the Aalto University or VTT. Moreover, Tekes has included Africa, Brazil, and India in its programs, with its information and communication technology (ICT), medical instrument, and bio-energy programs undertaking activities in these countries. Tekes's renewable energy program Groove has addressed internationalization and generated a wealth of information and material about the business and innovation possibilities in Africa, Asia, and Latin America, including targeted projects to network small Finnish companies with African counterparts. For more information, see the Tekes Groove website (http://www.tekes.fi/ohjelmat/Groove/Aineistot).

In addition, Finpro has initiated several projects exploring business and innovation opportunities in the developing countries and at the base of the pyramid. An important recent project was the Africa project implemented during 2010–11 by Finpro, which sought to raise Finnish awareness of opportunities in Africa for Finnish SMEs. For more information, see the Finpro, Africa project website (http://www.finpro.fi/web/english-pages/africa). Another project addressed BOP mobile ICT business and was closely aligned with the InfoDev's Creating Sustainable Business for Knowledge Economy, which was supported by the Ministry for Foreign Affairs.

This string of projects exploring developing-country and low-income market opportunities still continues, the latest one being Finpro's Weconomy Project, which offers tailored business development services for companies interested in BOP markets. See the Finpro Weconomy Start website (http://www.finpro.fi/web/english-pages/weconomy). Networking at the institutional level also continues, as the Ministry for Foreign Affairs and the Ministry of Employment and the Economy are collaborating with the World Bank on its Inclusive Innovation India Project.

Best Results through Joint Doing and Learning

Recognizing the importance of emerging-economy and developing-country innovation systems for Finland in the early 2000s, innovation policy makers faced two practical challenges. First, within the official public innovation system there were hardly any capabilities or expertise about what innovation is either in low-income markets or in developing countries. Second, there were no explicit policies or refined instruments in support of innovation aimed at developing-country markets or BOP markets in general. Yet a small nucleus of such expertise was being formed in a series of innovation and ICT-focused development cooperation programs funded by the Ministry for Foreign Affairs (Ainamo and Lindy 2013).

The learning and experience gained about innovation in developing countries have played an important role in the new globalization approaches of the Finnish innovation system since 2010, and policy makers have found practical solutions for forging new innovation partnerships between developed and developing countries.

Framing Development and Innovation

Finnish development programs that focus on knowledge, skills, innovation, and ICT for development commenced in the late 1990s and the first decade of the 2000s. By and large, this cluster of programs was created within the confines of development cooperation, and it did not attract systematic interest or support from government agencies until the early 2010s.

An important watershed in the approach to innovation and ICT in Finnish development cooperation occurred in 2004, when the themes of information society (IS) and communications technology emerged as a distinct sector in Finnish development policy (Ministry for Foreign Affairs 2004). The following year, the ministry issued "Development Policy Guidelines for ICT and the Information Society," which broadened the Finnish approach to include the concept of knowledge society (Ministry for Foreign Affairs 2005). The guidelines made explicit the departure from an infrastructure- and technology-focused IS, emphasizing the key objective of using ICTs to generate society-wide impacts. "Access to information, knowledge, and human welfare," the guidelines argued, were fundamental to all development issues.

The 2004 and 2005 development policy guidelines exemplified a solid understanding of how innovation unfolds and matters in developing countries. At the time, these conclusions were confined to development policy and not considered a part of innovation policy. They did, however, embody an important learning and stock-taking exercise that would eventually affect innovation policy as well. Development policy processes not only created expertise, but also directly funded programs that trained Finnish experts to understand and carry out innovation in developing countries. In addition to conceptualizing an IS and declaring its importance for development, the guidelines provided practical examples and recommendations on how to achieve this in fostering cooperation with developing countries. National poverty reduction strategies should make headway employing ICT as well as move broadly to benefit from IS strategies. In fact, according to the guidelines, "Partner countries receiving sectoral and budget support must also pay due attention to the mainstreaming of activities linked with the IS in development consultations" (Ministry for Foreign Affairs 2005, 13).

Establishing Capabilities in Developing-Country Innovation Systems

A wave of ambitious Finnish programming in the area of IS and STI took off in the closing years of the 1990s and expanded steadily throughout the early 2000s. Whereas Finland had previously supported these areas mainly through infrastructure programming, if at all, the Ministry for Foreign Affairs launched a series of programs that embodied practical learning about how to implement development cooperation focused on IS, ICT, and STI. The projects emphasized strategy, management structures, and leadership skills more than technological solutions per se, such as e-learning and e-health. In a sense, this set the Finnish approach apart, because at the time technological solutions often dominated project frameworks.

These programs generated a wealth of hands-on experience about innovation in developing countries, practical cooperation models between them and Finland, as well as understanding of the importance of public-private partnerships for innovation. They also created a growing pool of experts who could begin to influence Finnish innovation policy making. In this sense, they continued the tradition of earlier years, in which overseas development assistance investments in forestry or in health and education created a pool of experts in these domains.

Perhaps the most important initiative in this regard was a series of bilateral programs focused on ICT and innovation systems in South Africa—COFISA, INSPIRE, SAFIPA—totaling around €10 million in funding from Finland and substantial contributions from the South African government (Valjas, Farley, and Finlay 2010).

This cluster of programs functioned as a learning platform for both South Africans and Finns, and the project included an ambitious component of African and global dissemination. On the one hand, the programs strengthened nascent knowledge economy institutions and capacities in South Africa; on the other hand, they constituted a nexus of learning by doing about how to implement ICT- and innovation-centered development cooperation.

The programs were initiated at the request of the South African government, which had identified the strengthening of knowledge economy institutions as an important national development objective and then turned to Finland for advice and support (Government of South Africa 2002). The South African request for partnership arrived at a time when Finland was including ICT and innovation issues in its developing cooperation policy, thereby allowing for relatively quick funding, expertise, substantial programming, and learning by doing.

Running for about a decade, the program cluster created thematically and geographically the most substantial and distinct knowledge economy cluster in Finnish development cooperation thus far and ranks internationally as an important accomplishment. More important, it demonstrated to the South African government, the Ministry for Foreign Affairs, as well as South African, Finnish, and other stakeholders the advantages and challenges involved in a North-South learning exercise in building an innovation system.

The program cluster introduced a range of new instruments, intervention practices, organizations, and people into Finnish development cooperation. In particular, it fostered concepts such as user-driven innovation, co-creation, and living labs (box 8.3), which aimed to empower local people and users to shape technologies and innovations as they were being created. This type of activity, applied in this program cluster as well as in other Finnish-funded ICT and innovation programs, generated awareness about how to develop and introduce technology and innovations in developing countries and enabled local champions to do it instead of international experts.

Box 8.3 COFISA: How to Collaborate with Finland?

The collaboration between Finland and developing countries is based on *national agreements*. These agreements create and facilitate the framework for collaboration (including projects) and are drafted prior to start of the program. Outside of these frameworks, other individual projects and initiatives exist at the level of organizations, nongovernmental organizations, and enterprises.

Typically the agreements produce *targeted collaboration programs*. Traditionally these programs have been sectoral (that is, focused on specific sectors, such as agriculture or health care) and sometimes very narrowly defined (for example, gender equality).

One example is the Cooperation Framework on Innovation Systems between Finland and South Africa (COFISA), which was developed jointly by the government of South Africa, through the Department of Science and Technology, and the government of Finland, through the Finnish embassy in Pretoria. COFISA sought to enhance the effectiveness of the national system of innovation, thereby contributing to economic growth and poverty alleviation. COFISA focused on supporting innovation at the national, provincial, and rural levels as well as specifically in Sub-Saharan Africa. Some of COFISA's activities included provincially based forward planning (foresight) exercises in three target provinces (Gauteng, Western Cape, and Eastern Cape), focused on innovation and then on biotechnology.

Several *operational projects* fell within the program's framework. In COFISA, these included support for the development of science parks through awareness creation and feasibility studies and support for living labs to promote open user-driven innovation in rural information and communication technology services and applications. For example, the Siyhakhula Living Lab (SLL) in Eastern Cape was initiated by the University of Rhodes and the University of Fort Hare at the end of 2002 and was catalyzed in 2008–09 by COFISA. SLL has been pioneering new approaches to co-creation and user-driven innovation in Africa and has devised extended methods to involve and empower new user groups. Since its beginning, SLL has strived to advance innovation that benefits poor and marginalized groups, paying increasing attention

box continues next page

Box 8.3 COFISA: How to Collaborate with Finland? *(continued)*

to social innovation, rural populations, grassroots innovation, and more broadly to employing technology and innovation to empower disadvantaged people. As such, SLL has been instrumental in introducing and, indeed, creating co-creation practices in the context of rural South Africa.

COFISA's role as a catalyst for SLL enhanced its transformation into a recognizable living lab. An important component was the strengthening of SLL's link to the provincial system of innovation and its role in technology, EL Techno Park. Within COFISA, SLL seeks to provide "grounded and instrumented experimentation space" and to open commercial channels for innovation. Furthermore, SLL has been building a regional network of living labs and working within South African and international networks. COFISA strengthened its links to the Meraka Institute and established an association with the emerging living labs in the Southern Africa Network, also supported by COFISA, and the European network of living labs.

The Institutional Cooperation Instrument is an example of organization-level collaboration between higher education institutions in Finland and in developing countries. The Ministry for Foreign Affairs uses it to finance capacity development in higher education institutions. The aim is to strengthen developing-country higher education institutions by enhancing their administrative, field-specific, methodological, and pedagogical capacities through collaboration projects. The overall objective is to support higher education institutions in contributing to the development of society, to build competencies consistent with national development goals, and to contribute to achieving inclusive sustainable development and reducing poverty.

For additional information, see James (2010, 82–85) and the SLL website (http://siyakhulall.org/); higher education institution ICI website (http://www.cimo.fi/programs/hei_ici).

Observations from the case:

- The role of partners and the content of collaboration should be integrated thoroughly into the contract. Collaboration requires long-term commitment from a broad range of stakeholders.
- Programs should be seen as a coordinated and systemic set of complementary measures leading, step-by-step, toward common strategic ends. Instead of trying to fit existing solutions to other countries, all programs and projects should be based on an assessment and understanding of each country's situation and policies and planned from the bottom up.
- As part of larger coordinated programs, living labs, with their reasonably light structure, can foster multidisciplinary, open innovation when implemented well.
- Challenges may arise in implementation. In these cases, it is important to focus on the learning process itself rather than on concrete results.

Perhaps the most visible Finnish contribution to global ICT and STI programming is the World Bank's InfoDev Program, which seeks to foster ICT entrepreneurship and innovation in developing countries. This program typifies the possibilities and practical management of public-private partnerships in support of innovation in developing countries. In Finland, knowledge partnerships focused on mobile applications, private sector development, and direct involvement of the private sector, most notably the Nokia Group. Nokia contributed to the business and innovation expertise of the program and helped to build up its incubator and small and medium enterprise support activities. As defined in the program document, Nokia was expected to be "providing market and technology expertise to the mobile applications concepts and labs, for instance, through providing managers on secondment and a role on the advisory board; providing content for training courses to mobile entrepreneurs at Nokia's regional research centers; suggesting applications that could be profitably tried at the mobile applications labs; and assisting in developing social networking hubs in selected African cities" (Ministry for Foreign Affairs 2009). InfoDev collaboration enabled the Ministry for Foreign Affairs to access a global network of professionals and knowledge at a time when these capabilities were relatively scarce in Finland. Yet the program also illustrates some of the difficulties involved in developing public-private partnerships in a sector characterized by radical technological upheavals: Nokia's wholesale abandonment of its Symbian platform in early 2011 in favor of the Windows platform has had a notable effect on early builders of the Symbian mobile application.

Summary and Key Messages

Since the early 2000s, the proliferation of emerging economies and developing countries as central sources of global economic growth is transforming their relationship with the developed countries, which remain mired in a mix of slow growth and financial problems. One central theme in this unfolding transition, called here the new globalization, is the increasing development of innovations aimed at low-income markets across the developing world. Facilitated by efforts to reconceptualize the role of the private sector in global poverty alleviation and to underscore its ability to leverage change and reduce aid dependency, a range of new approaches to developing business and innovation for low-income markets has emerged.

To succeed in creating and introducing innovations for and in the low-income markets, a deep understanding of highly diverse user needs and requirements is needed. For developing countries, this phenomenon may offer a new competitive advantage, which they can exploit by upgrading their national innovation ecosystems and capabilities, and foster a new type of global network with innovation leaders. For developed countries, the challenge is to reorient their traditional internationalization strategies and establish new types of innovation co-creation models with partners from the developing world.

The economic importance of emerging economies and developing countries as sources of global economic growth and hosts to market segments that are growing rapidly is recasting the process of globalization, including the relationships between innovation leaders and those catching up. The international orientation of countries changes gradually, but the transition inevitably involves broad processes. It is yet to be seen whether the increasing importance accorded to emerging economies and developing countries in the global reach of rich-country innovation systems amounts to a substantial and lasting change, but an important turning point has been passed. Firms, universities, and governments around the world are placing great importance on the development of innovative products and services that can succeed in the global low-income market; they have realized that they must include the intended users in innovation processes.

The emergence of a new type of global innovation network presents specific opportunities and challenges for developed and developing countries, and both groups of countries need to adopt comprehensive public policy strategies in order to reap the benefits.

The incumbent global innovation leaders, such as Finland, must reevaluate their overall internationalization strategies and approaches and foster new policies, capabilities, and instruments enabling co-creation innovation and business models that extend between rich and low-income countries. This may involve targeting new populations of firms, such as the new emphasis on small and medium firms in Finland, generating a pool of experts in BOP business and innovation, and introducing new targeted instruments, such as the BOP activities within the FinNode network. Such strategies, approaches, and instruments will augment existing public policies in support of internationalization, not supplant them. For the time being, their weight will remain light in the context of a country's overall internationalization strategy.

For emerging economies and developing countries, low-income markets may gain a new competitive advantage. Firms, universities, and governments around the world are rushing to understand this market and to develop innovations that best serve its needs and preferences. It is essential that governments recognize this development and use it to leverage national innovation systems and capabilities.

Participation in co-creative innovation processes is premised on securing mutual benefits, and in this regard developing countries have a lot to gain by opening up for collaboration. Yet careful policies and regulation must be in place to insure against exploitation and harmful practices. More important, and probably more difficult, is to devise policies and practices that contribute to upgrading developing-country innovation systems and capabilities.

The best way for developing countries to benefit from innovation collaboration with rich-country partners is to implement active and forward-looking innovation policy, which includes a range of implementation instruments aimed at localizing benefits. These may include active scouting and selection of international collaboration partners, a strong vision and strategy to create locally strong living labs, harmonization and coordination of collaboration activities, and alignment of broader social objectives as well as higher education programs with collaboration programs. Global companies and universities are scouting for the best places to develop innovations for the low-income market, and national governments can make a big difference in setting up the right environment to innovate for the poor.

The character of developing countries' global interaction is critical in determining the extent to which they can exploit the growing interest in developing and marketing new services and products to low-income markets. With an increasing

Box 8.4 Key Messages

- The traditional roles of advanced economies as well as emerging and developing economies are changing rapidly. This development has prompted Finland, among other innovation leaders, to reconsider its strategies and approaches to developing countries.
- Development collaboration is about joint learning processes in which both sides should have an active role. Successful implementation of knowledge partnerships presupposes a deep understanding of user needs.
- The role of the various collaboration programs should be seen as a coordinated, systematic set of complementary measures leading, step-by-step, toward common strategic ends.

number of actors based in developed countries interested in developing technologies, products, and services for low-income markets, there is important potential for forging new types of partnerships between developing and developed countries, ones that go beyond traditional links between donor and recipient.

The promise of such innovation partnerships lies in mutual interest. Developed countries need to learn—and it is easy to underestimate the amount of learning required—to develop and introduce innovations in low-income markets. Developing countries need to upgrade their innovation ecosystems and capabilities. However, to gain momentum, the build-up of such collaborative mechanisms will take time and require considerable policy making from both developing and developed countries. Box 8.4 presents the key messages of this chapter.

References

Aiginger, K., P. Okko, and P. Ylä-Anttila. 2009. "Globalization and Business: Innovation in a Borderless World Economy." In *Evaluation of the Finnish National Innovation System: Full Report*, edited by R. Veugelers, K. Aiginger, D. Breznitz, C. Edquist, G. Murray, G. Ottaviano, A. Hyytinen, A. Kangasharju, M. Ketokivi, T. Luukkonen, M. Maliranta, M. Maula, P. Okko, P. Rouvinen, M. Sotarauta, T. Tanayama, O. Toivanen, P. Ylä-Anttila, 105–45. Helsinki: Taloustieto Oy.

Ainamo, A., and I. Lindy. 2013. "Lähetysseurasta kaupan tueksi: Suomalaisen kehitysyhteistyön institutionaalinen historia." *Yhteiskuntapolitiikka* 78 (1): 65–80.

Ali-Yrkkö, J., and C. Palmberg, eds. 2006. *Finland and the Globalization of Innovation*. Helsinki: ETLA.

Foster, C., and R. Heeks. 2013. "Analyzing Policy for Inclusive Innovation: The Mobile Sector and Base-of-the-Pyramid Markets in Kenya." *Innovation and Development* 3 (1): 103–19.

Government of South Africa. 2002. "South Africa's National Research and Development Strategy." Department of Science and Technology, Pretoria.

Halme, M., and T. Lehtonen. 2012. "Osallistavat innovaatiot BOP markkinoilla." Policy Brief 3/2012, Tekes, Helsinki.

Hart, S. L. 2010. *Capitalism at the Crossroads: Next Generation Business Strategies for a Post-Crisis World.* 3rd ed. Upper Saddle River, NJ: Wharton School Publishing.

James, T. ed. 2010. *Enhancing Innovation in South Africa: The COFISA Experience.* Pretoria: Department of Science and Technology.

Lundvall, B. Å., J. Vang, K. J. Joseph, and C. Chaminade, eds. 2009. "Innovation Systems Research and Developing Countries." In *Handbook of Innovation Systems in Developing Countries: Building Domestic Capabilities in a Global Setting.* Cheltenham: Edward Elgar.

Ministry for Foreign Affairs. 2004. "Development Policy." Government Resolution 5.2.2004, Ministry for Foreign Affairs, Helsinki.

———. 2005. "Development Policy Guidelines for ICT and the Information Society." Ministry for Foreign Affairs, Helsinki.

———. 2009. "Joint Program: Creating Sustainable Business in the Knowledge Economy." Draft program document, Ministry for Foreign Affairs, InfoDev, and Nokia, Helsinki.

OECD (Organisation for Economic Co-operation and Development). 2012. *Economic Outlook 2012/1.* Paris: OECD.

Prahalad, C. K. 2010. *The Fortune at the Bottom of the Pyramid: Eradicating Poverty through Profits.* 5th ed. Upper Saddle River, NJ: Wharton School Publishing.

Prime Minister's Office. 2004. *Strengthening Competence and Openness: Finland in the Global Economy.* Interim report. Helsinki: Prime Minister's Office.

Ramani, S. V., G. S. Sadre, and D. Geert. 2012. "On the Diffusion of Toilets as Bottom of the Pyramid Innovation: Lessons from Sanitation Entrepreneurs." *Technological Forecasting and Social Change* 79 (4): 676–87.

RIC (Research and Innovation Council). 2010. *Research and Innovation Policy Guidelines for 2011–2015.* Kopijyvä Oy. http://www.minedu.fi/export/sites/default/OPM/Tiede/tutkimus-_ja_innovaationeuvosto/julkaisut/liitteet/Review2011-2015.pdf.

STPC (Science and Technology Policy Council). 2003. *Knowledge, Innovation, and Internationalization.* Helsinki: STPC.

———. 2006. "Science, Technology, and Innovation." STPC, Helsinki.

Toivanen, H. 2011. "Finnish-Brazilian Research Collaboration and Strategic Interests: Bibliometric Analysis." Paper presented at "Innovation Potential and Possibilities in Brazil and Africa." Espoo, Finland. September 26. http://www.vtt.fi/sites/i4d/i4d_smartseminar.jsp?lang=en.

Toivanen, H., and B. Ponomariov. 2011. "Regional Aspects of the African Innovation System: Bibliometric Analysis of Research Collaboration Patterns, 2005–2009." *Scientometrics* 88 (1): 471–93.

United Nations. 2013. *Human Development Report, 2013: The Rise of the South; Human Progress in a Diverse World.* New York: United Nations, Department of Political Affairs.

Valjas, A., S. Farley, and A. Finlay. 2010. "South Africa: Evaluation of Programs in Science, Technology, and Innovation and in Information Society." Ministry for Foreign Affairs, Helsinki.

Wells, P. 2013. "The Tata Nano, the Global 'Value' Segment, and the Implications for the Traditional Automotive Industry Regions." *Cambridge Journal of Regions, Economy, and Society* 3 (3): 443–57.

World Bank. 2011. *Global Development Horizons, 2011: Multipolarity, the New Global Economy.* Washington, DC: World Bank.

CHAPTER 9

Conclusion and Lessons Learned

Kimmo Halme, Kalle A. Piirainen, and Vesa Salminen

The transition of Finnish society from an agriculture-based economy in the 1950s into one of the leading knowledge-based economies toward the end of the twentieth century offers an encouraging example for many developing countries undergoing similar changes. This report sets out in an analytical and informative way, how the transformation took place, what kind of issues it raised, as well as how it influenced government policies and structures.

The long transition into a knowledge economy continues, taking new forms and raising new kinds of governance and policy challenges. Most evident are the challenges brought by globalization and the new, broader nature of innovation. We call this new mode Knowledge Economy 2.0.

To a large extent, development of the Finnish knowledge economy has been driven by business and economic needs; at the same time, public policies and government measures have been important facilitators for the development and, in some respects, central to the process. The various chapters have described and analyzed development of the knowledge economy from the perspective of policy makers, drawing useful lessons for colleagues in other countries. In our experience, a well-functioning knowledge economy should be seen first and foremost as a result of conscious political choices and commitment, with inherent public-private collaboration throughout.

Several lessons can be drawn from Finland's experience. The report divides the lessons into six modules: (1) understanding and adjusting to challenges (ability for renewal), (2) recognizing the crucial importance of education, (3) establishing efficient governing and steering mechanisms, (4) implementing innovation policy at all levels, (5) monitoring and evaluating investments, and (6) building knowledge partnerships with developing countries (figure 9.1).

Understanding the Challenges from Global Trends

Crises and structural transformations occur, and they affect all economies that are integrated into the global markets. Hence, understanding the global trends and seeing the changes as opportunities are important for policy

Figure 9.1 Modules of the Finland Knowledge Economy

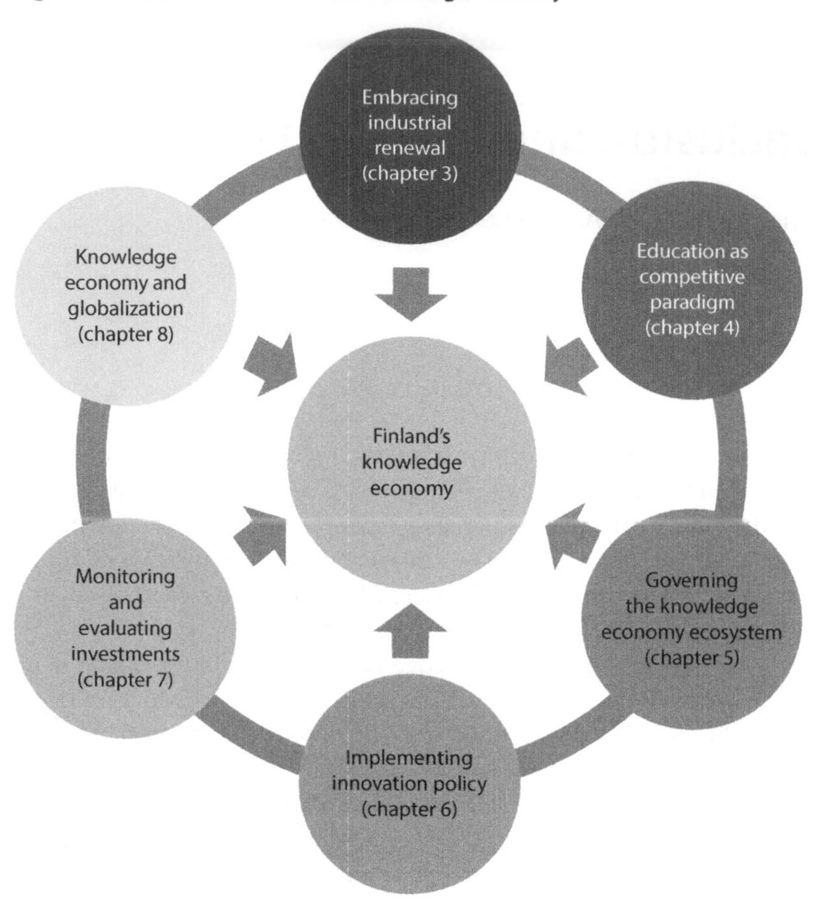

planning. The fortunes of countries are determined by how they prepare for and respond to the challenges. In times of change, national systems (research, innovation, education, economic policy) have to be prepared for the upcoming transformation. A country cannot emphasize a single sector of the economy and fail to prepare alternative scenarios. With the benefit of hindsight, the Finnish economy has been dependent on one industry and one enterprise—information and communication technology (ICT) and Nokia—but now that Nokia's contribution has declined, other enterprises have stepped up.

Conditions that promote and support entrepreneurship are hard to create through direct state action, but, as this report shows, the public sector can do much to create a desirable climate that supports multifaceted forms of entrepreneurship and encourages innovative companies to seek international growth. Hands-on examples of how this has been addressed in Finland are illustrated by the cases of Innovation Mill (box 3.2), the business accelerator Vigo (box 6.2), and the open innovation platform Demola (box 3.3).

Education as Competitive Paradigm

No country can jump into a knowledge economy without developing its base of knowledge and human resources through comprehensive and inclusive basic education, coupled with vocational training and tertiary education. This requires systematic long-term investments and commitment from all actors within the society.

The Finnish knowledge economy is based on a high level of education for both women and men. Key elements of the Finnish education system are its comprehensiveness and focus on equal opportunities, highly educated teachers, lifelong learning policy, and flexibility to adjust to new labor needs.

The Finnish case highlights the importance of adjusting to the need for new skills. In the future, actions are required to address the needs of an aging population, to enhance the efficiency of the education system, to speed up transition points, and to shorten study periods. Also an increasingly global labor market calls for closer international cooperation to develop models for anticipating the changing need for education and skills as well as closer collaboration between the education and private sectors. Cases on Aalto University (box 4.5) and the Aalto factories (box 4.6) shed light on some of the latest Finnish initiatives in this field.

Governing the Knowledge Economy Ecosystem

In countries like Finland with relatively limited resources, broad consensus, collaboration, and engagement among all actors from determining a national strategy to implementing hands-on governance are crucial, especially in the context of increasing global competition. A key characteristic of the Finnish approach to development of the knowledge economy has been the broad-based and engaging approach to formulating the education, research, and innovation policy agenda. Finland has been able to develop a wide and long-term consensus on the importance of adopting a national strategy to make the country a knowledge economy. The long-term perspective is also visible in how the government, parliament, and different agencies make use of forward planning (foresight) processes to support policy making (described in box 5.8). On a more practical level, the strategic coordination of education, research, and innovation policy, especially through a high-level coordination body (such as the Research and Innovation Council, described in box 5.4), should be examined more closely in other countries as well.

Enabling Innovation Policy

To implement the strategic choices and policies successully, a well-built structure of implementation and funding is needed. The Finnish model of decentralized implementation (described in box 6.3 on the Center of Expertise, Innovative Cities INKA, and the Center of Excellence programs) combined with centralized financial resources (such as Tekes, in box 6.1, and the Academy of Finland) may be of interest for countries seeking a model that combines a strategic overview with a diverse and viable research and innovation community. However, the Finnish context also provides food for thought regarding the effectiveness of policy instruments, as regional inclusiveness tends to bear an additional cost in the form of lower effectiveness or lower return on investment (see box 7.2 on the Tekes impact assessment).

The strategic centers for science, technology, and innovation (SHOKs) offer an interesting example of how Finland has responded to the need to implement innovation across sectors. All in all, while the Finnish system is far from perfect, the Finnish experience provides lessons for transparency, and illustrates the importance of clear roles and responsibilities (sometimes even through negative examples), as well as the need to strike a balance between planning and steering (chapter 5), implementation (chapter 6), and monitoring and evaluation (chapter 7).

Monitoring and Evaluating Investments

To be effective, policies need to be well-focused and efficiently implemented. In practice, improving the effectiveness of policy interventions is realized largely through systematic monitoring and evaluation of policies and the willingness of policy makers to learn from their own and others' experiences and to adapt policies accordingly. Moreover, monitoring and evaluation are crucial for transparency and legitimacy of the whole system.

The main lessons that can be drawn from the Finnish experience can be summarized in five key points. First, investing in building an open and critical evaluation culture pays in the long run: evaluations contribute little to learning from experience if they are not genuinely insightful and critical. Second, comprehensive and reliable basic data are the foundation of all evaluations. Third, it is essential to build policy learning into structures, for example, through guidance documents, key performance indicators, and benchmarking visits. Fourth, when drawing lessons, the evidence and political agendas should be separated. Fifth, evaluations and monitoring should be planned in advance.

Knowledge Economy and Globalization

The traditional roles of advanced as well as emerging and developing economies are changing rapidly. The emerging and developing economies are no longer merely a resource, but a true partner for collaboration and knowledge sharing. Increasingly a larger share of innovation is coming from outside the traditional advanced economies. This development has prompted Finland, among other innovation leaders, to reconsider its strategies and approaches to developing countries. While implementing this type of approach, Finland has learned a lot from the innovation systems of the developing and emerging economies. In fact, development collaboration is about joint learning processes in which both sides should have an active role. A deep understanding of user needs is also crucial.

Final Remarks

In many ways Finland is not a typical country, and some characteristics and contextual issues are important to recognize when considering the applicability of the practices and lessons described in this book. Understanding the surrounding framework and why an intervention works in those conditions is important. These characteristics include, among others, the following:

- Strong social cohesion and homogeneity of the population
- Low tolerance for unequal distribution of power in society and especially for perceived abuse of that power (short power distance) and a culture that prefers explicit and overt communication, where agreements are dependable even between strangers, focus on reliability and "delivery" is high, and relationships rely relatively little on personal and familial relations (low context and specific, "deal-focused" culture; see Nørmark 2013)
- Strong rule of law and good governance, very low corruption, and generally good trust in public institutions
- Small size and geographic and cultural remoteness
- Northern (partially Arctic) location, with an environment poorly suited for agriculture and relatively few exploitable natural resources besides forestry
- Recovery from wars and dependence on a very large economy (the Russian Federation) as a primary export market
- A pervasive public sector, including a welfare state with universal health care and education as well as a broad research, development, and innovation (RDI) policy, supported by relatively heavy taxation and driven by social cohesion and trust in government institutions
- Broad organization of labor and historically very strong role of labor unions in politics
- Strong orientation to seeking a broad consensus on (political) decisions, driven by social cohesion
- Significant role of the ICT sector, particularly from the 1990s onward
- Strong orientation toward globalization, especially after joining the European Union in 1995.

Particularly interesting is the interplay between a homogeneous population, a strong national identity and sense of community, good governance, and a consensus culture that enables and legitimizes the large public sector and the taxation that supports it. That is important because a firm tax base has enabled the government to develop and implement a comprehensive knowledge economy and RDI policies. Another facet is that Finnish policies have been stable and viewed as trustworthy both nationally and internationally. This stability is driven partly by consensus. Indeed, the mode of operation of the Finnish knowledge economy, which combines public and private, central and local, and interministerial collaboration, is based on a unique form of "social capital," national unity, and trust in relationships, even with people who are not related or otherwise part of one's inner circle.

Thus the Finnish knowledge economy has developed through a unique process, which may not be directly applicable to other countries, especially developing ones. To replicate it in a country without this kind of social capital might be difficult or produce unwanted outcomes. Therefore, attempts to implement the lessons and cases presented require a more in-depth case-by-case assessment of their feasibility. However, there are similar developments elsewhere in the world, particularly in Asia, where the "Japanese miracle" was evident in the 1980s and the East Asian miracle is evident today.

Regardless of the Finnish specificity, the lessons learned can provide policy makers with a good set of issues to be considered and even addressed. Of course, a healthy dose of careful consideration and adaptation is recommended. Real-life examples regarding the implementation of policies may be the most interesting and useful element. For this reason, we have illustrated each policy area with practical cases. Again, these cases are not ideal models, or directly replicable as such, but rather a source of inspiration and examples to develop, adapt, and build on.

The Big Lessons

When looking at the Finnish economic transition in the long run, and particularly the latest knowledge economy developments, several overarching messages can be drawn. The following are the most important for policy planning and governance:

- Finland has invested substantial time and funds in building its education system, which is the base of its knowledge economy. This is particularly relevant for developing countries.
- Determined policies and strategies for building a knowledge economy are important. Particular to Finland has been its systematic use of consensus mechanisms across all stakeholders in preparing and implementing these policies.
- Looking ahead (forward planning, impact assessment) and adjusting policies, governance, and instruments accordingly—even if sometimes during a crisis—are integral to societal evolution and economic growth. In this regard, policies and governance models should be flexible and enable cross-fertilization and horizontal collaboration.
- Finnish knowledge economy strategies have smartly aligned with and leveraged large corporations. Among the sectors, ICT has played an important role in Finnish development.
- The government has played an active role in the knowledge economy—as a coordinator and facilitator—while giving significant independence to the implementing agencies and regional or provincial organizations to allow for the efficient delivery of these strategies.

- In particular, government funding has been an important enabler and incentive for growth, development, and collaboration as well as for change and competition. The importance of smart funding mechanisms has been instrumental in driving and managing the transition.

Especially important is education. Kokkinen (2012) argues that a key enabler in Finland's catch-up from a poor agrarian society to a leading knowledge economy is the development of human resources through education, which has enabled both interaction and trade, as well as the adoption and assimilation of new knowledge, which has enabled innovation. In East Asian countries investment in stable, consistent economic conditions, good governance, and capacity building has given rise to economic "miracles" (Johnson 1982; Stiglitz 1996; Kniivilä 2007; Kokkinen 2012). Underlying education is the need to build trust in public institutions and good governance, which gives institutions and agencies legitimacy and the ability to implement programs.

How and Where to Apply These Lessons

Naturally the relevance of these lessons will need to be considered carefully and their application adjusted to the needs of each unique situation. Nevertheless, when possible, the lessons could be used in several ways.

For *policy-makers* in all economies, the Finnish examples should provide some inspiration for the benefits of committing to societal values and objectives related to the knowledge economy and some reference points for designing knowledge economy policies and strategies. Particularly useful are reflections on the reasoning behind such policies in Finland and on how the thinking has evolved over time and adapted to changing situations.

For *government officials*, it would be useful to study and benchmark Finnish governance models, institutional structures, and roles, especially regarding how to build mechanisms for enhancing collaboration within the system and how to assess the effectiveness and applicability of these mechanisms to one's own country, region, or organization.

For *development practitioners*, such as donor and funding agencies, the book should help to explain how the Finnish government has addressed its challenges and why. Here it might be useful to compare the experiences and practices to one's own country and perhaps benchmark with other countries as well, to see the full range of available approaches and their experience.

This report is not intended to be an academic study or analysis. Nevertheless, for *academics, researchers, and policy analysts*, it may shed light on the Finnish policy context and describe "case Finland," particularly in comparison with other economies, policies, and patterns of growth.

For others, such as companies, nongovernmental organizations, and innovation intermediaries, we hope that the Finnish example will highlight the *instrumental role that each societal partner*—whether the government, private sector, academia, or something else—has played in the joint development of the knowledge economy.

References

Johnson, C. 1982. *MITI and the Japanese Miracle: The Growth of Industrial Policy, 1925–1975*. Stanford, CA: Stanford University Press.

Kniivilä, M. 2007. "Industrial Development and Economic Growth: Implications for Poverty Reduction and Income Inequality." In *Industrial Development for the 21st Century: Sustainable Development Perspectives*, edited by J. A. Ocampo, 295–333. New York: United Nations, Department of Economic and Social Affairs.

Kokkinen, A. 2012. *On Finland's Economic Growth and Convergence with Sweden and the EU15 in the 20th Century*. Research Report 258. Helsinki: Statistics Finland. http://tilastokeskus.fi/tup/julkaisut/tiedostot/978-952-244-334-2.pdf.

Nørmark, D. 2013. *Cultural Intelligence of Stone-Aged Brains: How to Work with Danes and Beyond*. Copenhagen: Gyldendal Business.

Stiglitz, J. E. 1996. "Some Lessons from the East Asian Miracle." *World Bank Research Observer* 11 (2): 151–77.

List of Actors and Useful Links

Focus and institution	*Link*
Strategy and policy level	
Ministry of Education and Culture	http://www.minedu.fi/OPM/?lang=en
Ministry of Employment and the Economy	http://www.tem.fi/?l=en
Ministry for Foreign Affairs	http://formin.finland.fi/english
Prime Minister's Office	www.vnk.fi/english
Research and Innovation Council (RIC)	http://www.minedu.fi/OPM/Tiede/tutkimus-_ja _innovaationeuvosto/?lang=en
Government Foresight Report (online)	http://tulevaisuus.2030.fi/en/
Funding and implementation	
Academy of Finland	http://www.aka.fi/en-GB/A/
ELY centers	http://www.ely-keskus.fi/en/web/ely-en/
Finnish Industry Investment Inc.	http://www.industryinvestment.com/home
Finnvera	http://www.finnvera.fi/eng
Finpro	http://www.finpro.fi/web/english-pages
SHOKs	http://www.shok.fi/en/
Sitra	http://www.sitra.fi/en
Team Finland	http://www.teamfinland.fi
Tekes	http://www.tekes.fi
Vigo business accelerators	http://www.vigo.fi/frontpage
Agencies and research organizations[a]	
Foundation for Finnish Inventions	http://www.keksintosaatio.fi/en
Government Institute for Economic Research (VATT)	http://www.vatt.fi/en/
National Board of Education	http://www.oph.fi/english
National Board of Patents and Registration of Finland	http://www.prh.fi/en/index.html
Research Institute of the Finnish Economy (ETLA)	http://www.etla.fi/en/etla/
Statistics Finland	https://www.tilastokeskus.fi/index_en.html
Technical Research Centre (VTT)	http://www.vtt.fi/?lang=en
Platforms and open innovation	
Aalto Center for Entrepreneurship (ACE)	www.ace.aalto.fi
Aalto factories	http://www.aalto.fi/en/about/factories/
Demola	http://www.demola.fi/

table continues next page

Focus and institution	*Link*
Forum Virium	http://www.forumvirium.fi/en
Innovation Mill	http://www.openim.fi/eng/services.php
New factory	http://newfactory.fi/about
Protomo	http://www.protomo.fi/
Suuntaamo	http://www.suuntaamo.fi
Statistics and general information	
Center for International Mobility (CIMO)	http://www.cimo.fi
Finland in Figures (Statistics Finland)	http://tilastokeskus.fi/tup/suoluk/index_en.html
Finnish Education Evaluation Council	http://www.edev.fi/portal/english5
Finnish Federation for Communications and Teleinformatics (FiCom)	http://www.ficom.fi/ict/index.html
Finnish Higher Education Evaluation Council (FINHEEC)	http://www.finheec.fi/en
Finnish Information Security Cluster	http://fisc.fi/
Finnish matriculation examination	http://www.ylioppilastutkinto.fi/en/
Finnish Science and Technology Information Service	http://www.research.fi
General information about Finland	http://www.finland.fi
Key social indicators about Finland	http://www.findikaattori.fi/en
Neogames (Finnish game industry hub)	http://www.neogames.fi/en/
Teacher education in Finland	http://www.oph.fi/english/education/teachers/teachers_in_general_education
Global, indexes	
OECD Better Life Index	http://www.oecdbetterlifeindex.org
World Bank Institute	http://wbi.worldbank.org/wbi/
World Bank, Knowledge Economy Index	http://info.worldbank.org/etools/kam2/KAM_page5.asp
World Economic Forum, competitiveness	http://www.weforum.org/issues/global-competitiveness

a. Other publicly funded research institutes and agencies include, for example, the Finnish Environment Institute, Finnish Food Safety Authority (Evira), Finnish Geodetic Institute, Finnish Meteorological Institute (FMI), Geological Survey of Finland, National Institute for Health and Welfare, National Consumer Research Center, MTT Agrifood Research Finland, Finnish Forest Research Institute (Metla), National Research Institute of Legal Policy, and Game and Fisheries Research. A list of universities and polytechnics can be found on the website of the Ministry of Education and Culture.